AGENTS FOR CHANGE

AGENTS FOR CHANGE

Intelligence Services in the 21st Century

Edited by
Harold Shukman

ST ERMIN'S
PRESS

A *St Ermin's Press* Book

First published in Great Britain
in 2000 by St Ermin's Press
in association with Little, Brown & Company

Reprinted 2001

A CIP catalogue record for this book
is available from the British Library.

ISBN 0 9536151 9 7

Typeset by Palimpsest Book Production Limited
Polmont, Stirlingshire.
Printed and bound in Great Britain
by Clays Ltd, St Ives plc

St Ermin's Press
in association with
Little, Brown and Company (UK)
Brettenham House
Lancaster Place
London WC2E 7EN

CONTENTS

LIST OF CONTRIBUTORS AND PARTICIPANTS

Contributors

Professor Christopher Andrew – Cambridge University

Sir Rodric Braithwaite, GCMG – former Chairman Joint Intelligence Committee

General Shlomo Gazit – former Chief Israeli Military Intelligence

Sir Marrack Goulding, KCMG, Conference Chairman, Warden of St Antony's College

Sir David Hannay, GCMG – former Permanent British Representative to UN

Mark Heathcote – Deputy Chief of Security BP Amoco

Michael Herman – formerly GCHQ and JIO

Professor Loch Johnson – University of Georgia, USA

Ambassador Par Kettis – former Director General of Swedish National Defence Radio

General Vadim Kirpichenko – General Consultant Russian Foreign Intelligence Service

Admiral Pierre Lacoste – former Chief French Military Intelligence

Professor Brian Latell – Georgetown University, Washington, DC

John Lauder – Director, DCI Nonproliferation Center, Washington, DC

Admiral Fulvio Martini – former Head Italian External Intelligence

Sir Michael Quinlan, GCB – former Director Ditchley Park

Dr Andrew Rathmell – King's College, London

John Roper – College of Europe, Bruges

Paul Schulte – Director, Proliferation and Arms Control Secretariat, MOD

Dr Harold Shukman, Editor, Emeritus Fellow, St Antony's College and Conference Co-ordinator

Dr Dmitri Trenin – Carnegie Foundation Moscow

Colonel Oleg Tsarev – former Lieutenant-Colonel, Soviet External Intelligence Service

R. James Woolsey – former Director Central Intelligence, USA

Participants

Dr Richard Aldrich – Nottingham University, UK

Professor Martin Alexander – Salford University, UK

Major General Edward Atkeson – ex-US Army Intelligence

Stefan Backlund – Embassy of Finland, London

Claude Baker – Canadian Security Intelligence Service

Peter Baseby – St Antony's College

Michael Bates – Oxford Analytica

Klaus Becher – Research Institute for International Affairs, Munich

Dr Timothy Benbow – St Antony's College

Dr Mats Berdal – St Antony's College

William Birtles – St Antony's College

Christina Brendle – London University

A. David Brighty – former British Ambassador to Madrid

Professor Archie Brown – St Antony's College

James Burns – *Financial Times*, London

Anthony Campbell – Executive Director IAS, Ottawa

Sir Bryan Cartledge – former British Ambassador to Moscow

Anthony Cavendish – Author and business consultant, UK

Olda Cerny – ex-DG, Office for Foreign Relations and Information, Czech Republic

Sebastian Cody – TV executive and freelance consultant, UK

The late Gervase Cowell – former SOE Advisor at FCO

Professor Alex Danchev – Keele University, UK

Dr Philip Davies – Reading University, UK

Dr Anne Deighton – Wolfson College, Oxford

Brian Easey – former MOD

Fay Elliott – Director, St Ermin's Press, London

Geoffrey Elliott – Honorary Fellow, St Antony's College, and Chairman, St Ermin's Press

Sir Brian Fall – Principal, Lady Margaret Hall, Oxford
Professor Rosemary Foot – St Antony's College
Dr Roger Forder – Defence Evaluation and Research Agency (DERA), UK
Professor Michael Freeden – Mansfield College, Oxford
Timothy Garton Ash – St Antony's College
Polly Ghilchik – Student, St Antony's College
Roy Giles – Cody Fellow, St Antony's College
Dr Anthony Glees – Brunel University, UK
Dr Bulent Gokay – Keele University, UK
Dr Christina Goulter – King's College, London
Nik Gowing – BBC, London
Dr Robert de Graaff – Amsterdam University, Netherlands
Jan-Olof Grahn – Swedish MOD
Dr Max Gross – Dean, Joint Military Intelligence College, Washington, DC
Professor Robert Heibel – Mercyhurst College, Erie, PA, USA
Professor Peter Hennessy – Queen Mary and Westfield College, London
Andrew Hills – Director, BBC Monitoring Service
Alistair Horne – Honorary Fellow, St Antony's College
Dr Peter Jackson – University of Wales, Aberystwyth
Professor Rhodri Jeffreys-Jones – Edinburgh University
Aidan Kennedy – Student, St Antony's College
Dr Sheila Kerr – Joint Services Command & Staff College, UK
Dr Richard Kindersley – St Antony's College
Professor Baruch Knei-Paz – Hebrew University, Jerusalem
Professor Dr Wolfgang Krieger – Philipps University, Marburg, Germany
Terje Kristensen – Deputy Director General, Norwegian Intelligence Service
Major Donald Maclean – Defence Intelligence and Security Centre (DISC), UK
Lawrence Middleton – former HM Ambassador to Seoul
Mr Dan Mulvenna – Royal Canadian Mounted Police Security Services (Ret.)

Dr Kevin O'Brien – King's College, London
Professor Eunen O'Halpin – Dublin City University Business School
Robin O'Neill – former Chief of the Assessments Staff, Joint Intelligence Committee
Linda Osband – Editor, St Ermin's Press, London
Wing Commander David Oxlee – former Joint Air Reconnaissance Intelligence Centre, UK
Baroness Park of Monmouth – former senior British Intelligence Officer
Catherine Pawlow – Shell Services International, UK
Professor Hayden Peake – Joint Military Intelligence College, Washington, DC
Piers Plowden – St Ermin's Press, London
Alessandro Politi – Independent strategic and OSINT analyst, Italy
David H. Powell – UK Delegation NATO
Dr Alex Pravda – St Antony's College
Professor Olav Riste – Research Director, Norwegian Institute for Defence Studies
Dr Kenneth Robertson – Oxford Analytica
Dr Len V. Scott – University of Wales, Aberystwyth
Professor Avi Shlaim – St Antony's College
David Shukman – BBC, London
Colonel Tony Snook – late, The Parachute Regiment
Dr David Stafford – Edinburgh University
Duncan Stuart – SOE Adviser, FCO
Margaret Twomey – Australian High Commission, London
Professor Wesley Wark – University of Toronto
Sir Gerald Warner – former Intelligence Co-ordinator, Cabinet Office
Professor Donald Cameron Watt – London School of Economics
Nigel West – Author and Senior Commissioning Editor, St Ermin's Press, London
Professor H. Bradford Westerfield – Yale University, USA
Mark Wheeler – University of Derby, UK
Dr Cees Wiebes – Amsterdam University, Netherlands
Dr Christine Williams – United States Embassy, London

LIST OF ABBREVIATIONS

BND	German Intelligence Service
BTWC	Biological and Toxic Weapons Convention
CIA	(US) Central Intelligence Agency
CIG	Current Intelligence Group
CWC	Chemical Weapons Convention
DCI	(US) Director of Central Intelligence
DI	(CIA) Directorate of Intelligence
DIA	Defense Intelligence Agency
DDI	Director of Directorate of Intelligence
DGSE	French Foreign Security Service
DO	Directorate of Operations
FCD	(Russian) First Chief Directorate
FBI	(US) Federal Bureau of Investigation
FIS	(Russian) Foreign Intelligence Service
FRA	(Swedish) National Defence Radio Institute
GCHQ	(UK) Government Communications Headquarters
GPS	Global Positioning System
GRU	Soviet Foreign Intelligence Service
HUMINT	human intelligence
I&R	Bureau of Intelligence and Research
IAEA	International Atomic Energy Authority
IMINT	imagery intelligence
JIC	(UK) Joint Intelligence Committee
KGB	Soviet Committee for State Security
NATO	North Atlantic Treaty Organisation
NBC	nuclear, biological and chemical weapons
NIC	(US) National Intelligence Council
NIO	(US) National Intelligence Officer
NPIC	(US) National Photographic Intelligence Center

NPT	Nuclear Non-Proliferation Treaty
NSA	(US) National Security Agency
NSC	(US) National Security Council
OAU	Organisation of African Unity
ONE	(US) Office of National Estimates
OSS	Office of Strategic Services
SADC	South African Development Committee
SIGINT	signals intelligence
SIS	(UK) Secret Intelligence Service (MI6)
SISMI	Italian Foreign Intelligence Service
UNSCOM	UN Special Commission for Iraq
WEU	Western European Union
WMD	Weapons of Mass Destruction

FOREWORD

Sir Marrack Goulding

*S*ir Marrack Goulding, KCMG, (Warden of St Antony's College since 1997), served in the British Diplomatic Service from 1959 to 1985, working mainly on and in the Middle East, though his last post was as Ambassador to Angola. In 1986 he became an Under-Secretary-General in the UN Secretariat in New York. For his first seven years there he was in charge of UN peace-keeping, which expanded six-fold following the end of the Cold War. The operations he directed included those in Iran/Iraq, Namibia, El Salvador, Cambodia, Angola, Mozambique and the former Yugoslavia. In 1993 he became head of the new Department of Political Affairs, where he was responsible for the UN's efforts at preventive diplomacy and peace-making, as well as disarmament and electoral assistance.

This book is the record of a conference held at St Antony's College in the University of Oxford in September 1999. The conference was the brainchild of Geoffrey Elliott, an Honorary Fellow of St Antony's and a generous benefactor to the College. He is also the Chairman of St Ermin's Press, which has published this book with commendable speed.

It was entirely appropriate that St Antony's should be asked to organise and host the conference. It is one of the thirty-nine colleges of Oxford University, but it is unique among them in that it takes graduate students only, has a clearly defined field of specialisation (the modern history of, and social sciences related to, the main regions of the world), is highly cosmopolitan (less than 20 per cent of its students are British), and has always welcomed contact with practitioners in government and business.

Some of those contacts were with the world of intelligence, though their extent has sometimes been exaggerated by the media and in works of fiction. The College's first Warden, Sir William Deakin, was a distinguished historian who joined the British Special Operations Executive in the Second World War and was the first Allied officer to be parachuted into Yugoslavia to liaise with Marshal Tito and his partisans. Others of the first contingent of Fellows had had an adventurous war. Moreover, the College's interest, from the outset, in contemporary conflict, and especially in Europe and the Middle East, made it aware of the importance of intelligence.

So we were happy to organise the conference and host it at St Antony's. We were also happy because it was so topical. It came at a time when the end of the Cold War had made it possible for intelligence officers from both sides to talk openly, or reasonably openly, to each other about things whose discussion between them a decade before would have been close to treason.

The conference was also topical because it came when we in the West were realising, later perhaps than we should have done, that the end of the Cold War was not a simple movement from darkness into light, from night into day. By 1999 it had become evident that the post-Cold War world was different from what had preceded it but that that did not make it any easier to manage. Problems have become more diverse and complex in almost all areas of international activity – the prevention and resolution of conflict, the non-proliferation of weapons of mass destruction, economic relations, protection of the environment, and the control of international crime and migration.

In all these areas, governments continue to need covertly obtained information. But during this post-Cold War decade there have been technological changes that make the task of intelligence agencies even more difficult than it was. Our overwhelming reliance on information technology, at all levels of government but especially in the field of defence, makes our secrets more accessible to hackers from the other side – or other sides in the plural, for the gallery of potential enemies is rather more crowded than it used to be.

There have also been political changes in the environment within which the agencies have to work. Their activities, like the sexual *mores* of royal families, are no longer protected by a respectful taboo. Institutions and techniques which not so long ago were referred to only in whispers or by codeword have become daily grist to the media mill – the Secret Intelligence Service (or MI6, which takes less space in the headline), GCHQ, code-breaking, eavesdropping, satellite imagery and so on. Secrecy is more difficult to maintain – a fact which, of course, made our conference livelier and more informative than it would have been ten years ago.

This account of the conference's proceedings has been compiled and edited by Dr Harold Shukman, a historian of Russia and an Emeritus Fellow of St Antony's. His Introduction admirably signposts the issues discussed. I commend the book to all who are interested in the history of intelligence and in how the art of intelligence is adapting itself to the new demands of the post-Cold War world.

INTRODUCTION

Harold Shukman

*D*r *Harold Shukman, the Conference Co-ordinator and Editor of this volume, is an Emeritus Fellow of St Antony's College. He entered the College as a junior member in 1958 and, apart from research and teaching periods at various US institutions, including Harvard, Columbia, Stanford and UCLA, has spent his academic career at Oxford. He was University Lecturer in Modern Russian History until retirement in 1998. His publications include* Lenin and the Russian Revolution *(1966);* A History of World Communism *(with F.W. Deakin and H.T. Willetts [1975]);* The Blackwell Encyclopedia of the Russian Revolution *(ed. and contributor 1988);* Stalin's Generals *(ed. 1993);* Rasputin *(1997);* The Russian Revolution *(1998) and* Stalin *(1999). He has also edited and translated works by Dmitri Volkogonov, including* Stalin: Triumph and Tragedy *(1991);* Lenin: A New Biography *(1994);* Trotsky: The Eternal Revolutionary *(1996) and* The Rise and Fall of the Soviet Empire *(1998). He is Chairman of the Editorial Board of* East European Jewish Affairs, *and General Editor of Longman's* History of Russia *series.*

In the autumn of 1998 an informal discussion at St Antony's College, Oxford, on how the intelligence services were reacting to the end of the Cold War led a year later to a two-day conference, entitled 'Intelligence Services in a Changing World', and this volume is the outcome of the meeting. The organisers' intention had been to assemble practitioners from government and military intelligence agencies, as well as commercial experts, academics and writers on the subject, from the widest possible range of countries. Perhaps inevitably, and for reasons mostly logistical, the final assembly of one hundred participants was overwhelmingly British and American, and the result is reflected in the chapters of this book. Of equal importance, however, were the contributions, whether as prepared papers or in general discussion, from Australian, Canadian, Czech, Dutch, French, German, Irish, Israeli, Italian, Norwegian, Russian and Swedish participants, all of whose names and professional status appear below. Such a broad range of international representation at a conference on intelligence was possibly unique. It was certainly fruitful.

As one of the two chief adversaries in the forty-year confrontation of the Cold War – the Soviet Union – fell from superpower status, the questions arose whether the huge intelligence effort had been worth it, and what purposes, if any, intelligence might serve in the future. It soon became clear that the new political environment had not diminished the quest for information about other countries that most governments are prepared to pursue. What has changed is the number and diversity of 'targets': the 'unlicensed' producers of weapons of mass destruction, 'rogue states' which promote or protect international terrorism, drug barons and arms dealers. Moreover, new intelligence services have been created by most of the former Soviet republics, and Western agencies believe they require some monitoring.

It was to these themes that the conference was devoted. This book is virtually a transcription of the papers and the general discussion that followed them, and while some material was added by authors during the editorial stage, nothing was removed on any other grounds than comprehension.

Although the main aim of the conference was to discuss the future role of intelligence, it was also felt that some time should be devoted to the lessons of the past, and this was done in the opening session. Intelligence does not exist in a vacuum, its purpose is to inform government: 'telling truth unto power', to put it simply. The relationship between those who collect and evaluate intelligence and those who use it in the preparation of state policy – the providers and the consumers – is therefore of great importance. It is plainly the job of the intelligence services to influence policy, but are they likely to slant their evaluations to serve particular ends? Are they also likely to inflate a threat in order to inflate their budget, or even to stay in business? How far should governments dictate the tasks of intelligence in accordance with their transitory, perhaps politicised foreign policy aims? How far do governments want to accumulate knowledge on the principle that 'knowledge is power', or for more instrumental reasons? Ultimately, the national interest is the *raison d'être* of the intelligence services, not the other way round. How therefore are they to be controlled?

Different countries, with different needs, inevitably conduct the relationship between their intelligence services and their governments differently. The absence of a dividing line was characteristic, for instance, in the former Soviet Union under Stalin, as is illustrated in the opening chapter of the book. The intelligence leaders were part of the ruling élite, using intelligence as one of their weapons. In practice, Stalin's obsession with secrecy, and the literally terrifying climate of 'political correctness' that ruled in his era, meant that his officials were too scared to offer evaluations of the vast quantities of intelligence sent in by overseas agencies before they handed it over to the Leader, undigested, for his consumption. Lack of objective evaluation of material that had been 'hoovered up' in haste by a foreign agent and selected by the intelligence apparatus, must have made it impossible for Stalin to build an accurate picture of Western political realities and strategic intentions, even if it is also true that his pre-existing suspicions and hostility made objective assessment unlikely. Whether he discovered particular 'nuggets', and the question whether these ever affected his foreign or defence policies is a topic for further research.

The British model has been adopted by those who aim for the objective, policy-free collection of material from all sources and its collective evaluation at arm's length from government. Sometimes there is no dividing line between intelligence and policy-makers and decision-makers, even in democratic countries, and especially during time of war when national survival depends on the maximisation of the state's ability to focus all its resources. This diversity is reflected in several chapters; the Israeli case, in Chapter 4, is a particularly graphic example.

The future of covert methods is addressed in Chapter 2. The rule for tasking the Western clandestine services has always been to go after that which cannot be acquired better or more safely or more cheaply by any other means. The replacement of human agents where possible is desirable and natural. Human intelligence – HUMINT – used to be the norm because there was no alternative. Methods of collection have changed dramatically in the course of the twentieth century: satellite imaging and electronic interception are the most obvious evidence of this, and have become the tools of choice. Michael Herman, in his book *Intelligence and Power in Peace and War*, has estimated that as many as half a million people may have been engaged in spying for both sides during the Cold War. It is quite likely that the growing use of modern technology has led to an increase in that figure, along with vastly increased costs. In a world that is flooded with information, intelligence services are in danger of being overwhelmed by too much information, and therefore incapable of assessing it usefully. To illustrate this, the US National Security Agency – the American equivalent of the UK's GCHQ – recently revealed an 'intelligence gap' that has opened up as a result of information-overload brought on by the flow of e-mail and the vast increase in transmissions by other means. NSA failed, for instance, to detect increased activity or communications around Pokharan in India, when India set off the first round of nuclear tests in 1998. No less worrying, North Korea, using UN funds, has apparently bought encrypted mobile phones from Europe, high-speed switching-gear from Britain, and a state-of-the-art dialling service from the US, and succeeded in creating a system the NSA cannot easily read. A Senate intelligence committee was told by the NSA that unless it changes its intelligence collection system, 'it will go deaf'. Are the intelligence services faced by the paradox that too much data can mean too little understanding? Too much information may make it difficult to refine 'low-grade ore' to produce useful knowledge, while unbreakable encryption may be making it harder to access 'rich ore'.

This is a new element in the debate going on mostly outside the intelligence community between those who argue that open sources far outweigh in value the expenditure and effort devoted to clandestine methods. There is less, if any, such argument inside the intelligence organisations themselves, where it is understood that what is sought clandestinely is that which cannot be obtained openly, including confirmation, and that to identify the latter one must know the former. Another way of putting it would be: how reliable are open sources, or does the decision-maker want to be in the position of having to decide based on open-source information? This question is touched on in several other parts of the book. It is generally agreed that covert intelligence may only contribute a net gain of 5 or10 per cent of acquired knowledge for foreign policy, and that most of it is of no use for much of the time, but vital for perhaps 1 per cent of cases, especially for military purposes. Its main value is in anchoring the rest in reality. By analogy, vitamins provide only 1 per cent of the daily food requirement, but without them sickness will follow.

An issue that is addressed in Chapter 5 of the book is that of the role of intelligence on an international basis, specifically in the service of the United Nations and NATO. For virtually sixty years, as the 'special relationship' blossomed from the beginning of the Second World War and continued throughout the Cold War and into the present, British and American intelligence have

shared their knowledge: 'the jewel in the crown of British intelligence'. What might seem a natural extension of that co-operation to the defence establishments of other countries is in fact
a contentious issue. The UK-US nexus is viewed by the UK as
a precious asset, but the US may sometimes feel that its value
could be compromised by distribution to 'leaky' third parties.
International problems, such as proliferation, drug trafficking,
terrorism and ethnic wars that affect whole regions, call for
greater sharing of intelligence, and the issue is one that is unlikely
to go away.

The proliferation of weapons of mass destruction – nuclear,
chemical or biological – addressed in Chapter 6, is one of the
more recent targets for intelligence by countries that already
possess such weapons and do not wish to see others possess
them also. And since proliferant countries inevitably conduct
their activities in secret, all forms of collection, from satellite
imaging to human resources, are used against them. International
co-operation between government agencies is not merely desirable, it is also unavoidable, and the evolving modes of operation
are a subject that evoked much interested discussion at the
conference.

While military and political issues may remain the primary
goals of intelligence, globalised economic competition plays so
significant a part in national power status that economic espionage has become an important preoccupation. Indeed, it was
reported at the beginning of this year that French intelligence
is intercepting the telephone calls of British businessmen, after
investing massively in sophisticated listening stations. They are
presumably not the only ones so engaged. Clearly, the relationship between official and commercial intelligence agencies, which
is dealt with in Chapter 7, remains an area still to be defined.

A question that has long exercised the minds of practitioners
and observers alike is whether intelligence services should strive
to conduct their business using only 'just' or ethical methods: is

ethical intelligence a necessary corollary of an ethical foreign policy? This question was touched on by more than one speaker at our conference, and more extensively in the final paper. It is a subject that is particularly suitable for discussion in an academic environment, whether in the form of a further conference or a teaching medium.

Finally, against the background of the rapid changes in technology addressed in the chapters of this book, it may be assumed that the essential skills required of professional intelligence officers fifty years hence will probably not be so very different from those looked for by Mansfield Cumming, Allen Dulles, Felix Dzerzhinsky, or indeed William Pitt's 'Alien Office'.

Acknowledgements

The conference took place under the auspices of St Antony's College in association with St Ermin's Press, whose chairman, Geoffrey Elliott, generously sponsored both the conference and the publication of this book. The College owes him a debt of deep gratitude.

As the Co-ordinator of this conference, and Editor of this book, I chaired a small working group that was responsible for shaping the conference programme. It was made up of Geoffrey Elliott, Roy Giles, Michael Herman, Hayden Peake and Alex Pravda, all of whom contributed to shaping the programme and compiling the list of those to invite as speakers and participants, and to all of whom I express my thanks. Roy Giles not only provided the names of military intelligence officers to invite, but also assisted throughout the preparatory stage of organisation. Particular thanks are due to Hayden Peake, whose advice was most helpful, whether on whom to invite to the conference from the US and Russia, or in the final preparation of the book. Michael Herman deserves special thanks for the knowledge and experience – both as a former practitioner and teacher of intelligence – he brought to all stages of this project. I am also grateful to Linda Osband for her editorial help during the preparation of this book.

Finally, no conference can succeed as ours emphatically did unless the local administration gives full support. For this, we thank the Warden of St Antony's, who as chairman of the conference gave invaluable guidance throughout its preparation, and Polly Friedhoff, the College's Public Relations Officer, and her assistant, Janet Collyer, for their quietly efficient organisation.

ONE

INTELLIGENCE IN THE COLD WAR: LESSONS AND LEARNING

I

Christopher Andrew

*C*hristopher Andrew *is Professor of Modern and Contemporary History, and Chair of the History Faculty at Cambridge University. Professor Andrew is also Chair of the British Intelligence Study Group, founding editor of* Intelligence and National Security, *former Visiting Professor at Harvard, Toronto and the Australian National University, and a regular presenter of BBC radio and TV documentaries. His books on intelligence include:* Secret Service: The Making of the British Intelligence Community *(1987);* KGB: The Inside Story of its Foreign Operations from Lenin to Gorbachev *(with Oleg Gordievsky; 1990);* Instructions from the Centre: Top Secret Files on KGB Foreign Operations, 1974–1985 *(with Oleg Gordievsky; 1993);* For the President's Eyes Only: Secret Intelligence and the American Presidency from Washington to Bush *(1995);* Eternal Vigilance? 50 Years of the CIA *(with Rhodri Jeffreys-Jones; 1997); and* The Mitrokhin Archive: The KGB in Europe and the West *(with Vasili Mitrokhin; 1999).*

Sir Alexander Cadogan, Permanent Under-Secretary at the Foreign Office from 1938 to 1945, once described intelligence as the 'missing dimension of most diplomatic history'.[1] Though no longer wholly absent, it is still denied its proper place in studies of the Cold War. What follows is a preliminary attempt both to identify some of the most important gaps in our understanding of the role of intelligence and to suggest some tentative conclusions. Any rigorous attempt to learn lessons from the record of intelligence in the Cold War, however, will require a much better grasp of its history than we possess at present.

Intelligence Collection

Signals intelligence (SIGINT) provides perhaps the prime example of the failure of most academic research on international relations since the Second World War to come to terms with intelligence collection. Many studies of the Cold War still repeat the errors of the first generation of historians of the Second World War.

From 1945 onwards, almost all histories of the Second World War mentioned the American success in breaking the main Japanese diplomatic cipher over a year before the attack on Pearl Harbor. British success in breaking German ciphers during the First World War was also common knowledge; indeed, one well-publicised German decrypt produced by British codebreakers – the Zimmermann telegram – had hastened the US declaration of war on Germany in 1917. But, until the revelation of the ULTRA secret in 1973, it occurred to almost no historian of the Second World War (save for former intelligence officers who were forbidden to mention it) that there might have been major SIGINT successes against Germany as well as Japan.

At the end of the twentieth century, many of the historians who now acknowledge the significance of SIGINT in the Second World War still ignore it completely in their studies of the Cold War. The sudden disappearance of SIGINT from the historical landscape immediately after V-J Day has produced a series of eccentric anomalies even in some of the leading studies of policy-makers and international relations. Volumes 6 and 7 of Sir Martin Gilbert's epic biography of Winston Churchill, for example, rightly make much of his wartime passion for ULTRA. Volume 8, however, neglects entirely his interest in SIGINT as peacetime Prime Minister from 1951 to 1955. Nor is there a single reference to GCHQ, then as now the biggest and the most expensive of the British intelligence agencies. The reader is left to infer that Churchill's enormous enthusiasm for SIGINT, which had remained constant since 1914, had suddenly and improbably disappeared. Future research will probably show that it remained almost undimmed.

There are similarly startling lacunae in many of the best studies of United States policy in the early Cold War. Dwight D. Eisenhower, briefed personally by Churchill on ULTRA soon after his arrival in England in June 1942 as commander of American military forces, also became a SIGINT enthusiast. In July 1945 he declared that ULTRA had been 'of priceless value' to his conduct of the war, and sent to 'each and everyone' of the cryptanalysts at Bletchley Park 'my heartfelt admiration and sincere thanks for their very decisive contribution to the Allied war effort'. Ike's enthusiasm for SIGINT continued into the Cold War. The new US SIGINT agency, NSA, founded on the day of his election as President in November 1952, received much greater resources even than the CIA, in which Eisenhower also took a close personal interest. The basement of the 1.4 million square-foot NSA headquarters at Fort Meade, completed in 1957, contained the biggest and most sophisticated computer complex in the world. Remarkably, there is not a single mention of NSA in Stephen Ambrose's otherwise excellent biography of Eisenhower – or in almost any other studies of his, or any succeeding, administration.[2]

The Soviet Union put even more resources, though less advanced computer technology, into its SIGINT operations that were conducted on a massive scale by both the KGB and the

GRU. By the Gorbachev era, the Red Army had 40 SIGINT
regiments, 170 SIGINT battalions and over 700 SIGINT
companies. Since the launch of *Kosmos 189* in 1967, the GRU
Space Intelligence Directorate had put over 130 SIGINT satellites into orbit. More than 60 Soviet surface ships and over 20
different types of aircraft were used for SIGINT collection. The
GRU and KGB had between them over 500 SIGINT ground
stations in the Soviet Union and around the world. In all, the
GRU and KGB SIGINT network probably employed about
350,000 intercept operators, processors, cryptanalysts and other
technical specialists, a majority of them military personnel –
about five times as many as the NSA and US Service
Cryptological Authorities, which together had an estimated
60,000 to 70,000 personnel.[3]

Though the highest-grade cipher systems of the Cold War were
less vulnerable than those of the Second World War, the total
volume of SIGINT greatly increased in both East and West. The
KGB annual report sent to Khrushchev early in 1961 reveals
that during 1960 the Eighth Directorate decrypted 209,000
diplomatic cables sent by representatives of fifty-one states. No
less than 133,200 of these intercepts were forwarded to the
Central Committee (chiefly, no doubt, to its International
Department). By 1967, the KGB was able to decrypt 152 cipher
systems employed by a total of seventy-two states.

The KGB owed much of its success to penetration of Western
embassies in Moscow. The US embassy was penetrated virtually
continuously from the beginning of Soviet-American diplomatic
relations in 1933 until at least the mid-1960s. In 1952 the new
American Ambassador, George Kennan, ordered a thorough
search of both the embassy and his own residence. The security
experts sent from Washington asked him to dictate the text of
an old diplomatic despatch in his study in order to help them
discover any voice-activated listening device. As he continued his
dictation, one of the experts suddenly began hacking away at the

wall behind a wooden replica of the Great Seal of the United States. Finding nothing in the wall, he then attacked the Seal itself with a mason's hammer and triumphantly extracted from it a pencil-shaped bug which had been relaying Kennan's every word (and no doubt those of previous ambassadors) to Soviet eavesdroppers.

In 1953 work began on a new US embassy in Chaikovsky Street. During its construction American security personnel stood guard each day to prevent the installation of listening devices. The day-long security vigil, however, served little purpose since the guards were withdrawn at night, thus allowing KGB personnel ample opportunity to bug the embassy. During a heated discussion with US Ambassador Foy Kohler in 1962, Khrushchev made clear – to the dismay of the KGB – that he knew the Ambassador had personally opposed the supply of steel tubing manufactured in the West for the construction of natural gas pipelines in the Soviet Union. Though Kohler probably deduced that Khrushchev knew the contents of some of his cables to Washington, he seems not to have realised that the information came from the bugging of his own embassy. In 1964, however, acting on intelligence from the KGB defector, Yuri Nosenko, the embassy discovered over forty bugs concealed in bamboo tubes built into the walls behind the radiators in order to shield them from metal detectors.[4] Remarkably, most studies of US-Soviet relations continue to take no account of the almost continuous haemorrhage of diplomatic secrets from the Moscow embassy for more than thirty years.

Though security at the US embassy subsequently improved, that at many other embassies did not. According to Admiral Fulvio Martini, head of SISMI (Italian foreign intelligence) from 1984 to 1991, the attitude to security in Italian embassies in the Soviet Bloc frequently continued to be characterised by *'leggerezza e superficilità'*.[5] Few, if any, Western embassies escaped some degree of KGB penetration. Soviet SIGINT throughout

the Cold War was also greatly assisted by the penetration of a
number of Western Foreign Ministries. In 1945 the KGB's Paris
residency recruited a twenty-three-year-old cipher officer, code-
named JOUR, in the Quai d'Orsay who for the next forty years
became probably the KGB's most valuable French agent. The
large amount of French diplomatic documents and cipher
material supplied by JOUR were regularly despatched to Moscow
in what JOUR's file describes as 'a special container'. He also
talent-spotted other Quai d'Orsay cipher and secretarial staff. In
1957 JOUR was secretly awarded the Order of the Red Star. A
quarter of a century later he was awarded the Order of the
Friendship of Peoples for his 'long and fruitful co-operation'.
DARIO in the Italian Foreign Ministry had an equally long career
as both KGB agent and talent-spotter, and for most of the Cold
War was probably the most important agent run by the Rome
residency.[6]

The incomplete evidence currently available suggests that, at
a number of periods during the Cold War, France and Italy were
conducting towards the Soviet Union something akin to open
diplomacy. In 1983, for example, the French embassy in Moscow
discovered that bugs in its teleprinters had been relaying all
incoming and outgoing telegrams to the KGB for the past seven
years. According to Viktor Makarov, who served in the KGB
Sixteenth (SIGINT) Directorate from 1980 to 1986, the
European states whose diplomatic traffic was decrypted with
varying frequency during these years included Denmark,
Finland, France, Greece, Italy, Sweden, Switzerland and West
Germany. There was, he believes, no penetration of high-grade
British cipher systems during that period.[7]

An inner circle within the Politburo – consisting, in 1980, of
Brezhnev, Andropov, Gromyko, Kirilenko, Suslov and Ustinov –
were sent a daily selection of the most important intercepts. A
larger selection was forwarded each day to the heads of the KGB
First and Second Chief Directorates.[8] Though neither selection

is yet available for research, both will one day be sources of major importance for historians of Soviet foreign policy. In the meantime, though there are some excellent histories of the Soviet Union, it is difficult to think of a single one which devotes as much as a sentence to the enormous volume of SIGINT generated by the KGB and GRU.

The most obvious lesson to be drawn from the SIGINT evidence already available is that the consequence of its virtual exclusion from the history of post-war international relations has been to distort our understanding of the Cold War in significant ways. That point is illustrated by the very first Cold War SIGINT to be declassified: the approximately 3,000 intercepted Soviet intelligence and other telegrams (codenamed VENONA) for the period 1939 to 1948, mostly decrypted by American and British codebreakers in the late 1940s and early 1950s. The decrypts have large implications for American political history as well as for Soviet-American relations. VENONA provides compelling evidence of the reliability of the previously highly controversial testimony of Whittaker Chambers and Elizabeth Bentley, the two leading defectors from pre-war and wartime Soviet spy-rings in the United States. There is no longer any reasonable doubt, for example, that Harry Dexter White, who became Assistant Secretary of the Treasury in January 1945, was a Soviet agent codenamed JURIST, or that Alger Hiss, who was a member of the US delegation at the Yalta Conference and was personally congratulated afterwards in Moscow by the Deputy Foreign Minister, Andrei Vyshinsky, was Agent ALES.[9]

By the standards of the Cold War, VENONA was a rather small-scale operation, never involving as many as a hundred people. Many much larger SIGINT operations of the 1950s remain classified. Among the most important decrypts from the early Cold War which have still to be declassified are those for the Korean War. It is already clear, however, that the SIGINT failure at the outbreak of war was a direct consequence of the failure to learn the lessons of past mistakes. The rivalry between US service SIGINT agencies which had helped to make possible the success of the Japanese surprise attack at Pearl Harbor on 7 December 1941 reappeared in an even more confused form before the North Korean invasion of the South on 25 June 1950, once again with disastrous results.

Before Pearl Harbor, the bitter turf battles between military and naval cryptanalysts had been contained, though not resolved, by an absurd compromise which gave each the right to Japanese diplomatic messages in the high-grade PURPLE cipher on alternate days. By the time of the Korean War, the number of service SIGINT agencies had doubled. The air force, like the army and navy, now had its own independent cryptanalytic agency. An inter-service SIGINT body, the Armed Forces Security Agency (AFSA), set up in a vain attempt to co-ordinate the work of the three rival agencies, merely added to the confusion. Had the US intelligence community had to face the scrutiny of Congressional intelligence committees, the pressures to resolve the confusion would surely have been much greater.

Largely as a result of the lack of co-ordination, North Korea did not became a priority SIGINT target until after it had attacked the South. Had it been targeted before the invasion began, it is difficult to believe – given the success of SIGINT operations after the outbreak of war – that no warning would have been obtained of the massing of over ninety thousand North Korean troops and 150 T-34 tanks at 'jump-off' points north of the 38th Parallel. A later CIA study concluded that in the course of the war, with improved co-ordination between the 'shame-faced' service agencies, SIGINT became 'a critically important source of information'.

Research on all subsequent crises of the Cold War remains similarly handicapped in varying degrees by the continued classification of the SIGINT files. On some occasions SIGINT doubtless made little difference. On others, however, it was of the first importance. During the 1956 Suez Crisis, for example, the Foreign Secretary, Selwyn Lloyd, sent a personal letter to the Director of GCHQ congratulating him on the 'volume' and 'excellence' of the decrypts it had supplied 'relating to all the countries of the Middle-East': 'I am writing to let you know how valuable we have found this material . . . .'

When historians are finally allowed access to the decrypts, they will find them valuable too. It is already clear that SIGINT will force us to modify our understanding of the Suez Crisis in significant ways. Britain shared none of the Middle Eastern SIGINT generated by GCHQ with France, her co-conspirator in the Suez operation. All of it, however, was shared with the United States, who was the prime mover in bringing the whole operation to an end. There are few better illustrations of the astonishing closeness of the Anglo-American intelligence alliance. The text of the 1948 UK-USA Agreement – the corner-stone of the SIGINT alliance, which also involves Canada, Australia and New Zealand – still remains classified. (The few studies of the Cold War that notice its existence usually date it wrongly as a 1947 accord.)[10]

Even today, despite the fact that the perfectly accurate phrase 'special relationship' is considered too embarrassing to use in public, Britain and the United States share more secrets than any other independent powers have ever done in peacetime history. Despite the active intelligence liaison between Britain and a number of her continental partners, there is at least a potential conflict of interest between Britain's membership of the European Union and her intelligence alliances. For the fore-seeable future, Britain will continue to share with four powers outside the European Union SIGINT denied to other members of the Union.

Intelligence Analysis and Use

The experience of the Cold War suggests that, with all its faults
(notably the tendency to blandness that invariably results from
the quest for consensus), the British Joint Intelligence Committee
(JIC) may be the best assessment system available. The CIA has
high-level representation on it; past representatives have included
former Deputy Directors for Intelligence and Deputy Directors
for Operations. The only point at which the 1996 report of the
Commission on the Roles and Capabilities of the United States
Intelligence Community (better known as the Aspin-Brown
Commission) concludes that there is anything which US intelligence might learn from the experience of the rest of the human
race concerns the JIC. The Aspin-Brown Commission argues –
over-optimistically perhaps given the traditional turf battles that
divide Washington's much larger, more powerful and less co-
ordinated bureaucracy – that 'the concept embodied in the JIC
can also be made to work in the United States'.[11] The Commission may well have been unaware that during and immediately
after the Second World War an attempt was made to get the JIC
concept 'to work in the United States' – and that the attempt
failed.[12]

Throughout the Cold War the JIC proved better than the NSC
or any other American body at resolving turf battles, co-ordinating assessment by Intelligence, Foreign Office, Defence and
Treasury representatives, and gaining the confidence of policy-
makers. The JIC Red Book almost certainly attracts greater attention from consumers than US National Intelligence Estimates,
which some policy-makers appear not to read at all. The
Twentieth Century Fund Task Force on the Future of US
Intelligence (of which the author was a member) found that,
outside the Defense Department, most US government officials
'do not much value the [intelligence] analysis they receive'.[13]
The first of the measures proposed by the Aspin-Brown
Commission to improve 'the performance of US intelligence'

was directed at policy-makers rather than the intelligence agencies: 'Policy-makers need to appreciate to a greater extent what intelligence can offer them and be more involved in how intelligence capabilities are used.'[14]

Though the important role of the JIC in the Second World War has been clear for over twenty years, its role in the Cold War has until recently curiously failed to attract scholarly attention. Alan Bullock's magisterial study of Ernest Bevin's tenure as Foreign Secretary is one of many standard works which make no reference to the JIC – despite the fact that Bevin was clearly influenced by JIC assessments. The recent Cambridge PhD thesis by Alex Craig on the role of the JIC from 1945 to 1956 argues persuasively that, despite occasional eccentricities (such as the belief that London 'jitterbug clubs' were potential centres of Soviet subversion), 'the JIC was the most effective organisation on either side of the Atlantic conducting intelligence analysis in the early Cold War', based on both open and secret sources. Though intelligence collection in the late 1940s did not compare with the astonishing successes of the Second World War, the JIC made generally effective use of limited resources. Its picture of Soviet intentions, unlike many other assessments of the time, was broadly in line with those of post-Cold War historians who are now able to draw on better sources than those available to the JIC half a century ago and who remain unaware that some of their own conclusions were anticipated by the JIC.[15]

Alex Craig also shows convincingly that planning for the greatest fiasco in British post-war foreign policy – the Suez adventure of 1956 – was so inept largely because the JIC was excluded from it, for fear no doubt that it would take a dim view of the whole exercise. The most absurd adventure in Cold War US foreign policy – the Bay of Pigs catastrophe in 1961 – similarly derived largely from the fact that, unknown to Kennedy, the CIA Directorate of Operations (then known as 'Plans') deliberately excluded the analysts of the Directorate of Intelligence from having any say in preparations for the landing, for fear once again that the analysts would object. On the eve of the operation, the DDI, Robert Amory, who had had more Second World War experience of amphibious operations than anyone else in the CIA but had been told nothing about the Cuban operation, asked the DCI, Allen Dulles, 'What should I do if anything comes up?' Dulles replied sharply, 'You have nothing to do with that at all.' As so often, 'intelligence failure' derived far less from the collection and analysis of intelligence than from the use made of it.

The bypassing of the JIC in 1956 and of the DI in 1961 would have been far less likely with present systems of Parliamentary and Congressional scrutiny. Though the case is controversial, the need for such scrutiny – despite its inevitable limitations – is arguably one of the intelligence lessons of the Cold War.

As the Cold War progressed, the JIC became both more powerful and more influential. Margaret Thatcher, whose passion for intelligence seems almost to have equalled Churchill's, made the Chairman of the JIC, Sir Percy Cradock, her Foreign Policy Adviser.[16] At present, however, so little is known in detail about JIC assessments from the 1960s onwards that it is premature to draw detailed lessons from them. Alex Craig's thesis will need to be followed by many more.

It is arguable, but in our present state of historical ignorance not certain, that the quest for inter-departmental consensus within the JIC system has left too little place for dissenting opinions. Co-ordinating all-source information in a form which makes it accessible to and usable by policy-makers, while at the same time giving appropriate weight to dissenting opinions, is the intelligence equivalent of squaring the circle. So far no fully satisfactory method for achieving this miracle appears to have been devised. The Israeli establishment after the Yom Kippur War of the office of the Devil's Advocate, charged with picking holes in major intelligence assessments, is intellectually interesting but apparently hard to make work in practice. It has, allegedly, frequently proved difficult to fill the office.

How the US intelligence cycle works in practice changes with every administration.[17] When a President who is well-informed and enthusiastic about intelligence is succeeded by one who is poorly informed and little interested (or vice-versa), the consequences for the intelligence community and the use of its product are profound.

The first Cold War President, Harry Truman, arrived in the Oval Office both profoundly ignorant of intelligence and deeply suspicious of the whole idea of US espionage in peacetime. (As Vice-President, he was unaware even of the existence of ULTRA.) Roosevelt, unlike Truman, would not have closed down OSS without establishing a peacetime foreign intelligence agency to take over from it.[18] Eisenhower, however, had experience of using the best SIGINT and IMINT (imagery intelligence) in the history of warfare (though the wartime experience of special operations behind enemy lines led him to draw a false analogy with peacetime covert action). His wartime experience was responsible for his peacetime enthusiasm for intelligence in all its forms.

The transition at the end of the Cold War from Bush to Clinton was almost as dramatic as the shift forty years earlier from Truman to Eisenhower. With the arguable exception of George Washington, Bush was the first DCI to become President, regularly rang up the desk officers at Langley, raised morale within the Agency, and provided the regular feedback which all intelligence agencies require from policy-makers if they are to do their jobs effectively. Clinton, by contrast, has found it progressively more difficult to find suitably qualified candidates willing to become his DCI. If he has maintained morale at Langley, the secret has been well kept. The lesson, though simple and obvious, is rarely drawn. Political leaders whose interest in and understanding of intelligence predate their arrival in office are, with inevitable exceptions, likely to handle it better than those who are introduced to it on or shortly before their elevation. In intelligence, as in all other walks of life, experience counts.

Ike's experience of wartime IMINT was directly related to the stabilisation of the Cold War between the mid-1950s and the early 1960s. Throughout the Cold War, Western policy to the Soviet Union was profoundly influenced by the availability and reliability of intelligence on its nuclear weapons and delivery systems. Shortage of intelligence in the early 1950s contributed to the dangerous American myth of the 'bomber gap', later followed by that of the 'missile gap'. In 1955 US air force intelligence estimates calculated that by the end of the decade the Soviet Long-Range Air Force would be more powerful than US Strategic Air Command, whose head, General Curtis Le May, became dangerously attracted by the idea of a pre-emptive strike to prevent the Soviet Union achieving nuclear superiority.

The first step in stabilising the nuclear Cold War was the IMINT revolution of which Eisenhower was one of the prime movers. The introduction of the U-2 spy-plane in 1956, followed four years later by spy satellites scanning Russia from above, provided proof that the Soviet nuclear strike force was not overtaking that of the United States. The U-2, wrote Eisenhower in his memoirs, 'provided proof that the horrors of the alleged "bomber gap" and "missile gap" were nothing more than the imaginative creations of irresponsibility'.

A few days before he left office in January 1963, Ike established the National Photographic Intelligence Center (NPIC), under CIA administration, with Art Lundahl as its director. Of critical importance to the resolution of the 1962 Cuban Missile Crisis was not merely the availability of U-2 photographs of the missile sites under construction but also the confidence shown by President Kennedy and his EXCOMM advisers in NPIC's interpretation of them. Among the many honours later bestowed on Lundahl was an honorary British knighthood. IMINT, however, depended on HUMINT. NPIC was conscious that the success with which it identified the various stages of missile site construction in Cuba owed much to secret documents (code-named IRONBARK) supplied by Colonel Oleg Penkovsky, an agent in the GRU run jointly by SIS and the CIA in what one senior NPIC analyst described as 'one of the most productive intelligence operations in history'. Significantly, the 'Evaluations of the Soviet Missile Threat in Cuba' supplied to the President and EXCOMM during the crisis carried the codeword IRON-BARK to indicate their use of Penkovsky's documents. Had the United States, as Khrushchev intended, discovered the presence of the missile bases only after they became operational, the prospects for a peaceful resolution of the crisis would have been dramatically reduced.

Studies of the Cold War sometimes forget the truth of Eisenhower's dictum that intelligence on 'what the Soviets *did not* have' was often as important as information on what they did. If all Presidents had possessed as little intelligence on the Soviet Union as Truman, there would have been many more missile gap controversies and much greater tension between the superpowers. During the 1970s and 1980s, IMINT, together with electronic and telemetry intelligence (ELINT and TELINT, varieties of SIGINT), gave the superpowers the verification systems which enabled them first to control, then to limit, the nuclear arms race through the SALT and START agreements.[19]

As usual in the history of intelligence, what CIA analysts found hardest to judge during the Cold War were the intentions of the opposing leadership. In 1982–3, for example, the Directorate of Intelligence found it difficult to credit the entirely accurate warn-ings provided by Oleg Gordievsky, a British agent in the KGB London residency, of the extent of Soviet fears of Western surprise attack.[20] Intelligence failures, however, usually become public knowledge well before intelligence successes. The achieve-ments of the Directorate of Intelligence during the Cold War are still frequently underestimated. As Robert Gates, DCI from 1991 to 1993, has argued:

> The great continuing strength and success of the analysts of CIA and the intelligence community was in describing with amazing accuracy from the late 1960s until the Soviet collapse the actual military strength and capabilities of the Soviet Union . . . . And these numbers and capabilities would be relied upon, with confidence, by the Executive Branch (including the Defense Department), the Congress, and our allies both in arms control negotiations and in military planning.[21]

The Soviet Union was, almost invariably, far worse at intelligence analysis than at intelligence collection. Authoritarian regimes have an in-built advantage (of which, admittedly, they do not always take advantage) over open societies in collecting human intelligence. Throughout the Cold War it was always easier for a hostile intelligence agency to operate in London and Washington than in Moscow or Beijing. By contrast, authoritarian regimes in general and one-party states in particular have an in-built disadvantage by comparison with parliamentary democracies in intelligence assessment.

Soviet political intelligence assessment suffered from two serious inherent defects. The first was a paranoid tendency, institutionalised during the Stalinist era. In the middle of the Second World War the Centre absurdly concluded that Kim Philby and the rest of the Cambridge 'Magnificent Five', probably its most gifted agents, were part of an elaborate deception run by British intelligence. Though intelligence analysis after Stalin's death never again descended to quite such paranoid depths, at moments of crisis in the Cold War the KGB tended to fall back on conspiracy theory. In both the early 1960s and the early 1980s, the Centre reported – with horrendous inaccuracy – that the United States was planning a nuclear first strike against the Soviet Union.

Secondly, Soviet intelligence analysis was also seriously distorted by political correctness. Though the Soviet leadership never really understood the West until the closing years of the Cold War, it would have been outraged to have its misunderstandings challenged by intelligence reports. As one political intelligence officer later admitted, 'In order to please our superiors we sent in biased information, acting on the principle, "Blame everything on the Americans, and everything will be OK."'

There is no more convincing evidence of Gorbachev's 'new thinking' towards the West during his first year as General Secretary than his denunciation of the traditional bias of Soviet political intelligence. The fact that the Centre had to issue stern instructions at the end of 1985 'on the impermissibility of distortions of the factual state of affairs' is a damning indictment of its previous political correctness.

Leonid Shebarshin, who succeeded Vladimir Kryuchkov as head of the First Chief Directorate (FCD) in 1988, insists that foreign intelligence reports were by then free from past, politically correct distortions. As the Soviet system began to crumble in 1990–1, however, some of the old, anti-American conspiracy theories began to resurface. The United States and its allies were variously accused by Kryuchkov and other senior KGB officers of infecting Soviet grain imports, seeking to undermine the rouble, plotting the disintegration of the Soviet Union, and training agents to sabotage the economy, administration and scientific research.

The Soviet system found it far easier to digest scientific and technological (S & T) intelligence than political intelligence. By the Second World War, S & T was seen as crucially important. Nothing did more than intelligence on British-American plans to build the first atomic bomb to bring home to Stalin and the Centre the necessity of S & T in ensuring that Soviet military technology did not fall behind the West. The first Soviet atomic bomb was an exact copy of the American original.

The enormous flow of Western (especially American) S & T throughout the Cold War helps to explain one of the central paradoxes of a Soviet state which was once famously described as 'Upper Volta with missiles': its ability to remain a military superpower while its infant mortality and other indices of social deprivation were at Third World levels. During the early 1980s, probably 70 per cent of all Warsaw Pact weapons systems depended on the theft of Western technology. Both sides in the Cold War depended on American know-how.[22]

Governments and Intelligence Communities

Future research on declassified files of the Cold War is likely to demolish the common assumption of a basic symmetry between the roles of intelligence in East and West. The Cheka and its successors were central to the functioning of the Soviet system in ways that intelligence communities never were to the government of Western states. The construction and survival of the world's first one-party state in Russia and its 'near abroad' depended on the creation after the October Revolution of an unprecedented system of surveillance able to monitor and suppress all forms of dissent.

The war against dissent was also an important part of KGB foreign intelligence operations. The failure by many Western historians to identify the KGB as a major arm of Soviet foreign policy is due partly to the fact that many Soviet policy aims did not fit Western concepts of international relations. Surveys of Stalin's foreign policy, for example, invariably mention the negotiations on collective security against Nazi Germany, which were conducted by Maksim Litvinov and Soviet diplomats, but commonly ignore entirely the less conventional operations against the White Guards in Paris, the plan to assassinate General Franco early in the Spanish Civil War, the liquidation of the leading Trotskyists in Western Europe in the late 1930s, and the plot to kill Tito in 1953 – all of which were entrusted to the foreign intelligence service.[23] Even after Stalin's death, much of Soviet foreign policy – though far less homicidal – was not cast in a Western mould.

The greatest achievement of the MGB (the immediate predecessor of the KGB) in the aftermath of the Second World War was its central role in the creation of the new Soviet empire in Eastern and Central Europe. That role, according to a sanctimonious Soviet official history, was to 'help the people of liberated countries in establishing and strengthening a free domestic form of government' – in other words, to construct a series of obedient one-party states along the Soviet Union's western borders. Throughout the Soviet Bloc, security and intelligence services, newly created in the image of the MGB, played a crucial part in the establishment of Stalinist regimes. Informers in the German Democratic Republic were seven times more numerous even than in Nazi Germany. As in East Germany, many of the leaders of the new one-party states were not merely loyal Stalinists but also former Soviet agents. In the immediate aftermath of the suppression of the Hungarian Uprising by Soviet tanks in 1956, and again after the destruction of the Prague Spring in 1968, many Western observers doubted whether the genie of freedom could be quickly returned to its bottle. Thanks mainly to the KGB and its Hungarian and Czechoslovak allies, one-party states were restored with remarkable speed and success.[24]

The sanitised history of Soviet intelligence currently propagated by the SVR, the present Russian foreign intelligence service, claims that the First Chief Directorate (FCD), the KGB's foreign intelligence arm, 'honourably and unselfishly did its patriotic duty to Motherland and people'. The FCD, it insists, was not involved in the persecution of dissidents and the abuse of human rights. In reality, it was centrally involved in both. As head of the FCD, Kryuchkov collaborated closely with the KGB Fifth (Ideological Subversion) Directorate in the war against dissidents at home and abroad. During 1977 a total of thirty-two 'active measures', jointly devised by the FCD and the Fifth Directorate, were implemented in an attempt to destabilise and destroy the reputations of the leading dissident, Andrei Sakharov, and his wife, Elena Bonner.

So far from being a mere adjunct to more conventional foreign operations, the FCD's war against the dissidents was one of its chief priorities. Among its most important operations in 1978 was to prevent the dissident, Yuri Orlov, receiving the Nobel Peace Prize – as Sakharov had done three years earlier. Mikhail Suslov, the Politburo's chief guardian of ideological orthodoxy, was woken in the middle of the night by the KGB's Oslo residency to be told the good news (for which it falsely claimed much of the credit) that the prize had gone instead to Anwar Sadat and Menachem Begin. There are few better indications of the importance attached by any intelligence service to a new intelligence report than the decision to wake a minister to inform him or her of it.

It was chiefly because of the immense time and resources expended in the war on all fronts against 'ideological subversion' during the Cold War that the KGB was many times larger than any Western intelligence or security agency. The importance of the KGB's vast system of social control to the survival of the Soviet system only became fully apparent once it began to be relaxed in the late 1980s.

The new freedoms of the Gorbachev era went far to justifying the KGB's earlier fears of the potential damage to the Soviet regime if political dissidents were allowed to proceed with their 'ideological subversion'. In 1989, less than three years after Sakharov was freed from internal exile and allowed to return to Moscow, he established himself, as – in Gorbachev's words – 'unquestionably the outstanding personality' in the Congress of People's Deputies. Almost all the main dissident demands of the early 1970s were now firmly placed on the political agenda.

The manifesto of the leaders of the August 1991 coup, led by Kryuchkov, which attempted to overthrow Gorbachev, implicitly acknowledged that the relaxation of the KGB campaign against ideological subversion had shaken the foundations of the one-party state: 'Authority at all levels has lost the confidence of the population . . . . Malicious mockery of all the institutions of state is being implanted. The country has in effect become ungovernable.'

What the plotters failed to realise was that it was too late to turn back the clock. 'If the *coup d'état* had happened a year and a half or two years earlier,' wrote Gorbachev afterwards, 'it might, presumably, have succeeded. But now society was completely changed.' Crucial to the change of mood was declining respect for the intimidatory power of the KGB, which had hitherto been able to strangle any Moscow demonstration at birth. Large crowds, which a few years earlier could never have assembled, gathered outside the Russian White House to protect it from attack and later circled the Lubyanka, refusing to go home until the giant statue of the founder of the Cheka, Feliks Dzerzhinsky, was toppled from its plinth in the middle of the square outside KGB headquarters.

At the time the speed of the collapse of the Soviet system took almost all observers by surprise. What now seems most remarkable, however, is less the sudden death of the Communist regime at the end of 1991 than its survival for almost seventy-five years. Without the systems of surveillance and repression pioneered by Lenin and Dzerzhinsky, without the KGB's immense Cold War campaign against ideological subversion, the Soviet experience would have been much briefer. The KGB's most enduring achievement was to sustain the longest-lasting one-party state of the twentieth century.[25]

The post-war success of the KGB and the allied agencies created in its own image in imposing one-party states on the peoples of the Soviet Bloc for over forty years provides one of the most depressing lessons of the Cold War. In the course of the twentieth century, intelligence services with unprecedented power to monitor and suppress dissent in all its forms have become central to the structure of authoritarian states. From Iraq to North Korea they are indispensable supports for the world's most unpleasant regimes.

II

Oleg Tsarev

Oleg Tsarev completed his studies in international economics at the Moscow Institute of International Relations (MGIMO) in 1970, and intelligence school in 1971. From 1971 to 1989 he served in the First Chief Directorate of the KGB as a journalist engaged on political intelligence. He served in the Press Bureau of the KGB in 1989–91, and in 1991–2 in the Press Bureau of the SVR (Russian Foreign Intelligence Service). He retired in 1992, becoming a part-time consultant until 1998. He is currently the chairman of a business security consulting company. In 1990 he began research on intelligence history and has published Deadly Illusions *(with the late John Costello; published in USA, Britain, Germany, Russia, 1993), and* Crown Jewels *(with Nigel West; published in Britain and USA, 1998, and forthcoming in Poland and Russia).*

I fully agree with Professor Andrew that, before we can draw lessons about Cold War intelligence, we should know what it was all about. In my paper, which I call 'War or Peace', I shall address this issue and we shall know a little bit more about Stalin's favourite reading, which was intelligence in its raw form.

The Second World War delivered a devastating blow to the countries involved in it. With a little imagination one can easily formulate the vital questions that world leaders faced as hostilities drew to a close. Is there going to be a new war? If so, who with? When is it going to happen? What is it going to be like? What is the enemy's strategy going to be? If there is to be no war, what kind of peace are we going to have? As British military and political leaders tried to find answers to these questions they unwittingly satisfied the curiosity of Soviet leaders. In the post-war years, Soviet intelligence obtained and submitted to Stalin several important documents prepared by British strategists on the subject. Having become familiar with the peace-loving rhet-oric of Anthony Eden, in September 1945 Stalin detected the first call for war in a British document titled 'The Security of the British Empire'. Note that all the quotations that I am using are re-translations from Russian, as the English originals did not survive in the archives.

Eden's apprehensions predictably came true in the form of a memorandum prepared by the post-war Planning Staff with the Chiefs of Staff, who, as Eden had informed Duff Cooper in his 1944 letter, had been studying the problem. This principal docu-ment laid the foundation of British foreign and military policy for many years to come. Dated 29 June 1945, it secretly proclaimed the Cold War at a time when the Alliance was still in being and the Allies were about to take joint action against Japan. The authors of the memorandum, Allen, Curtis and Warburton, said in the preamble that they had reviewed issues of global imperial security for the period 1955–60 and formu-lated their objectives of Britain's general strategy. The memo-randum was intended to serve as a guide to strategy for the Foreign Office and the essential strategic background for the War Office, Admiralty and Air Ministry in planning post-war mili-tary measures. For the purpose of this paper I shall deal only with those paragraphs of the total number of 153 which relate mainly to the Soviet Union. The memorandum opens with the following self-explanatory statement:

Imperial security is in essence an issue of preventing the

possibility of other powers imposing their will on us.
Diplomacy can deal with certain threats and help in
acquiring allies whose territory and military assistance are
important in war, but diplomacy alone cannot be successful
if it does not rely, or if it does not know that it does rely,
on military might sufficient to convince both our friends
and our potential enemies of our capability and resolution
to carry out our obligations. Military might therefore
becomes essential for success in diplomacy and for preventing its failure.

I think it is beautiful and that is why I have decided to quote
it. Having made the case for military power, the authors go on
to assess potential enemies. They wave away Germany, Japan,
France and China as countries which would hardly constitute a
serious threat to the Empire. Paragraph 10 deals with the USA
and the USSR.

Both the USA and the USSR have sufficient potential to
pose a serious threat to the security of the British Empire.
In the case of the USA, taking into account our common
heritage and common language, we think we have the right
to rule out the possibility of war as a result of differences
or conflicts of interests. It is reasonable to admit that Britain
and the US will keep their present unity in the main defence
issues. We don't have such ties with the Soviet Union. The
Soviet Union proved to have a military potential capable to
pose a threat to the British Empire. Therefore in our assessment of Imperial security we, out of mere prudence, have
to take into account the Soviet potential. A certain military
policy can become the most effective deterrent for the USSR
if it thinks of aggression.

In paragraphs 23 and 74, summing up the deliberations on
the Soviet threat, the authors were more outspoken. 'The hostile
USSR poses a maximum threat to the British Empire.'

Discussing measures to counter the Soviet threat, the authors first turn to offensive measures and come to the conclusion that the USSR would be invulnerable to a blockade, its industry and resources would be safe from a land attack and relatively inaccessible to air strikes. It was unlikely that Britain could disrupt Soviet internal communications by offensive actions and the defeat of the USSR could be achieved only in the course of a prolonged war.

Defensive measures included the creation of a West European bloc, as a means to give more depth to British defences in Europe. It was to include France, Holland, Belgium, Norway, Ireland, Iceland, Portugal, Spain and Italy. To improve the morale of this group and to strengthen its joint resources, American support would be invaluable. To protect British communications in the Atlantic and Mediterranean, Britain would need to have naval and air bases on the Continent, in Ireland, Iceland, Atlantic islands, Canada, Newfoundland, Spanish Morocco, Tangier, the Azores and the Balearics.

Protection of India and the Indian Ocean, which after the metropolises ranked second in the British system of strategic values, would also require a whole chain of naval and air bases dispersed in the region with Ceylon as the main operational base. Large land forces should be deployed in the north-west of India and the spread of Soviet influence in Afghanistan stopped. Since the United States had interests in the oil-producing region of the Middle East, number three on the British scale, they should be made to share military obligations for its defence against the Soviet threat. In South-East Asia and the Pacific, moved to fourth place by the authors of the document, another string of forward bases should be stretched with the co-operation of the USA and China from Formosa through the Philippines, Caroline and Marshal Islands to the Island of Midway. The Soviet Union should be prevented from gaining more influence in China than Britain and the USA had.

In the armaments field the authors recommend that Britain

should be ahead of other countries in terms of the military application of scientific and technical progress, especially with the
appearance of, I quote here, 'An explosive many thousand times
more powerful than conventional ones'. Obviously the atomic
bomb was not mentioned directly for security reasons.

Immediate attention was to be paid to other important issues
in connection with the preparation of the Empire for war. Among
them, organisation of an effective intelligence service, use of
propaganda both in peace and wartime, creation of organisation
for underground operations.

There was not much for Stalin to interpret in this document.
It was pretty straightforward, business-like and in essence
amounted to nothing less than a secret declaration of hostilities.
What had been seen by Eden in 1942 as an undesirable possibility – namely, a strong and victorious Russia independent of
Britain and America, and described by him as a disaster in 1944
– the substitution of Russia for Germany and Europe split into
two hostile camps, evolved in 1945 into a blueprint for a global
confrontation. Stalin had to face the fact and whatever his plans
for Eastern Europe could have been, he was only encouraged to
implement them more likely than not for the same reason as the
British would try to implement theirs.

Even a very brief account of the memorandum shows to the
modern reader that it held all the principal and recognisable
components of the Cold War: definition and identification of the
main adversary, military blocs, later to get their appropriate
names, military bases all over the world, arms race, intensified
intelligence activity, propaganda and subversion.

One can also make the curious observation that the origins
of the Cold War were neither ideological nor political. The memorandum is expressly devoid of politics and ideology. First came
the simple fact that the Soviet Union was the only country that
was physically capable of doing harm to the British Empire.
Disregarding the question of whether the Soviet Union really

intended to use its capability, merely being in possession of it was enough for the authors to call it a threat.

Reading the memorandum one can get an impression that the Soviet Union could just as well be a capitalist country, but with an equally awesome potential to justify its being declared a threat to the British Empire. The authors of the memorandum, in a very professional way, left it to politicians to decide on the seriousness of Soviet intentions. In paragraph 4 they say: 'We do not say that a war with the USSR is likely. We decline to make any political forecasts.'

From a number of British documents which later found their way on to Stalin's desk, it could be seen that politicians, especially the Labour politicians who replaced the War Cabinet, rather liked the idea.

Stalin's policy in Europe, encouraged by his assuredness of Western concessions and dictated by similar geo-political principles, in the disguise of Communist rhetoric, provided the necessary political and ideological dressing for the so-far naked truth of the military. Ideas of the Security memorandum were later echoed in Orme Sargent's memorandum on the outcome of war, dated 11 July 1945, in the Joint Intelligence Sub-Committee memorandum of 26 July 1945, that got down to the task of creating an efficient, scientific and technical intelligence service, and in Foreign Secretary Bevin's private talks with his deputies McNeal and Redesdale, when they discussed how to go about creating a West European bloc.

Other British documents of strategic importance which now and then landed on Stalin's desk testified to the fact that with very few alterations the guiding principles of the Security memorandum remained Whitehall's political thinking at least into the early 1950s. It may be a far-reaching conclusion to say that the Western role in the Cold War grew out of the British perception of the Soviet Union's potential and Stalin's policy alone, but this seems to be true at least for the first period of the Cold War.

The fact remains, and later events show, that the recommendations for the security of the British Empire were duly implemented in co-operation with Britain's allies.

Alas, they fell short of their objectives. The British Empire
ceased to exist for reasons other than the Soviet military threat,
and the Cold War lingered on for a little bit longer. Soviet intelligence made sure that the security of the British Empire memorandum did not look like a stray cat, and they provided Stalin
with a stream of similar documents that confirmed and developed the principal considerations of the above.

The question of who the war was going to be with, that is,
who the main adversary was, was answered in another memorandum, titled 'Strategic Position of the British Empire', reported
to Stalin, Molotov and Beria on 17 October 1946. It was put
together by Alan Brooke, former Chief of the General Staff,
Tedder, Chief of the Air Force Staff, and Roderick McGregor,
Chief of the Naval Staff, and it said among other things: 'Recent
events have shown that Russia is our most probable potential
enemy, much more dangerous than a restored Germany. In a
conflict with Russia it would be a vital necessity to seek the
wholehearted participation of the USA on our side from the very
beginning of hostilities.'

On 6 August 1949, after a spell of nearly three years, yet
another fundamental document landed on Stalin's desk. It was
titled 'Strength and Structure of the British Armed Forces', dated
28 February 1949, a 186-page memorandum written by a
working group of representatives of the three Services on orders
of the Chiefs of Staff Committee. Although it was trying to show
how to use £2.5 billion sterling allocated for 1950–3, it
contained, apart from practical things, some important and more
mature strategic evaluation. In the section 'Instructions by the
Chiefs of Staff', there were quoted the working groups' suppo-
sitions. One, there can be no war without US participation in it

as a British ally. The USA will conduct a war against the Soviet Union with all available means. The US contribution to the war against the Soviet Union will be decisive. Two, the old British dominions should take upon themselves a greater responsibility for the defence of all British Commonwealth territory, especially the Indian Ocean and some regions of the Pacific Ocean, in peace and wartime. The Continental countries of the Western Alliance, France and Benelux, will engage their human resources and military potential in the future war, which in particular will create a greater depth of defence for Britain, weakening the efficiency of air strikes against its territory.

Finally, there was one more document, this time by the Chiefs of Staff's joint group. A seventy-page document, dated 1 May 1950 and called 'Defence Policy and Global Strategy', it was submitted to and approved by the Cabinet Defence Committee on 25 May 1950. It found its way on to Stalin's desk on 15 August 1950, that is, less than three months from its approval. In paragraph 2 it gave a more expanded view of who was going to fight Russia: 'Continental Europe cannot fight Russia at war without the US. In their turn, the US cannot fight Russia without the British Commonwealth's assistance. It is senseless to view British or West European strategy as something independent and self-sufficient. Full co-operation with the US is of vital importance both in policy planning and determining means of war. Cold War against Communism is a Global War. Inevitably a Hot War will be the same.'

It did not take a great mind to realise from such pretty straightforward statements that in the case of war the Soviet Union would face a collective adversary and be attacked from every possible angle.

The same bunch of documents dealt of course with the question of when a war was going to be. The question of when seems to be a wider issue than just a date. It's an issue which includes why and under what circumstances, that is, apart from the time factor, it requires an examination of the pre-conditions that are self-sufficient for the start of hostilities.

Orme Sargent, in his 'Summary of the War Results' memorandum, dated 11 July 1945 and reported to Stalin in September 1945, did not believe in an immediate threat. In July 1945 he wrote, 'At present the Soviet Union is so weak that Stalin will hardly be able to pursue his policy of ideological penetration by force, if he has to face obvious resistance. One can say with certainty that he cannot afford to unleash a new war in Europe, it is also doubtful that he should try to conquer new territories.'

A year later Orme Sargent's view was echoed by the military in 'Strategic Position of the British Empire', written by Brooke, Tedder and McGregor, quoted above: 'Russian policy seems to consist in spreading its influence to more distant strategic areas by any means, excluding a big war.'

As in obtaining atomic secrets, Britain's special relations with the USA would, from time-to-time, give Soviet intelligence unique access to what the Americans thought about the contemporary situation. In May 1948 this opportunity came in a letter from Geoffrey Harrison, Russian Section, British Embassy – it's not clear in which country – to R.M.A Hankey, Northern Department, Foreign Office. The letter was dated 1 April 1948 and was reported to the Soviet leadership on 31 May 1948. Harrison wrote,

> The local US Embassy has just finished a memorandum on Soviet intentions and I have had a chance to see it. The American analysis seems to be similar to ours, their conclusions are: the Soviet Union will try to achieve its objectives by all means except war. However, Soviet leaders are watching the situation very closely and have not yet taken the final decision. It will not be taken until the Kremlin is convinced that a) it will not achieve its objectives by means other than war and b) the military potential of the Western

democracies is effectively increasing. This moment may come this year but the odds are that it will arrive next year or the year after, that is 1949 or 1950.

Although the American assessment repeated the British belief that the Soviet Union would try to avoid a big war, it gave the run-up danger period of just under three years, but placed responsibility for any aggressive action on the Kremlin decision-makers and in turn on their assessment of the consequences. It appears that the Cold War mentality, as we know it – we think that they think that we think – was gradually conquering the minds of the main players in the game of too many ifs.

In contrast to such a qualified approach, 'the strength and structure of the British Armed Forces', which was reported to Stalin in August 1949, was much more specific and therefore sounded alarming to the Soviet leadership. The memorandum stated that

further development of British Defence Policy should take into account the following considerations: the possibility of being involved in an unpredictable war in the nearest future, the necessity to create a base for a rearmament programme meant to enable us to conduct a predictable war in about 1957. It was taken into account that the probability of an unpredictable war in the nearest future was less than the possibility of a predictable war in 1957 or later.

The fact that the document mentioned the specific date for a breakout of hostilities was good intelligence, but it did not explain why. Still, here we have a rare opportunity to learn how the analysts in the Committee on Information, a joint intelligence body created by the Politburo in 1947 and disbanded in the early 1950s, commented on the date. Their conclusions were attached to the summary of the British memorandum and equally reported to Stalin. They said,

It follows from the memorandum that Britain bases its war plans on the probability of a war with the Soviet Union in

1957. It should be noted that the same date was mentioned
in a Foreign Office telegram of 28 June 1948 sent to
Washington by the British delegation participating in talks
on the North Atlantic Pact. Taking into account that Britain
could hardly plan a war without considering US intentions
and war plans, one can suppose that 1957 was the tentative date scheduled by the Anglo-American bloc for unleashing a war against the USSR.

The Korean War was the first real test of the big powers in a
local conflict. Britain was seriously alarmed by the American
behaviour, and even more so by the lack of information and co-
ordination of Western foreign and military policy. The Cabinet
decided that urgent talks should be held with the Americans to
resolve the problem. The Foreign Office instructions, as they
were called, were issued to Air Marshal Tedder and Assistant
Deputy Foreign Secretary Denning for military political negotiations with the Chief of Joint Chiefs of Staff Group Bradley, and
the State Department's Special Counsel Jessup, which took place
at the end of July 1950. The fifty-page document was reported
to Stalin on 6 August 1950, that is, in about two weeks. The
instructions were not of an ad hoc but of a long-standing character and permanent value. In the preamble it was especially
noted that they were to be used in any such talks with the British
allies. It expressly stated that Britain wanted to localise the
Korean situation in order to prevent transformation of the
Korean conflict into a world war. It also required of the two
countries to foresee new Soviet bloc advances and try to prevent
the possibility of them achieving success by such actions that
did not include open war.

Giving an assessment of Soviet intentions, the instructions
again touched on the subject of a big war. As an optional Soviet
reaction to American behaviour in the Korean War, the Foreign
Office thought that they may decide that a global conflict was
now inevitable, and would start to concentrate their forces

accordingly. But, the document continued, 'American nuclear superiority makes it unlikely that Russia would intentionally try to be involved now in a World War.' The instructions also assessed the probability of a Western military intervention should the Soviet Union invade Turkey and Iran, 'conditionally, yes, Finland no, Germany and Berlin, unconditionally yes, Yugoslavia, unlikely to be invaded, Greece, unlikely to be invaded'.

The Foreign Office instructions was one of those documents that by way of a reference gave a most valuable insight into another British paper. In Appendix B, which dealt with Soviet intentions in general, it quoted from the Joint Intelligence Committee memorandum, 'Probability of a war with the Soviet Union and the date when the Soviet leaders may be ready to start the war'. It was approved in the spring of 1950 and contained, as the author said, the following well-considered conclusions:

a) Soviet policy is based on the conviction that the world victory of Communism is inevitable and this can be achieved without the Soviet Union being involved in a world war with the non-Communist world if the Soviet Union is strong enough to thwart capitalist aggression. b) Therefore it is not in the interests of the Soviet Union to start a world war intentionally, especially in view of the enormous hardships that the Soviet Union would suffer from use of the atom bomb; thus, it is unlikely that they should wish to unleash a world war . . . . d) However, the time may come when the Soviet leaders think they are strong enough to repel any military strike by Western powers, and then they may speed up implementation of their plans for expansion of their influence and control, ignoring Western reaction. Under such circumstances, Western powers will be forced to start a war in order to protect their vital interests. e) On the other hand, we may not exclude the possibility of the Soviet leaders coming to believe that Western states intend to attack the

USSR, and therefore they will decide to strike first. f) The Soviet Army and Navy are probably sufficiently prepared for a big war now. By 1952 the Soviet Union will have a considerable number of atom bombs, but, without an economic crisis in the West, it is unlikely that the Soviet leaders will decide to provoke a war until the Soviet Air Force and the economy are adequately prepared. The available data indicates that this will not happen before 1955.

Well, to sum it up, at the end of the decade, the West, or at least Britain, believed that the likely date for the Soviet Union to attack its adversary was 1955, while Stalin was left to solve the puzzle of 1957 as the co-ordinated Anglo-American date for unleashing a war against the Soviet Union.

As early as summer 1945, Stalin could be satisfied that Britain was not aware of his intentions. This clearly followed from Orme-Sargent's summary memorandum of the results of the war. With some irony, the author stated that, unlike Hitler and Mussolini who publicly disclosed their intentions, 'Stalin will not do us such a favour, and that is why we should ourselves try and find out his plans and the tactics that he is going to use for their implementation'.

In 1946 Brooke, Tedder and McGregor, in their 'Strategic Position of the British Empire', must have been more assured in saying that Russian policy seemed to consist in spreading its influence to more distant strategic areas by any means, excluding a big war. To avert the Soviet threat and to secure Britain's main strongholds, the authors suggested that Britain

> should make sure that in any conflict we have a sufficient depth of front in our main strongholds, which will enable us to mobilise our main forces and activate US resources, not agree to Russia having a possibility of gaining large additional human resources and war materials in peacetime, keep the necessary bases from which Russian vital territories can be attacked by air or by long-range weapons. These bases

can serve us as one of the powerful deterrents and the only means of defence available in a period of hostilities.

At the end, Brooke, Tedder and McGregor stressed the long-standing character of their strategic assessments and recommendations. They said, 'the above strategic considerations are based on geographical facts and information on the allocation of human and natural resources that are not changeable, therefore we believe that the main principle of our strategy will not undergo radical changes, due to the development of new war methods.'

About three years passed and 'The Strength and Structure of the British Armed Forces' memorandum recommended a much more modest and realistic military policy. It plainly stated that the main task of the British Armed Forces was defence of British territory:

Our prime responsibility should be security of the United Kingdom and preservation of its territories, a base for an allied defensive. This task includes air defence of Britain, defence of our territorial waters and naval communications, and limited assistance to the armed forces of the Western Alliance as a measure taken in our own interests. At the same time the British Armed Forces were to defend the Middle East to make possible deployment of Allied Forces in this region.

Having singled out defence of British territory as the main task, the authors insisted on building a strong defence system, rather than providing the Armed Forces with offensive weapons. In the authors' view, intelligence was no less important than scientific research and experiments. Intelligence funds were to be increased by £4.5 million sterling. This meant better working conditions and higher salaries for intelligence officers, more information-gathering on the Soviet Union and East European countries, including science and technology, SIGINT and use of open information.

When reporting the summary of this almost 200-page document to Stalin, the Committee on Information analysts added
their conclusions. They rightly noted that the memorandum
contained recommendations that could be altered by the Chiefs
of Staff Committee, and they went on, 'while Britain is concentrating on economic problems, the main financial burden in the
war preparations in the British view should be carried by the
USA. While the Americans want a greater mobilisation of British
and West European resources, this will lead to sharpening of
contradictions between Britain and the US.' Then came the
inevitable ideological note: 'As Britain wants to stay away from
active military operations, limiting its war effort to the defence
of the metropolis, the main war effort, in their calculations,
should be taken by the USA, West European continental countries and the British dominions.'

While the above paper was a gift to Soviet military planners
and media propagandists, the next one dealt with the much more
serious matter of a Hot War and the role of atomic weapons.
For the first time the Defence Policy and Global Strategy memorandum by the Chiefs of Staff Joint Group, submitted to Stalin
on 15 August 1950, defined the Western objective in a war with
the Soviet Union.

So, what was the objective of a 'Hot War'? According to paragraph 9, 'if a Hot War is forced upon Western countries, then
its objective remains in principle the same as that of the Cold
War. Our main concerns should be to survive, withstand and
outlive the first attack. Our final military objective should be to
bring the war to an end in the shortest possible time, without
allowing Western Europe to collapse, and to defeat Russian military might and the present regime.'

From the above it is clear that the kind of peace that East and
West were going to have between themselves was in fact balancing on the verge of war, with the war itself taking place between
1955, the estimated Russian attack, and 1957, the estimated

Western attack, or anywhere from then on, circumstances permitting. The kind of peace was merely preparation for a war or a peaceful confrontation, better known as the Cold War.

Orme-Sargent's thirty-page memorandum, summarising the results of the war, was the first document to reach Stalin that called for a stand-down with the Soviet Union:

6. . . . Stalin will not necessarily consider strengthening his position by way of conquering territories. He can achieve his objectives in the countries he thinks important by conquering what one may call ideological living space . . . .

9. If we have to confront Russia, it is just the right moment for us to challenge Russia in the above-mentioned six countries (Finland, Poland, Czechoslovakia, Austria, Yugoslavia and Bulgaria, even if we have to agree to Russia having the upper hand in Romania and Hungary) instead of waiting for Russia to threaten us farther in the West and South – in Germany, Italy and Turkey.

Almost five years separated Orme-Sargent's views and the Chiefs of Staff Joint Group's seventy-page memorandum on Defence Policy and Global Strategy, dated 1 May 1950, submitted to and approved by the Cabinet Defence Committee on 25 May 1950, and seen by Stalin on 15 August 1950. The latter gave a much better thought-out presentation, since its authors had more experience of East-West confrontation. Outlining 'Allied defence policy and global strategy', this document formulated its objective as 'making Russia and its satellites give up further military and ideological aggression and at the same time creating conditions under which nations with different methods of government will be able to co-exist peacefully'.

At the same time, in a paragraph titled 'Cold War objective', the authors struck the familiar confrontational note that was hardly compatible with peaceful co-existence proclaimed a few lines earlier: the Cold War objective, 'which is to be achieved possibly without real military action, requires, first, stabilisation of the anti-Communist front in the modern free world and then, when the Western powers become less weak in military terms, intensification of Cold War measures aimed at loosening Russia's control over the satellite countries and eventually at achieving their complete independence from Russian control'.

The authors said that in their view there were three possible stages in the Cold War. Their timing would be determined by the correlation of conventional armaments and the scientific and technical capability of the Western powers and Russia.

a) Stage 1, where we find ourselves now, is a stage of restraint . . . . The military might of the Western powers on the whole is so weak that purely from the military point of view Russia is able at any moment to advance to the Atlantic. The fact that it has not yet done so can be explained by its understanding that the definite consequence of aggression will be a war with the United States that will mean an immediate counterattack with atomic weapons.

b) Stage 2 (near parity between Russia and the US) will come when Russia has a stock of atomic weapons big enough to be of decisive importance in a war against the United Kingdom which the Russians must see as the key to Western defences . . . . We reject the very idea of a preventive war against Russia. Our Cold War policy at that stage will require more than ever an efficient defence against atomic attack.

c) Stage 3 will come when scientific methods of defence make the use of conventional bombers so expensive that it will be impractical. The West may become invulnerable first. Russia, because of the large territory it has to defend, may remain vulnerable. If Russia stops being vulnerable to conventional bombers then we shall return to a period which preceded the epoch of strategic bombing. The West will become relatively weak.

During Stage 3 we should develop a radio-controlled type of supersonic bomber, or some other machine that is capable of carrying atomic or other weapons to the heart of Russia, despite the most modern means of defence.

In terms of military research the memorandum recommended an early version of the arms race:

'15. The allies should concentrate their efforts on the research and development of defence weapons in order to guarantee their survival and offensive weapons for attacking distant areas of Russia.'

Conclusion

At the beginning of this paper I posed questions that Western and Soviet leaders were likely to ask of the intelligence services. And they certainly did, maybe wording them differently, because with the coming of the Nuclear Age those were questions of life and death. Now we know that the Soviet intelligence service provided Stalin with a rare opportunity to have a much better look at his opponents' plans and intentions than merely watching and interpreting the superficial course of events would have allowed. The intelligence that landed on Stalin's desk gave two dates, 1955 and 1957, for a possible Western attack. The first date was calculated by Western analysts, subject to the Soviet leaders having concluded that the Soviet Union was strong enough to win a war with the West. Therefore the first date was conditional. There are good reasons to believe that so was the second date. Plainly speaking, precise dates were not important; the question of when was rather a matter of circumstance and military superiority.

Who is it going to be with? The available documents gave a clear answer: it will be a global war with the United States participating in it from the very beginning. The number of countries involved on the Western side could be easily calculated by adding those of the North Atlantic Treaty and British Commonwealth. What is it going to be like? A nuclear war with air attacks deep into Soviet territory and guided from the Middle East. The war's objective would be to destroy Soviet military power and the regime, but even so, Britain admitted that at least up to 1950 the West was weak enough to let the Soviet army occupy the whole of Western Europe. Stalin was not tempted.

The likelihood of war being dependent on military superiority, the arms race was spurred on up to a point that the Soviet economy could not withstand. If it was not losing the arms race, it was losing on the economic front. Communist ideals became bleaker and bleaker. Enormous changes have taken place since. Former adversaries have become partners, more areas of government and military activity have become open, new challenges are inviting a joint intelligence effort: non-proliferation of nuclear weapons, terrorism, drugs, organised crime, ecology.

But whatever changes are taking place, as long as secrets remain intelligence services will try to penetrate them, not because they are staffed by evil men, as some with second-hand knowledge of intelligence may think. Their governments ask the same old questions: if there is a secret, is there not something that may mean danger to my country? No? Then why keep it secret? True, we are partners and may exchange our military plans, but how do I know that the other side has given me genuine plans? In a changing world, intelligence services will be kept busy, though their priorities, as seen by various governments, are changing with the world.

GENERAL DISCUSSION

Opening the discussion, the chairman of the session, Professor Donald Cameron Watt, stressed that assessors often submitted alarming reports, not so much to frighten the enemy, as to extract more money and resources from their governments. This view was indirectly reinforced by James Woolsey, a former Director of Central Intelligence, who remarked that it was doubtful that the British had serious plans to launch a strike against the Soviet Union with the aid of the British Empire, if only because within two years after the war they began to dismantle that very Empire. As for the support of the USA, regarded as essential in the Foreign Office papers handed over to the Russians, this, in Woolsey's view, would have to have been wilfully abandoned by Britain when it joined with Israel and France in attacking Suez and alienating its principal ally. An analogous point was made by a former member of British Military Intelligence, who noted that, while the Chiefs of Staff paper by Brooke, Tedder and McGregor clearly identified the Soviet Union as the future enemy and included the comment that Britain should prevent war materials being accrued by the Soviet Union, the Attlee Government in 1946 made the extraordinary decision to present to the USSR the most reliable and most powerful jet engine in the world. Twenty-five Rolls-Royce Nene engines were sent just in time to be fitted into the prototype MiG15, turning it into a world-beating aircraft, superior to the F86 Sabre in the Korean War. This necessarily cast doubt on the influence of the Chiefs of Staff paper.

Oleg Tsarev replied that Stalin was given raw intelligence and read it voraciously. The absence of evaluation and assessment, which would have involved political judgements his aides were too afraid to make, meant that such materials lacked depth and background. Bellicose contents in such seemingly high-level documents could obviously have unfortunate consequences.

Another former member of British Military Intelligence suggested that paranoia and political correctness were two causes of the Soviet failure of intelligence analysis. Noting that Oleg Tsarev had mentioned a figure of nearly a quarter of a million decrypts for 1961 alone, he added that the KGB must have been simply swamped by the sheer volume of information, and that much of it was speculative rubbish of the kind that might have been found in the *Economist* or *The Times* at the time.

Following up this point, Christopher Andrew noted that Soviet practice had changed with time. He agreed that analysts had been too afraid to give Stalin their analyses; they had given him documents and snippets from documents, and the same was largely true of Khrushchev. This only changed under Andropov, who was himself a long-standing former head of the KGB. Despite this change, Gorbachev's damning indictment of the analyses provided to him in 1985 carried a larger implication than for that particular year.

As for the paranoia, Andrew pointed out that this too changes over time. Documents that he was given in 1990–1 show that in December 1990 the Soviet press reported a speech by KGB chief Kryuchkov – who had been chief of foreign intelligence for fourteen years – in which he warned of the deliberate infection of Soviet grain imports from the USA. The same document had been classified a few years earlier and brought out by Oleg Gordievsky in 1984. Similarly, in January 1991 Prime Minister Pavlov talked about Western plans to destabilise the rouble. The last speech by Kryuchkov in a closed session of the Supreme Soviet on 18 June 1991 declassified on the spot an assessment of 1977, where he revealed a CIA master-plan to teach young Soviet leaders sabotage of various kinds, to lead the economy into dead ends and to lead scientific research into dead ends. The two elements, of paranoia and political correctness, Andrew concluded, were a constant, and indeed that political correctness is an inevitable feature of authoritarian regimes to a greater degree than in the West. It is institutionalised in authoritarian regimes.

Tsarev recognised that a lot of intelligence could be found in newspapers and magazines of good reputation, and recalled that the question of whether or not Hitler was going to attack Russia was widely discussed, the newspapers were full of it. But the question for Stalin was to know which of the two options was true. Is he going to attack or is he not going to attack? Is it a bluff or is it a real threat? And he was unable to make the right choice. The intelligence supplied to him pointed in both directions. There was no analytical service at that time. He took a more recent example: will the Western forces bomb Kosovo or will they not bomb Kosovo? It was discussed, the newspapers carried arguments for and against, but for an analyst to make an intelligence assessment he has to know which answer is correct. If he makes the right choice, he has provided good intelligence.

A Canadian academic asked Oleg Tsarev whether the documents show any indication that the KGB was aware of major differences of strategic assessment in the intelligence field in this period between the British and Americans? More broadly, he asked both speakers if they thought it was yet possible to say whether or not the contending intelligence services knew of the abilities and role of their counterpart services, and whether anybody ever raised the issue of whether such abilities, or lack of them, in the intelligence field was a danger to international security.

Oleg Tsarev replied that he had not seen any comparative assessment of the intelligence capabilities of either side. He noted that the Soviet agency networks at that time were virtually frozen, both in Britain and America, with information coming only from Kim Philby and occasionally Anthony Blunt. Soviet intelligence therefore had some knowledge of current developments in the British and American intelligence worlds, such as the creation of the CIA and the agreement on co-operation between SIS and the Central Intelligence Bureau. The main supply of documents began only in 1948, when Guy Burgess was reactivated and contact with John Cairncross was re-established.

Christopher Andrew noted that he too had seen no comparative assessment of British and Soviet intelligence for the period of the early Cold War. All the evidence points to the fact, he said, that the KGB did not produce assessments of the kind that are made in the West by, say, the JIC. For instance, all the material on the Cuban Missile Crisis has been analysed, yet the KGB Chairman, Semichastny, never once made an assessment of the possible US reaction to the placing of missile bases in Cuba. What is provided day in and day out are either full-length documents, as Oleg Tsarev said, or else snippets which are assembled, but with very little assessment related to them.

On the sources of his British documents, Tsarev said that 'Security of the British Empire' was supplied by Philby, although this could only be deduced from the circumstantial facts supplied by the agency. Everything connected with British military planning and armaments was supplied by Cairncross. The Korean document he cited, concerning instructions for the negotiations between the British and the Americans, was supplied by Burgess, probably the last document he supplied before leaving London. The sources, in other words, were the 'Big Five'.

Donald Watt pointed out that Chiefs of Staff documents would have existed in at least fifty copies, that they circulated fairly widely within the various centres which would include heads of sections in SIS, and would certainly have covered heads of commands. They would come from the Planning Staff and the Joint Planning Committee and would then circulate to the Cabinet, and actually identifying who leaked a particular document would have been as difficult then as it is today.

Notes to Christopher Andrew's paper

1. Christopher Andrew and David Dilks (eds), *The Missing Dimension: Governments and Intelligence Communities in the Twentieth Century* (Macmillan, London, 1984).
2. Christopher Andrew, 'Intelligence and International Relations in the Early Cold War', *Review of International*

Studies, no. 24 (1998), pp. 321–2.

3. Desmond Ball, *Soviet Signals Intelligence (SIGINT)* (Australian National University, Canberra, 1989); Desmond Ball and Robert Windren, 'Soviet Signals Intelligence (Sigint): Organisation and Management', *Intelligence and National Security*, vol. 4, no. 4 (1989).

4. Christopher Andrew and Vasili Mitrokhin, *The Mitrokhin Archive: The KGB in Europe and the West* (Allen Lane, The Penguin Press, London, 1999), ch. 21.

5. Admiral Fulvio Martini, *Nome in codice: ULISSE* (Rizzoli, Milan, 1999), pp. 19–20.

6. Andrew and Mitrokhin, *The Mitrokhin Archive*, pp. 200, 361–2, 459, 601, 603, 608–9, 621, 628, 630, 718. On DARIO, see the additional information in the Italian edition, *L'Archivio Mitrokhin* (Rizzoli, Milan, 1999), pp. 693–4.

7. *Ibid.*, pp. 458–9, 625–6.

8. David Kahn, 'Soviet Comint in the Cold War', *Cryptologia*, vol. 22 (1998).

9. The growing literature on VENONA includes: Daniel Patrick Moynihan, *Secrecy: The American Experience* (Yale University Press, New Haven, 1998); Allen Weinstein and Alexander Vassiliev, *The Haunted Wood: Soviet Espionage in America – The Stalin Era* (Random House, NY, 1999); John Earl Haynes and Harvey Klehr, *VENONA: Decoding Soviet Espionage in America* (Yale University Press, New Haven, 1999); Christopher Andrew, 'The Venona Secret', in K. G. Robertson (ed.), *War, Resistance and Intelligence: Essays in Honour of M. R. D. Foot* (Leo Cooper, Barnsley, 1999).

10. Andrew, *For the President's Eyes Only: Secret Intelligence and the American Presidency from Washington to Bush* (HarperCollins, London/NY, 1995), chs 5, 6; Andrew, 'Intelligence and International Relations in the Early Cold War', pp. 329–30.

11. *Preparing for the 21st Century: An Appraisal of US*

Intelligence, Report of the Commission on the Roles and Capabilities of the United States Intelligence Community, 1 March 1996.

12. On the decline and fall of the US JIC, see the forthcoming Cambridge PhD thesis by Larry Valero, due for submission in 2000.

13. *In from the Cold: The Report of the Twentieth Century Fund Task Force on the Future of US Intelligence* (Twentieth Century Fund Press, NY, 1996).

14. *Preparing for the 21st Century*, p. xv.

15. Alex Craig, 'The Joint Intelligence Committee and British Intelligence Assessment, 1945–1956', unpublished Cambridge PhD thesis, 1999.

16. Sir Percy Cradock, *In Pursuit of British Interests: Reflections on Foreign Policy under Margaret Thatcher and John Major* (John Murray, London, 1997).

17. That proposition is argued in detail in Andrew, *For the President's Eyes Only*.

18. *Ibid.*, chs 4, 5.

19. *Ibid.*, chs 6, 7, 13.

20. Ben Fischer, *A Cold War Conundrum: The 1983 Soviet War Scare* (CIA Center for the Study of Intelligence, Washington, DC, 1997). This otherwise very valuable study contains a somewhat inaccurate Appendix B on Gordievsky himself (in particular on his interpretation of the role of Harry Hopkins in the Second World War).

21. Robert Gates, *From the Shadows* (Touchstone, NY, paperback edition 1997), p. 562.

22. Andrew and Mitrokhin, *The Mitrokhin Archive*, Conclusion.

23. *Ibid.*, ch. 5, pp. 462–6.

24. *Ibid.*, chs 15, 16.

25. *Ibid.*, pp. 16–17, chs 19, 20, Conclusion.

AFTER-DINNER SPEECH

R. James Woolsey

R. James Woolsey is a partner at the Washington DC law firm of Shea & Gardner, where he has practised at various times since 1973. He served as Director of Central Intelligence from 1993 to 1995. His other US Government appointments include: Ambassador to the Negotiation on Conventional Armed Forces in Europe (CFE), Vienna, 1989–91; Presidential Delegate at Large to the US-Soviet Strategic Arms Reduction Talks (START) and Nuclear and Space Arms Talks (NST), 1983–6; Under-Secretary of the Navy, 1977–9; General Counsel to the US Senate Committee on Armed Services, 1970–3. During military service in the US army, he served as an adviser on the US delegation to the Strategic Arms Limitation Talks (SALT I), Helsinki and Vienna, 1969–70. He has been a member of the following official bodies: the Commission to Assess the Ballistic Missile Threat to the US (Rumsfeld Commission), 1998; the President's Commission on Federal Ethics Law Reform, 1989; the President's Blue Ribbon Commission on Defense Management (Packard Commission), 1985–6; and the President's Commission on Strategic Forces (Scowcroft Commission), 1983. He is currently a Trustee of the Center for Strategic & International Studies and Chairman of the Advisory Committee of the Clean Fuels Foundation.

Looking around the room, this may be the finest collection in modern times of brilliant minds considering intelligence issues, with the exception (and here I'll borrow a formulation of President Kennedy's) of those times when R.V. Jones dined alone.

I was in a group a year or so ago hearing a panel that included the Holocaust survivor and human rights spokesman, Elie Wiesel. The panel was asked what the major challenges of the twenty-first century were to be, and the other panel members each said something rather predictable. They talked about the challenges of the information revolution and the challenges of the globalised economy and the challenges of this and the challenges of that. But when it came to Elie he said, 'No, the principal challenge of the twenty-first century is going to be exactly the same as the principal challenge of the twentieth century: how do we deal with fanaticism armed with power?'

I want to talk tonight about the role of intelligence in facing Elie Wiesel's challenge. Because although there are other challenges for intelligence, and there are other useful things that intelligence can do, unless we can deal decisively and effectively with fanaticism armed with power – all of us from the Western democracies, and I include our friends from the new democracy of Russia in this – nothing else really will matter.

From 1914 into the 1990s, fanaticism armed with power was principally situated in the governments of authoritarian and totalitarian states. The weapons which the democracies used, the military forces, the sinews of war, the intelligence, all were designed in one way or another principally to deal with that problem: the armed authoritarian or totalitarian state. Whether the focus of intelligence was decyphering the Zimmerman Telegram, breaking the German and Japanese codes in the Second World War, stealing the war plans of the Warsaw Pact, or learning about potential Soviet developments in stealth aircraft, whatever we focused on was principally the work of a powerful state – a state that had a doctrine, serious military and other capabilities, and, from the point of view of the democracies, clearly hostile intentions.

These struggles really had two principal characteristics.

First of all, there was a certain predictability to much of the conduct of the authoritarian or totalitarian state. The way that the Soviet Union self-destructed was for most observers not highly foreseeable. There were a few notable exceptions such as Ronald Reagan and Daniel Patrick Moynihan, but I guess what I think about that is that perhaps the Irish just hear voices that the rest of us don't hear. But in their day-to-day operations the authoritarian and totalitarian states had important secrets that were available to be stolen and that we needed to steal, and that was the principal purpose of the collection of intelligence. Certainly those stolen secrets might be put together with openly available material, but stealing these states' secrets was at the heart of what we were doing, and the key point is that these states were somewhat predictable in the way they went about what they did. If you watched seven test ranges with your tele-metry collection and your reconnaissance satellites, and you used as a template the developmental schedule that our spies had stolen from the Soviet military, you would be able to track Soviet developments rather precisely and even to design your own weapon systems to enter production in exactly the right year, so that they could be deployed in time to counter, for example, a new Soviet jammer when it came on-line.

In addition to there being a certain degree of predictability in their day-to-day behaviour, the imminent threats posed by the dictatorships were episodic. When an enemy, whether it was the Kaiser or Hitler or the Japanese military or Stalin's Soviet Union, glowered, and especially when it had a success, the Western democracies tended to rally and rally rather well – not always, but most of the time they rallied rather well. If you began unre-stricted submarine warfare against the Western democracies, or cornered them at Dunkirk, or initiated the Blitz, or bombed Pearl Harbor, or attacked South Korea, or conquered Kuwait, we did not always come through, but in the vast majority of circum-stances, in one way or another, we got mobilised and, in the vernacular, slightly cleaned up, handed the opponent his hat, his *derrière* and his overcoat.

We were really rather good at mobilising for crises. But in between those challenges it was a different story. I believe this difference in performance when there is a clear challenge and when there is not is a general characteristic of democracies. Certainly preparedness was not at the heart of this fine country's agenda in the years of the 1920s and the early 1930s. But let me illustrate the episodic nature of what we did principally by referring to the United States. And I want to use as a metaphor something that Dwight Eisenhower talked about all of his life. It was an example that had been used to him by his teacher at Staff and Command School, at Leavenworth, Kansas, when he was a young major after the First World War. His teacher said to him that if you want to understand how we, and he meant the United States, deal with really serious problems, you have to understand the wagon train.

What I would surmise Ike's teacher meant was the following: a wagon train is a unique institution. People are going about their daily business in the East, as farmers, ranchers, shopkeepers, ministers, and an objective comes up, say to get to California. A temporary society is then pulled together. It's a remarkable society in its way. It's voluntary. It's a meritocracy – it doesn't matter what your name is, or how much money you have, or what your status is, if you are the best person to lead the wagon train you will lead the wagon train. It's almost familial in its nature – for the time that it exists everyone pulls together, all for one and one for all. It accomplishes remarkable things – crossing the plains, fighting off Indian attacks, going through blizzards, climbing mountains, fording rivers – but when it gets to California, hey, it's beach time. The wagon train disbands, and everyone goes off to be a shopkeeper or a rancher or a minister or a farmer.

Those who crossed the continent on a wagon train often looked back on the experience as marking the best years of their lives, because of the sense of commitment, the sense of common purpose, and the accomplishments. But no one – and this is the point – believed it's the way anyone should live all the time. It was an exception. It was an episode.

The United States and many other Western democracies – this country as well – have dealt with these crises over the last century by organising, in a sense, a wagon train. Recall with me for a moment, though, what one important period in between wagon trains was like. Focusing, since I am going to be critical, on my own country, recall with me an earlier era from American history, the last time we had a full decade of peace and prosperity, having, with our allies, won a major war: the First World War. Unlike the Cold War, that war was hot – the war to end all wars. The period that immediately followed was the roaring '20s of course. Over across the Atlantic, we roared with jazz, we roared with talkies, we roared with speakeasies, the stock market roared – beginning to sound familiar? – and while we were roaring and while we were happy and prosperous, we blew it.

We blew it, at least in my country, because of a propensity for material self-indulgence in such times, and we also exhibited our remarkable national capacity for naïveté. The President of the United States in the 1920s at one point said, 'the business of America is business', suggesting that the business of America was only business. To our French and British allies who had suffered so terribly in the First World War, and to whom we had lent substantial funds for recovery, when they asked for some relief from the debt, the President growled, 'They hired the money, didn't they?'

We put heavy faith in those days into arms control agreements. After all, if you have the Washington and London Naval Agreements that cover the biggest strategic weapons at the time – battleships – and you put numerical and length limitations on battleships, certainly there would never be any more strategic wars, right? We also signed the Kellogg-Briand Pact. Germany and Japan signed it. It was a lovely agreement. It outlawed war.

How could you ever have war again if you had such an agreement?

But my favourite example of the spirit of the times is from the field of intelligence. A wonderful man, a hard-nosed, tough, able, crusty old Republican, Henry Stimson, who was Woodrow Wilson's Secretary of War in the First World War and Franklin Roosevelt's in the Second World War, in between, in the late 1920s, was Secretary of State. And Stimson, when he was Secretary, closed down the State Department's codebreaking because, he later explained, after all 'gentlemen don't read one another's mail'. Well, Stimson I'm sure was very pleased when he was later Secretary of War to realise that some British codebreakers had been less than gentlemanly with respect to German codes during the inter-war years and some American naval codebreakers had been less than gentlemanly with respect to Japanese codes.

But it is not really fair to blame Stimson, Coolidge, Hoover or any of the politicians of this inter-war era for not being clairvoyant. Even Churchill in the 1920s didn't really see what was coming in Germany. Until the Depression of the early 1930s, no one did. But it is fair to blame these men because they weren't careful. And their lack of care, I fear, bears some resemblance to the behaviour of most of the leaders of the Western democracies in today's safe and comfortable mood.

As in the 1920s, the threats that we face today are vague and inchoate, at least in terms of not being embodied clearly in one or two powerful ideological foes. The fanatic – North Korea, Iraq, Osama bin Laden – are not that powerful, and the powerful, at least those that could destroy us within the flight time of an ICBM – China and Russia – are not fanatic. But the question is, how can we better see the potential of fanaticism being wedded with power in the days to come, the months to come, the years to come, and how can we prepare to deal with that possibility better than our grandfathers' generation did in the 1920s?

I would submit that there are three sets of actors on whom we really need to focus by way of intelligence collection and assessment. The first are two major states, powerful states still with their important military forces. One, China, is still a Communist dictatorship, although a complicated one that is improving and modernising its economy in a sporadic but in some ways impressive way. The other, Russia, is a fellow democracy, but a very troubled one. One of the key problems in both countries is the propensity of both military industrial complexes, to some degree influenced by corruption and to some degree, in Russia at least, involved with organised crime, for disseminating weapons of mass destruction and the wherewithal for making them and carrying them – everything from missile guidance systems to fissionable material.

It is important and helpful that the central governments of both Russia and China are willing to work with us on these questions of proliferation, but it is still an extraordinarily serious problem for the entire world. Also, particularly with respect to China, we need to be concerned that economic development and especially the disestablishment of the large state-owned enterprises may produce unemployment so great that the Chinese leaders will begin to feel that they have to play the nationalism card in order to keep things from getting out of hand. The obvious focus for expressions of nationalism is Taiwan, because Taiwan as a free economy and a political democracy is a living, breathing affront to the rulers in Beijing, much the same way that Solidarity Poland was an affront to the Soviet Union at the end of the 1980s. And the tension between China and Taiwan could potentially drag us into a confrontation or, even worse, hostilities with a nuclear armed state.

Second, we need to focus on rogue states, I would say especially Iraq and North Korea, although Iran, and in some circumstances perhaps Libya, could conceivably play a vigorous rogue-state role. Iran seems to me to be now a much more complex case after President Khatemi's election two years ago, and Libya is relatively weak. I would think the principal focus ought to be on Iraq and North Korea, the first ruled by a very rigid and evil man, and the second ruled by a gentleman who is sort of a cross between Caligula and Baby Doc Duvalier.

The third major subject and set of actors on which I think we need to focus is terrorist groups. The terrorist groups that most of us began looking at in the 1970s generally wanted a place at the table: ETA, the Basque group in Spain, is one good example. They sometimes did very brutal things and killed a lot of people unnecessarily, but ultimately they had some type of a political objective.

The newer terrorist groups that we now need to deal with – whether it's Osama bin Laden and his friends in the Middle East, Aum Shenrikyu, or a red, white and blue terrorist such as Timothy McVeigh, the bomber of the Murrah building in Oklahoma City – do not want a place at the table at all. They want to blow up the table and pretty much all of us, including themselves if need be, who are sitting at the table. And that type of terrorism, although it's not altogether new in the world, nevertheless in terms of the number of groups involved and the degree of fanaticism presents a difference in degree from the past that approaches a difference in kind.

Secondly, the vast expansion of available information through the internet and the world-wide web, means that virtual groups may come together and that expertise in the technology of, say, biological weapons, can be transmitted to the fanatics using e-mail and web sites. So people are able to come together to do things in new and creative terrorist ways, just the way lots of us come together in new and creative ways in the same medium for positive purposes.

For each of those three types of entities – major states, rogue states and terrorist groups – I would suggest that the instrumentalities that might be used to arm fanaticism with power are several, and these instrumentalities ought to be our principal intelligence focus. The first is, of course, weapons of mass destruction, including particularly nuclear and biological, and the materials and technical knowledge for constructing such. Second, the wherewithal to deploy long-range systems that can carry such weapons, especially ballistic missiles, but cruise missiles as well. It is worth noting that even without weapons of mass destruction, and with only commercially available hardware and software, missiles having GPS guidance – together with 1-metre resolution imagery, available within hours on the web from commercial reconnaissance satellites for a few hundred dollars – will be able to be used very effectively against many targets.

I don't believe that the conventional military threats with which most of our militaries are principally designed to deal are likely to be the instrumentalities through which we are going to suffer damage from fanaticism armed with power, at least for many years. These threats are not irrelevant and certainly we have to be able to deal with them, and this is made especially difficult in circumstances in which nuclear or biological weapons might also be involved. This might be the case, for example, if Iraq possessed one or both types of weapons and then again took Kuwait, or if North Korea attacked South Korea and threatened using ballistic missiles and weapons of mass destruction against Japan and perhaps also portions of the United States, or if China moved with conventional forces against Taiwan and threatened us with weapons of mass destruction in the midst of such hostilities. So conventional weapons and conventional forces are far from irrelevant, but increasingly they are only likely to be used by a state to challenge us if that state can also threaten us and others with weapons of mass destruction.

Two types of economic weapons might well also be used by fanaticism armed with power to the great disadvantage of the Western democracies.

One is the denial of oil. As more and more of the world's

proven reserves come to be concentrated in the Mid-East – probably about two-thirds in the Persian Gulf and another several per cent in the Caspian Basin – it is becoming apparent to the International Energy Agency of the OECD, to the authors of recent major articles in *Science Magazine* and *Scientific American*, and to many others, that much of the rest of the world is going to see production start to turn down within the next few years. I'm not talking about heavy oil or tar sands, I'm talking about conventional oil. That production decline in the rest of the world in turn is going to produce a situation in which, according to *Fortune* magazine last year, approximately $1.5 trillion over and above the current level of flow will go to the Middle East over the course of the next fifteen years. To use only one example, again according to *Fortune*, as Asia comes back on-line after its economic problems of the last few years, by 2010 Asia alone through economic growth will add 9 billion barrels a day to world oil demand. That is more than Saudi Arabia pumps every day. The second type of economic weapon on which we need to focus is information-system attacks. The information infrastructure of our country and certainly of many Western democracies is highly vulnerable, and it does not require a major effort by a major state to create very substantial problems in such things as pipelines, electricity power grids, and the like.

I have not put on this list a number of other challenges – such as those posed by the situations in Somalia, Haiti, Bosnia, Kosovo, East Timor – not because involvement in those areas is unimportant, but because I don't believe that such problems are what drives, or should drive, the design and operation of our intelligence systems, nor should they be our major focus in trying to keep ourselves from suffering at the hands of fanaticism armed with power.

If weapons of mass destruction and the delivery systems for them, including terrorists, and economic weapons in the form of oil deprivation or information-systems attacks could be said to be the major issues, then the next thing to ask is what are the secrets about them that intelligence needs to steal and how should we go about doing the stealing?

I would add that for the reasons I have set out I favour some movement towards ballistic missile defence for all of us, and I also favour moving towards substitutes for petroleum, a subject that Senator Richard Lugar and I examined in *Foreign Affairs* magazine this past January. But this is not a policy discussion, it is an intelligence discussion, and I close by talking for just a moment about what all this means for intelligence.

First of all, if you look at the military's distinction between force planning and operational planning – deciding what to buy, on the one hand, versus deciding how to use what you have on the other – the most important lesson from assessing this pot-pourri of problems we face is that intelligence-collection systems need to maintain maximum flexibility. This is true for all three types of collection networks: photo-reconnaissance satellites, signal intercept systems and espionage.

To give an example of what I mean by flexibility, let me mention briefly what happened in the Pacific in the Second World War with naval forces. All three of the main types of ships which the US Navy used in the Pacific in the Second World War – aircraft carriers, battleships and submarines – were initially designed for a completely different purpose than they were used for. The battleships were designed and purchased to be ships of the line, to re-fight naval battles such as those of the First World War. The carriers were designed and purchased to be scouts for the battleships. And the submarines were designed and purchased to be fleet submarines, sort of advance underwater destroyers proceeding in front of the battleship groups.

But these systems were virtually never used in these ways in the Pacific in the Second World War. There was only one major naval battle in which the opposing fleets even saw each other. Instead, the carriers became the ships of the line, the battleships became the shore bombardment systems against the Japanese-held islands, and the submarines became devastating commerce raiders, operating alone far from any fleets. But the US Navy in the 1930s had been designed by people who, happily, weren't too sure that they were right about the specific purposes of the systems they were designing. Consequently they designed the systems flexibly enough so that they could be used for a number of purposes. We have to have that sense of humility and that same type of attitude towards all three of our types of intelligence-collection networks today.

I believe that major reforms are necessary to foster flexibility in these networks, and I'll mention two very quickly with respect to espionage. One is that, as long as one is going to be concentrating on such targets as organised crime, terrorist groups and rogue states, one is not going to be able to count on potential recruits coming to embassy cocktail parties. We are going to have to move very substantially into a world of non-official cover officers, NOCs – our Russian friends call them illegals. It is dangerous but necessary.

Secondly, in my own country we have done some very strange things with respect to the guidelines we use for espionage. As a result of some of the criticisms about events in Guatemala several years ago, in 1996, after I left the Agency, a decision was made to put out new guidelines. These do not actually bar CIA case officers from recruiting as informants those who are guilty of human rights violations, but they do deter such recruitments and make them somewhat harder. Now, if you don't know what is going on inside Hezbollah, the problem isn't that you have too many human rights violators on your payroll as informants, it's that you don't have enough. If you recruit only nice persons as spies, let's say in the Middle East, you will be able to do a dandy job of understanding what is going on in the churches and, say, in the Chambers of Commerce, but if you want to understand what is going on inside Hezbollah you will be out of luck.

These types of barnacles have built up on some of our policies and intelligence-collection systems over the years, and they need to be scraped off in order for us to do even an adequate – much less what is needed, a superlative – job against these very difficult intelligence targets.

Well, you may have a different list. The concrete measures are certainly debatable. What we have to realise, however, is that if we don't take particular care to tend to our security by reducing our vulnerabilities when we can, and by focusing our intelligence capabilities on the most important tasks, then we are flirting with tragedy at the hands of fanaticism armed with power.

Democracies' weakness is that inherently they tend to believe that there is always going to be time to get back from the beach party and to organise a wagon train. But without some forethought, this next time around we may not have the time to do that. The first terrorist event using a weapon of mass destruction, biological or nuclear, may well produce not only a Pearl Harbor's worth of deaths, around 5,000, a Vietnam's worth, for American forces around 50,000, but conceivably even a Second World War's worth of deaths, for us around half a million. It's not at all inconceivable that a clever use of weapons of mass destruction in a major city could produce casualties approximating what we suffered in the Second World War.

So as our democracies roar into the twenty-first century, full of pride, some more troubled than others, but all hoping for peace and prosperity, we need to keep in mind that the last time we were here, the last time we had a decade of relative peace and prosperity three-quarters of a century ago, we blew it. The history of the late 1930s and the 1940s was horrible, but there are ways now that the consequences of self-indulgence and naïveté could be more horrible still in a world of weapons of mass destruction. This time we really ought to try to get it right.

TWO

THE FUTURE OF COVERT INTELLIGENCE

Sir Michael Quinlan

S ir *Michael Quinlan was a United Kingdom civil servant from 1954 to 1992. Most of his career was spent in the defence field, including a tour of duty at NATO Headquarters in Brussels. At the Ministry of Defence he was Deputy Under-Secretary (Policy) from 1977 to 1981, and Permanent Under-Secretary from 1988 to 1992. After retirement from the Civil Service, he was Director of the Ditchley Foundation from 1992 to 1999. In 1994 he undertook a special study for the UK Government on the post-Cold-War need for secret intelligence and on arrangements for setting its tasks and budgets. In 1997 he mounted a major conference on the future of intelligence in democracies. He has written numerous articles on international security issues, especially those concerning nuclear weapons, and on public-service questions including ethics.*

I propose to lay the ground for this session of our conference by surveying – at what some of you may find a rather elementary level – reasons why covert intelligence may remain useful, and then by touching briefly upon some limiting or qualifying factors.

During the Cold War, the orientation and allocation of intelligence effort was dominated, for countries involved in the East/West confrontation, by the perceived needs imposed by that confrontation. Sceptics now ask whether the massive apparatus thus generated remains necessary at all; and some further suggest that the huge increase, largely beyond the control of governments even if they are restrictively inclined, in the flow of information made possible by the technological revolution is an additional and powerful reason why we could and should now dispense with most of it. So there is, at least at a surface level, a case which intelligence communities have to address.

The defence starts from the simple proposition that to frame sound public policy and action (including inaction where appropriate) requires a basis of relevant, accurate and timely information. In modern circumstances a huge volume of policy-relevant material – far more than before – is readily available. But we cannot assume that everything we want will be thus available. Some of the countries or other actors with whom we are dealing, or may one day need to deal, may have even now no habit of providing information openly on matters relevant to our concerns; some indeed may have no dependable or adequate systems for providing it systematically even to themselves, to their own leaderships. Beyond this, however, the central consideration is that we often want information about matters in which our interests may diverge from those of others, or at least cannot be assumed to be identical; and such divergence, actual or potential, inescapably creates an incentive to those others to withhold from us, temporarily or permanently, information which we might use in order to advance our interests at the expense in some degree of theirs. That can apply even in respect of countries whose general character and policies are usually congenial to us – we cannot automatically take at face value everything they may tell us. In brief, therefore, we may want, for the pursuit of our interests, to know things which others do not want to tell us, or at least not tell us yet.

Now some of these things may nevertheless, in open societies, be available to us easily even when governments would really rather they were not. But across the world's wide and diverse spectrum of countries and of other relevant actors we shall often find that that is not so, and that accordingly if we want the information we must somehow dig it out. And because, *ex hypothesi*, the actors do not want it to be dug out and would so far as possible obstruct the digging process if they knew exactly how it was being conducted, we have to keep the operational details of the process, if not the fact of its existence, as secret as we reasonably can.

That, at its most general, is the basic case for covert intelligence in support of policy. In other words, it seeks – whether by unearthing specific nuggets of information, or by building up patterns of understanding to help our ability to interpret what we observe – to offset gaps, uncertainties and distortions in what we can find out openly, in order that we may judge more wisely, explain more pertinently, and act more confidently and successfully (or sometimes, as I hinted earlier, refrain from acting – secret intelligence may valuably help us to decide that we need not worry much about some conceivable eventuality, or conversely that some situation is so much more dangerous than it initially looks that the prudent course is not to get our fingers caught in the mangle).

I pause for a moment on that adverb 'confidently'. I have heard distinguished diplomatic practitioners, of long experience, say – and I am wholly prepared to believe them – that it is pretty rare for secret intelligence to uncover facts so sure, so unexpected and so significant as actually to reverse outright the course which decision-makers would otherwise have been minded to take. But confidence matters in policy action; and information which has not passed through the filter of an adversary's selection and presentation can be of especial value in that regard.

Secret intelligence can moreover still have a useful role even in situations and subjects where the flow of open information is very copious. It can help us to sift the flow – to validate and calibrate more open sources in respect of balance, veracity and completeness. And there are various more particular scenarios in which secret intelligence may enhance our efficacy. It may, for example, aid us in tough negotiations where our interlocutors or competitors do not realise how much we know; almost conversely, if we are known or are reputed to have an effective intelligence capability, potential opponents may in some degree be kept honest in adversarial dealings, or deterred from actions which we would find unwelcome by a fear that we may have clandestine knowledge exploitable to foil them.

All this so far is very general. Let me make it at least one stage more specific, in three assorted respects. First, for reasons that need no spelling out, the countries in relation to which the West – I use that term as political, not geographical, short-hand – is most likely to have to contemplate difficult external-policy decisions against the wishes of others will more often than not be precisely those whose character makes sure and timely information hardest to come by openly, especially in time of crisis. Second, the West increasingly recognises a need to deal with formidable non-state actors, often operating globally or at least across some borders, in fields – notably terrorism, narcotics, illegal armaments trade and financial wrongdoing – where the attempted concealment of information is at the centre of the business. Third, secret intelligence may have special value in support of international treaties and other agreements, as in arms control, trade bargains or sanctions regimes. In the initial negotiation secret intelligence may not only help us bargain more confidently and aptly but may even be essential if we are to feel able to come to the table at all. Would United States leaders have been prepared to strike bargains about strategic nuclear arms if they had depended solely upon what their Soviet interlocutors chose to tell them about the armoury? And the utility of intelligence bears also upon both the trustworthiness and the policing of the deals struck. Countries breaching agreements are not usually going to make a public present of the fact; it often has to be detected against their will. Detection is obviously an essential precondition of acting to deal with breaches (if, I observe wryly in passing, we truly have the will to do so – consider Iraq), and the perceived possibility of detection can moreover be a valuable deterrent supporting due observance of agreements.

And there is of course one other and special field in which the acquisition of information against the wishes of its 'owners' is crucial – that is, in the actual or potential use of armed forces in conflict. War and warlike situations are the supreme expression of competition, and adversaries are not going to co-operate in yielding information to improve our chances of prevailing; so covert intelligence is of key importance. And that importance is all the greater if, as is increasingly the case, our societies are deeply sensitive to costs of all kinds incurred in conflict; and also if, as is again increasingly so, we seek to rely not on mass-levy conscript forces but on smaller professional forces which depend for their success upon operating with very high efficiency. The Kosovo conflict reminded us moreover, sometimes rather uncomfortably, that our societies nowadays expect high precision and discrimination in the application of force; and that requires accurate and up-to-date knowledge.

What I have put before you so far is a collection of reasons – none of them peculiar to the Cold War setting, though their particular weight may have shifted – why covert intelligence can be valuable. Let me turn now to qualifications and constraints.

The first qualification is that even the most successful covert intelligence capability cannot find out what is not available to be known. The distinction between secrets and mysteries is, I think, well established in intelligence discourse; but I am not sure that publics and Parliaments always grasp the difference between finding out existing but concealed facts and divining the likely course of future events amid the caprices and uncertainties of world affairs. It is foolish to expect, or to claim, too much in the latter respect.

The second qualification is that whether a country needs the potential benefits of covert intelligence, or how badly it needs them, plainly depends on its position in the world and its view of its role. If you are the United States, you will be interested in all the benefits; if you are (let us say) Togo or Tonga, your rating of them will be rather different. I note that, as indeed with the provision of armed forces, you may elect to rate them worth more effort and resource than narrowly national needs might indicate, in order to make a contribution or secure influence in wider settings, such as alliances or the United Nations; but there will remain vast differences between countries in the value attached.

And that brings me to costs – first and most obviously, public-expenditure costs. Not many countries – at least not the larger ones – declare just how much they spend on covert intelligence, and differences of classification and definition would anyway make it hard to establish internationally consistent figures. But, just for example, though UK expenditure on intelligence has almost certainly declined in real terms since the end of the Cold War, we know from published figures that the three intelligence agencies cost around three-quarters of a billion pounds per year, and we may reasonably suppose that the two collection agencies, GCHQ and SIS, take up most of this. US figures would of course be many times higher. Amid constrained public finances the opportunity cost of sustaining such efforts – and they have to be sustained if they are to be useful, since covert intelligence is not a tap easily turned on and off – is not trivial.

And there are other sorts of cost – at least three other sorts. The first 'other' sort is political. It is in open democracies a disadvantage, and so in a real sense a cost, that we have to maintain a substantial set of activities, with matching resource expenditures, about which we cannot be fully candid with our publics and Parliaments, and which accordingly cannot be as fully and healthily accountable as is or should be the norm elsewhere in public business. There may well be proper scope for stronger patterns of oversight than hitherto in many of our countries, but the covers cannot come off entirely without stultifying the business. And the political cost is sharpened, and extended to the external as well as the domestic arena, when (as is humanly bound to happen from time to time, however careful we are) something goes wrong – an operation is embarrassingly botched, or an adversary catches us out in something which for one reason or another we would have preferred to remain undiscovered. Covert intelligence cannot be made a risk-free enterprise.

My second 'other' cost is also political, but of a different kind. The needs of covert collection capability may require us to maintain facilities and relationships of kinds, or in places, that constrain our policy freedom in other respects – we may, in order to protect the contribution to our capability, have to shape our dealings with particular countries or situations in ways that we would not otherwise have regarded as ideal.

My third 'other' cost is one not much talked about, so far as I know, and I admit to having nothing very clear or concrete to say about it, particularly within an introductory contribution which can be no more than a broad survey of factors. It is, in a certain sense, a moral cost. I do not at all say that secret intelligence is an immoral activity. I do not believe that. But like any other human activity it cannot claim total dispensation from moral evaluation. To take the obvious analogy, the use of armed force in war involves individuals doing things – harming other people – which in ordinary contexts would be deeply wrong; and the concepts of just war and the international law of war have been evolved to set boundaries to what is legitimate in the context of this special activity. I am not aware that there has been comparably developed any conceptual structure for just espionage – hardly an easy subject, but there are surely some limits to what a decent country may engage in even for the pursuit of worthy interests.

I am very ready to accept that in a good many countries, and certainly in my own, there are constraining codes of conduct and indeed elements of relevant statute law; and I recognise also that it would be unrealistic to expect the detail of the constraints to be the subject of wide public debate, still less of international law. But we have nevertheless to acknowledge that effective espionage – at least and especially the HUMINT component of it – involves doing things which would normally be reprehensible – concealment, untruth, subterfuge, intrusion, illegality at least abroad, co-operating with or employing disreputable people, suborning individuals from their formal responsibilities. Secret intelligence cannot be conducted without all or anyway most of these actions, and I am not minded to condemn it accordingly; it would seem to me manifestly contrary to moral common sense to hold that, for example, we were not entitled to do certain of these things in order to penetrate and weaken murderous clandestine organisations in Northern Ireland. But in themselves such activities surely have to be assigned to the debit side of the ledger, just as does the fact that soldiers may have to kill. For the soldier's environment there have been developed ethical doctrines disciplining both recourse to war – *jus ad bellum* – and how war may be fought – *jus in bello*. I would be minded to look for something of the same conceptual pattern in the intelligence field – some concept of what it is morally legitimate to seek, and how it may properly be sought. We cannot say – in the West I know we do not say – that anything goes. (And, in passing, I note that that must apply also and perhaps even more to what is customarily called covert action, which is not the subject of our conference but is often assigned, for reasons of partly related aspects of expertise, to intelligence agencies.)

I have flagged up these various aspects of cost to set alongside or against the possible benefits I sketched earlier. But before we can bring the two sets together into cost-benefit evaluation to underpin decisions by governments on their future provision for secret intelligence, we need to note a set of questions or caveats which complicate or obscure the picture. I offer five main points.

The first point is that it is mostly hard even with hindsight – and policy, alas, has anyway to be made looking forwards, not back – to measure the reality and scale of the possible benefits in any concrete way and to bring them into a common calculus with the costs. Much intelligence effort is directed towards insurance against events whose probability, importance and cost cannot themselves be measured. The most measurable things about the value of intelligence are usually to be found in its failures; successes are more generally a matter of things that did not happen, and that gets us into alternative histories and the near-impossibility of proving the prime causes of non-happenings. This is not to say that we should despair of evaluation; it has to be attempted by one route or another, and I am sure that in many countries constant efforts at improvement are being made; but their limitations will remain formidable.

The second point is that however valuable some aspect of information may rightly be judged to be, if it simply cannot be obtained, or only at disproportionate cost of some kind, financial or other (for example, in the face of mounting technical difficulty, though I shall not try now to get into comment on how the offence/defence balance in the technological arena may evolve in future), it is not sensible to invest in the effort. There is of course another problem here, short of the case of absolute impossibility: disproportionate to what? – which often takes us back to that awkward problem of benefit-valuing. I used often to be told in my Ministry of Defence days, in respect of some weapons system or another, that the last 5 per cent of performance accounted for 50 per cent of the cost. But if the 5 per cent is the Spitfire's margin over the Messerschmitt 109, and thus the difference between winning the Battle of Britain and losing it, is the 50 per cent disproportionate? Intelligence too is largely in support of potentially competitive activity, and the costly extra bit of output may have huge leverage. (Or it may not.)

My third point – another familiar one to most of you, I know – is that the product of secret intelligence, however pertinent, may simply not be usable; we may have to sit on our hands and let something nasty happen rather than risk exposing a unique informant in breach of our protective promise, or revealing to the opposing commander that we can read all his tactical communications and so forfeiting even greater long-term advantage. Sometimes unavoidable, I know; but it has to be scored as potentially a limitation to intelligence value.

The fourth point is adjacent to that, but not quite identical. It is little use putting effort into intelligence that tells us things we do not truly want to know, or which we are not prepared to act upon. Many of us will be able, I suspect, to think of instances where governments preferred to look the other way when arms-control agreements were breached; and when that is so, the intelligence effort which found the breach is largely – perhaps not wholly, but largely – wasted (and incidentally, which may also matter, those who did the collecting may be undermined or disheartened).

My fifth point is of a rather different and wider kind. However splendid the covert intelligence we collect, it has in practice to operate through various gears or filters, which, if they are not up to the job, may gravely dilute or even destroy eventual value. We will, I am sure, be discussing these filters later in the conference. I observe briefly however that our covert collection efforts and their costs stand to be wasted if they are not well tasked to fit the real needs of policy-framers and decision-takers; if we lack the skills to evaluate the material sensibly and promptly alongside other inputs of information, neither understating nor overglamorising it; if we lack the organisation and channels then to disseminate the product of evaluation effectively to those who might act upon it; or if we lack thereafter the attitudes, procedures and structures in decision-making actually to exploit it. There are, I suspect, wide variations even among advanced countries in their capacity to put all these together and so get a good bang for the intelligence buck; and it is bad economy to maximise collection effort yet skimp on, or neglect, these other elements.

At least the second half of what I have put before you, as a provocation to discussion, may have sounded like a long recital of 'buts'. If so, let me make clear, by way of *envoi*, that I remain a firm believer in covert intelligence as a proper and necessary support to legitimate interests and policies, and so as fully entitled to public acceptance and approval, domestically and internationally – including in support of the UN – in the world of the twenty-first century. But we shall need awareness and care – heightened, if anything – in its scale, its management, its application and its scrutiny.

DISCUSSION

Admiral Fulvio Martini

Admiral Fulvio Martini graduated from the Leghorn Naval Academy in 1943. During the Second World War, 1944–5, he served on escort vessels. He was assigned in 1958 to the Naval Intelligence Department, where he served until 1968. From 1965 to 1968, as a Commander, he was Assistant Naval Attaché in Belgrade, and was then made a member of the Brosio Study Group in Norfolk, Virginia. From 1969 to 1972 he was assigned to the Military Intelligence Service as Head of the Analysis Division. From 1974 to 1978, as Rear Admiral, he was Head of Operations, including those concerning Middle East terrorism, and of the Analysis Branch. He became Deputy Secretary-General of Defence and Deputy Director of Armaments in 1981. From

1984 to 1991 he was Director of the Italian Military Security and Intelligence Service. After retirement in 1993, he was appointed the Prime Minister's adviser on National Security. He published his memoirs as Nome in Codice Ulisse *in 1999.*

I spent about twenty-two years in the intelligence sector, seven of them as Director of the Italian External Intelligence Service. Therefore, I believe I can describe myself as a professional.

I agree with the ideas expressed by Sir Michael Quinlan. I, too, am convinced that covert intelligence will have a crucial role in supporting any government's foreign policy in the future. There will always be a need for intelligence that is not openly available. Such intelligence is useful both in normal relations among states and in international and trade agreements, as well as to tackle the local conflicts which seem bound to scar the future (Kosovo, Somalia, Bosnia).

Covert intelligence is an enterprise that requires an equally efficient system of analysis that can enable government authorities to exploit its products to the full. At this point, I would like to introduce a new approach to the main problem. Given that covert intelligence will continue to be necessary in the future, I would like to examine more closely the issue of what kind of intelligence it will be.

Referring to the United Kingdom, Sir Michael mentioned the GCHQ and the SIS, and he stated that the budget for both could be £750 million. The UK, however, has world-wide interests. Let us focus on the case of the Italian service, an intermediate service that operates regionally.

During the Cold War my area of responsibility, as it had been defined by the Government, included the Mediterranean, the Balkans, the Danube area and the Horn of Africa. In that time, and until my retirement in 1991 at the end of the Gulf War, I was able to avail myself of US satellites and the Allied SIGINT network as a support to my own. I do not think that the climate of intensive information exchange that existed during the Cold War, when we faced powerful adversaries, such as the Soviet Union and Warsaw Pact, still continues.

In fact, our current targets are of a much smaller scale, are more diversified and less technically sophisticated.

I do not think my country can afford to spend large amounts of money to produce intelligence technology, which, in my opinion, would only yield limited results. Therefore, we have no choice but to rely on HUMINT, which can yield very effective results in our area of interest and at sustainable cost.

In short, I believe that intermediate-level regional services will continue to operate as they did in the past, even though, on the basis of a cost and objective evaluation, they will foster their HUMINT sectors, using the new technologies wherever possible.

Countries with global interests may have different points of view. The example of Kosovo, however, would seem to confirm my opinion. The main efforts of Allied intelligence activities concentrated on interpreting the Belgrade leadership's decision-making processes. Within that context, data collected with HUMINT techniques played a pivotal role. Moreover, in Kosovo, the total of actual hits on targets bombed during NATO air-raids was much lower than the forecasts on the basis of NATO's technical intelligence data, since an electronic eye can be deceived by certain devices, if the data are not cross-checked with information from dependable human sources.

Lastly, recent experience in different sectors, such as terrorist or destabilising activities, confirms that important decisions are taken in very restricted contexts and derive from logical processes that are deeply affected by human and emotional factors. In conclusion, it is my personal opinion – and it is therefore of course open to criticism – that HUMINT has recovered a central role within covert intelligence activities.

Ambassador Par Kettis

*Ambassador Par Kettis is Senior Councillor of the Atlantic Council
of the US and an international consultant in Washington, DC. A
major participant in the development of a long-term strategy for the
Swedish Intelligence Service, he was a member of the Government
Commission on the Future of the Intelligence Service 1997–9. A
concluding Report was published in April 1999. His diplomatic post-
ings include Deputy Chief of Mission, Washington; Assistant Under-
Secretary for International Organisations, MFA; Warsaw and Addis
Ababa. He has also served as Swedish Ambassador to India in
1989–94 and Iceland in 1994–8; and was a Visiting Fellow at the
Hudson Institute, Washington, between posts. He was Director General
of the National Defence Radio Institute (FRA) in 1985–9. He was
Deputy Secretary-General of the Nordic Council. He has negotiated
agreements in the political, economic and legal areas, especially assistance programmes to India, Sri Lanka, Nepal and Bhutan, and
conducted crisis management of terrorist situations in Kashmir and
Sri Lanka. He has a Law degree from the University of Stockholm,
has studied in Lausanne, Grenoble, Bordeaux and London, attended
the Swedish Defence College and its Senior National Security
Programme, and studied cultural restoration at Göteborg University.*

I agree with everything Sir Michael has said and will limit myself
to adding emphasis to a few points.

Before I do that, however, I will say something about the official inquiry into the Swedish Intelligence Service. It started in
1997 and the Report was published in April of this year.[1] The
Government is expected to send its proposal based on the Report,
I hope, to Parliament this coming winter.

The study was non-partisan in accordance with expressed
wishes of the politicians, government and opposition alike. The
study was conducted by Judge Johan Hirschfeldt (President of
the Svea Appeals Court, former Attorney General of the

Government, a non-political function); Professor Kerstin Fredga (Director General of the Swedish Space Agency); and myself as former Head of the National Defence Radio Institute, better known as FRA. Government experts also played an important role in producing and evaluating the material. Two years may seem long for such a study, but we all maintained our normal functions. In addition, the Defence Minister had made it clear that, owing to the domestic agenda, he did not want to have our proposals earlier.

The Report is public in its entirety and there are no secret appendices. One expected result of this open attitude is that the Report is an overview and as such does not go into great detail. Under the circumstances, we did not feel that there was any special disadvantage in this approach.

A basic premise for the work was the dramatic changes that had taken place in the world, not least in our own part of it, and that had brought about a new focus for the intelligence service. This has entailed a shift away from traditional early warning against military attack in the form of invasion, and comprehensive operative and tactical military intelligence, and towards more strategic and political intelligence, with increased emphasis on long-term analysis, new external threats in the form of non-military intelligence, covering ethnic unrest, domestic instability, terrorism, drug traffic, proliferation of weapons of mass destruction, trans-boundary crime, ecological threats, a more selective follow-up of military activities in the vicinity and, finally, support for international peace operations.

You may ask why the Swedish inquiry came so long after the global changes that followed the end of the Cold War. The explanation is mainly domestic. An earlier valuable study of the intelligence service, commissioned by former Prime Minister Carl Bildt, was shelved after he lost an election and resigned. That report had discussed the pros and cons of forming a National Security Council and an organisation like the CIA, both definite

non-starters in Sweden: the former, because the appointment of
non-elected officials to a body deciding vital issues would run
counter to the Swedish constitution, which is based on the
common responsibility of all members of the Government; the
latter, because Swedish public opinion is hostile to the kinds of
covert political action believed to have been used by the CIA
against left-wing regimes. One benefit in delaying the inquiry
was that we could take advantage of the experiences of other
countries. The committee visited many foreign intelligence organisations, which were very helpful in sharing their views with us.
Some were old partners, and some were new contacts.

One reason for including new countries in our contacts was
our wish to pursue intelligence co-operation in non-military
areas, such as international crime, drugs, etc., as noted above,
and for peace operations.

I will comment on a few of the points just mentioned. We all
agree that the risk of a big war is very low, and in any case necessary rearmament will take at least ten or fifteen years. Instead,
we have a global situation with widespread instability and internal armed conflicts in many regions. Two of the most dangerous conflicts have been located in Europe: in former Yugoslavia
and in south-east Russia. There does not seem to be any hope
of stabilisation in the near future.

We are all adapting our defence forces to this new situation.
This modernisation has been long overdue and much antiquated
Cold War thinking is still in place. The mobility and flexibility
of modern forces as planned are intended to satisfy the need for
participation in global peace forces and to deter limited military
actions in our own neighbourhood.

What do we know about the future? It would be irrespons-
ible of us to base our national security on the vague theory that
we have finally reached the stage of a lasting peace in the North
Atlantic-European context. That is our hope, but in the present
circumstances an effective defence force adapted to the existing

situation is the best insurance that peace will prevail. A contin-ued presence of the US in Europe and a well-functioning NATO are vital for maintaining this peace in the coming years.[2] In addi-tion, NATO is an effective restraint on the re-nationalisation of European defence, and is the ultimate guarantor of security and stability on the European continent.[3] An indispensable compo-nent in support of a modernised national defence is a top-class intelligence service which should be tasked to do as much as possible with available resources.

The value of good intelligence increases as military forces grow smaller. Sufficient time is needed to adapt the defence forces, if that will ever be necessary again. Very early warning to detect possible emerging threats is therefore a necessity.

In addition, the intelligence service must at all times be able to detect and warn of external threats or attacks, other than inva-sion.

In the Report, we say that more selectivity is now possible than during the Cold War. There are still large military forces and hardware in Europe, although their status in many cases is doubtful. The general readiness is low but may change. We want to see a stable and prosperous Europe everywhere, but that is not what we have, and our planning must take this into consid-eration.

Plus ça change, plus c'est la même chose. The more things change, the more they remain the same. We concluded our report by stating that, in order to be able to warn of a military build-up in our area or other military-related threats, the intelligence service must follow, or retain the ability to follow, basically the same targets as before. For this purpose, its capabilities will largely be maintained, but modernised and made more efficient. On the other hand, the task of reporting military movements could be reduced. Therefore, it should be possible to free resources that could be reallocated to the new areas of threat.

Far-reaching technological changes are taking place.

Nowadays practically all advanced thinking, information and planning is stored electronically. If a need arises and the resources are available, the potential is there for retrieving this information, even if it is protected. What this means is that SIGINT could be very useful in the future.

The analysis should be focused more on intentions than actual movements and capabilities. To find out what others are going to do is of course extremely difficult. During the Cold War, the reactions of the two sides were predictable. Of course, there were exceptions when the West was provoked, as in Berlin and during the Cuban Missile Crisis.

The rogue states of today, international terrorists, drug networks, ideological fighters and other non-state offenders, have made the problem of predicting what their next move is going to be many times more complicated. All means have to be exploited to try to find usable information about the organisations, resources, connections, movements, communications and plans of these widely diverse groups.

Often those we target may have a long-term goal but do not know what they will do in the immediate future. For example, it has been said of Milošević that, in spite of having detailed plans for the armed forces, he was largely reacting day by day to what NATO was doing. When trying to make forecasts, an analyst needs both the open sources and covert intelligence of all kinds.

The civilian and military communication systems are rapidly converging and the new threats are generally of a civilian nature. The intelligence organisations, not least SIGINT, are wise to adapt to this change by substituting a unified approach for the traditional division between military and civilian.

Support for international peace operations is very important. Protecting own forces and personnel from danger must be a priority. Well-organised SIGINT and HUMINT should go a long way to satisfy this need. An important by-product is often a good tactical overview of the surrounding areas. The political deliberations that are nearly always crucial to the success of peace operations are greatly assisted by detailed intelligence on the parties involved from all kinds of sources and levels. Often these actors say one thing and do something very different, and knowledge of such double-talk is vital for establishing conditions under which a peace force can enter the area and fulfil its mission.

New non-military threats and international operations are opening the way for more advanced co-operation between security and intelligence organisations from participating and interested countries. One reason is that nobody can effectively cover the whole world where such activities may take place. The efficiency and economy of such intelligence work could be greatly enhanced through co-operation between intelligence organisations. The reservations that traditionally have been setting limits for co-operation in the military field do not have the same weight in the new context.

The SIGINT and military intelligence organisations of three Scandinavian countries – Denmark, Norway and Sweden – have signed open agreements on co-operation in Bosnia. The Committee Report clearly states that previous limitations for foreign co-operation in the intelligence area have become too restrictive in the new situation. There is value in itself in increasing the exchange of intelligence between nations. In addition, a degree of specialisation and division of labour may be worthwhile. We are all aware of the need to move step by step to secure confidentiality and trust. Even if the cloak has been lifted for certain types of intelligence co-operation, it is vital that specific information remain highly classified.

In the past the Swedish Intelligence Service has not been regulated by law. The Report contains draft legislation laying down some general principles. It suggests codification of the principle that only external military or other serious threats fall under the competence of the intelligence service. It is specifically mentioned that the intelligence agencies may establish co-operation in intelligence matters with foreign nations and international organisations, as the Government decides. A clear division is drawn up between the activities of intelligence agencies and police work.

The Committee did not suggest any major change in the existing intelligence organisations. On the other hand it proposes creation of a secretariat for the co-ordination of intelligence in the Government Office. From a Swedish perspective this is an important step. The Government has traditionally kept intelligence administration separated and at arm's length, although they have been very interested readers at times. (Former PM Carl Bildt was foremost in showing the greatest interest in intelligence in all its forms, including raw.) The secretariat for intelligence co-ordination has been so designed that it can be located in the Government Office wherever desired. The decision is left to the Government of the day, but natural locations would be the Prime Minister's Office, the Foreign Ministry, or the Defence Ministry.

The Committee also describes the activities of a still secret and highly informal group of senior officials who are responsible for security matters. It is suggested that this group continue as a Preparatory Group for Intelligence on Secretary of State level, including also the heads of the main intelligence agencies. The Group will direct and be assisted by the Secretariat for Co-ordination of Intelligence.

There is a body for oversight of the intelligence service – the Defence Intelligence Commission, whose members are appointed by the Government and are senior MPs and a judge. It is suggested that this oversight body shall not, as hitherto, evaluate the intelligence budget, a duty for which it is not qualified in its present form. Instead, it is suggested that the Commission concentrate its inquiries on the performance of the intelligence agencies. One essential element would be to review how the agencies execute the numerous directives laid down by Parliament, the Government and the Commander-in-Chief, and to ensure that those activities are performed in a correct way. The Committee suggested that the oversight body and the two main agencies publish annual reports about their work, something that would seem natural at the present time.

The Committee follows the trend in support of more use of open sources. There is a Centre for open information in the Military Intelligence Organisation. The Centre produces an excellent daily media summary, using advanced software and computers. Readers can easily obtain additional specialised information from the system. The Centre maintains contacts with similar institutions in other countries and exchanges material with many of them. Practically all Swedish intelligence workers use this product and complain loudly when for some reason the information is not forthcoming. Evidently this system is a valuable tool in the hands of intelligence analysts. It seems certain that this or similar methods will soon be in widespread use wherever there is a need for the effective collection and handling of information. The Committee utters an obvious warning about the risk of misinformation and limited availability, especially when the need is great, as in times of crisis.

Having outlined the Swedish Report, I will now turn to Sir Michael's very interesting and thoughtful presentation.

To begin with I will continue my discussion about the use of open sources. The amount of information has indeed increased significantly. Of course, it should be used to the fullest extent. However, this information is not as limitless or overwhelming as commentators sometimes seem to believe.

For intelligence purposes, it is evident that if we focus on a concrete area or problem, the number of real, original contributors – journalists, freelance writers, scientists – who are telling a story or describing facts, is usually quite limited. I may add that one reason for the success of the Swedish Open Sources

Digest is that its authors use original reports, statements, etc., as much as possible, rather than newspaper articles that are only rewrites or repetitions of the original piece. If one eliminates all rewrites that use the same original information, the quantity of information is reduced considerably.

According to an American study, published in *Warp Speed*[4] under the auspices of a Committee of Concerned Journalists, one conclusion is that 'the classic function of journalism to sort out a true and reliable account of the day's events is being undermined'. Another observation is that 'People lie now in a way that they never lied before – and the ease with which they lie . . . . This word-spinning . . . is a nice uptown way of saying lying.'

One more finding in *Warp Speed* is that 'the new media outlets are engaged in commenting on information rather than gathering it. The rise of twenty-four-hour news stations and Internet news and information sites has placed demands on the press to "have something" to fill the time.' The authors call this 'a new journalism of assertion, which is less interested in substantiating whether something is true and more interested in getting it into the public discussion'. The book tries to quantify the process by using the Clinton-Lewinsky story: the result was 'that a remarkable 41 per cent of all the reportage in the first six days of the story was not factual reporting at all – here is what happened – but was instead journalists offering their own analysis, opinion, speculation, or judgements – essentially commentary and punditry'. Another report analysing a longer period is said to have found the percentage to be over 50 per cent.

So volume does not equal real information. Evidently the information revolution covers a lot of misinformation, second-guessing, repetition and speculation, all under the guise of real information. The good news is that experience tells us that the intelligent analyst soon finds out who is a reliable source and what is garbage. But he will still need as much covert intelligence as may be available to verify or correct the version distributed by the media.

It is generally believed that a worsening of the overall security situation will be preceded by fairly clear public signs of what is going on. These will no doubt be reported by the media and available for anyone interested in drawing conclusions. It is a general assumption that a deteriorating world climate will be analysed and reported by the media and diplomats. I agree that this is a likely scenario for an overall, global deterioration. But what about regional disturbances? Can we trust that the media will cover those for us as well? Probably not, or at least not early or deeply enough.

The larger question remains of whether we are willing to rest our future security on what the media can find out, e.g. that they will detect and report the sinister plans of a new dictator so well in advance that proper precautions can be taken. The conclusion is obvious. We can and should take advantage of whatever material the media reports. At the same time states have an absolute obligation to their people to make sure that new and serious threats are detected in time to counteract and prevent death and destruction, if at all possible. To this end, covert intelligence is needed to discover what is really happening.

On the subject of continuity, in my experience this aspect is quite often undervalued. It is of particular importance for small countries. Most people – politicians, officials without much exposure to production of intelligence – think they understand: if you discontinue competence this year, it is not possible to recover that competence with much hope of success some years later. However, they often do think that the agencies can mothball the whole thing and keep it going on the backburner for bad times. In most cases, however, this is not a possibility. Even less understood is the fact that, if you are not alert when a new technology is introduced, it is very difficult and often impossible to catch up later. At least in the technical field, the truth is almost always that if you don't hang in there, you risk being left out in the cold for a very long time, even if your government is willing to spend a lot of money. Many services have had to bite this particular bullet. What you need to succeed is continuity and friends.

In Sir Michael's words, closely connected to the issue of continuity 'is that the product of secret intelligence, however pertinent, may simply not be usable'; or that intelligence 'tells us things we do not truly want to know, or which we are not prepared to act upon'. Such a discussion is possible only if one knows beforehand what the likely outcome will be of a particular intelligence operation.

But the discussion will be very difficult, if not impossible, in cases where you cannot know beforehand what is going to come out of a concrete investment. This is especially true with technical means of different kinds, for example, satellites and signals intelligence. What agencies harvest today may be the result of investments sown decades ago and carefully nurtured over the years. The content of a decrypt given to principals on a certain day may have been written the same morning, but the system that made it possible to produce that piece of intelligence may have been nurtured during the lifetime of the agency. Hence the many 'UNCLOSED' files in the Public Record Office and similar institutions in other states. In short, either you have it, or you don't. And if you have it, you have to live with a certain amount of unwanted knowledge and deal with this problem as it arises. If decision-makers had opted not to have it, we might have had to live without the Zimmerman Telegram, the fourteen paragraphs in the Japanese telegram before Pearl Harbor, and MAGIC and ULTRA.

The cost factor is interesting and the Swedish Committee also discussed this problem. There are some obvious difficulties. For example, what is the value of an insurance policy against surprise attack? What is a reasonable *per diem* rate for air and sea surveillance of potential trouble-spots? The Swedish Committee soon found that our principals were more interested in receiving relevant and timely information about areas of concern to them than in minimising cost. A reasonable cost for intelligence in relation to the total cost of defence was not a problem. Personally, I was much encouraged by the wise approach to these matters by the politicians. Their perspective on these issues was far superior to that of most of the officials we were dealing with, who were often entrenched in their never-ending budget games.

There is a moral cost, naturally, but I think this is less a problem for small organisations than for the big ones, which also have a historical burden in this respect. Nobody expects any Nordic intelligence service to send out lethal missions, but everybody knows about the plans to assassinate Castro. The answer in democratic countries, of course, is that Parliamentary oversight provides as good a check as we can expect to have. Problems seem to arise when these oversight rules are bypassed.

Finally, and in connection with the previous discussion, I want to mention a piece of information that seldom finds its way into the books on intelligence history. When the Second World War broke out, the Swedish General Staff ordered a build-up of its signals intelligence operations. These soon reached an impressive volume and were targeted against German diplomatic and military traffic. Sweden had a definite advantage in that Germany had leased telegram cables through Sweden to its occupation forces in Norway and later also to German forces in Finland, as well as to the German embassies in Finland and Sweden. Copies of the numerous German telegrams were immediately delivered to the Swedish SIGINT. The codebreakers managed to read many lower systems, but the traffic on the strategic level from Hitler and the General Staff on the *Geheimschreiber* (secret writer) in Berlin through Sweden could not be decrypted. Among the staff was a conscript who was a mathematician. After working with the unsolved telegrams for some time, he stuffed a big bunch of them into his briefcase, went home and stayed there for several days. Finally he came back and presented a blueprint to his colleagues: 'If you build this machine,' he said, 'I think we can break the code.' And it worked.

For the most critical war years, Sweden had access to the German strategic traffic in a similar way to that being used by the Allies. The decrypts included German instructions for difficult negotiations in Berlin and Stockholm about the concessions Sweden had to make to stay out of the war. The Swedish breakthrough came some time before the Allies managed to read corresponding systems on their fronts. It was mostly the work of one man, Arne Beurling, who later became a professor at Princeton. The security, however, had not been strict enough and somebody told the Germans in Helsinki that Sweden was reading their encrypted traffic. Fortunately by this time the tide of war had turned and the risk of a German invasion was diminishing. The Germans changed the keys and gradually Sweden lost this traffic.

GENERAL DISCUSSION

Referring to the recent media exposure of British nationals as agents of the East German Stasi, a former British Military Intelligence officer, noting Sir Michael's remarks about 'just' espionage, asked whether we were entering an era of politically correct traitors. Is it possible under the new concept therefore that, if you worked for a disgraceful left-wing regime, at least the United Kingdom would not take serious actions against you?

For lack of current information, Sir Michael Quinlan declined to comment on the recent revelations, but suggested as a perfect example of 'just' espionage that of Oleg Gordievsky, who deserved very high moral approbation, and yet there was in formal terms a breach of trust there. Sir Michael saw the need for a theory of just espionage to parallel that of the theory of just war.

A British academic, commenting on the question of SIGINT versus HUMINT that had been referred to, and the cost limitations of collection noted by Fulvio Martini, drew attention to an area of collection of particular interest to a conference on the problems facing intelligence in a changing world, but that had not been mentioned, namely, intelligence gathered by the penetration of information systems, or what he dubbed HACKINT. This potential growth area of intelligence was also far less expensive than conventional SIGINT. It is, he added, much cheaper to hack into a computer system than to try, for example, to intercept the digital uplink-downlink data streams between a user and a satellite. He concluded by asking whether the use of information technology as a method of intelligence-gathering, particularly for middle-sized and smaller intelligence agencies, was a solution for the near future.

Admiral Martini responded that the cost of keeping up with the development of technical intelligence is very high in the Italian context. The cost of improving HUMINT was more acceptable for the Italian Government. He pointed out that Italy's targets were of a smaller scale, noting illegal immigration from Albania or Montenegro as examples, and that technical support in such cases is expensive but not effective. The most effective intelligence gathered by the Italian service, whether on the Balkans or Middle East terrorism, had come from human sources.

A British academic suggested, in response to Admiral Martini's comments, that to rely on HUMINT required a much more long-term view. It is generally accepted that intelligence's most successful HUMINT operations have come about through one of three ways: bribery, walk-in intelligence and long-term cultivation of sources, as happened particularly in Britain in the 1930s. Any of these three are going to be difficult to apply against

the sorts of targets that have emerged now, unless there is much
more serious thought devoted by the intelligence agencies to
where likely targets are going to arise. This kind of risk-
assessment requires an agency that can bring together the different sources of intelligence agencies to make a judgement as to
where a risk may arise. On technical intelligence, he noted that
it depended on the society one was observing, citing Central
Africa as an example where radio SIGINT could hardly have
done much good.

Admiral Martini agreed that an assessment department was
essential for providing the kind of analysis that was capable of
identifying new risks. He stressed the cultivation of human intelligence because he was a user. He believed that, even with the
help of sophisticated technical intelligence, the target required
deep study. A human network, he noted, would function on
average for three to five years, and this was still less expensive
than operating technology for the same period. He added that
at least 80 per cent of Italy's intelligence successes during the
latter years of the Cold War came from human sources, and 20
per cent from Italian technical sources which were themselves
using GCHQ, NSA and US satellites.

Sir Michael added that, for example, members of the Security
Council aspiring to be global players in the field had to cast
their nets extremely wide. From his experience in Defence, he
cited the example of planning armed forces and expressed his
scepticism that it was possible to say exactly what one would do.
For example, it would have been impossible to keep the aircraft
carriers in port in case they were going to be needed in the
Falklands, or keep an armoured division where it was because
we might need it for the recovery of Kuwait. Am I not right in
thinking, he asked James Woolsey, that the US had switched off
its intelligence effort in Africa? (The response was, 'It was an
amber light!') In other words, it is not possible to say you are
willing only to concentrate, say, in the Mediterranean. You may

have to invest very widely on a very long-term basis in the things that may never get used.

Admiral Martini admitted that one target against which technical intelligence can be more effective than human intelligence was weapons proliferation. But against terrorism or Muslim extremists, technical intelligence is quite useless.

A British academic raised the question of disinformation, citing two cases. The first concerned Harold Macmillan, who was often accused of being lax on intelligence security matters and uninterested. On more than one occasion in private conversation he had said that the damage done by Philby and Co. was not so much the intelligence gained by the KGB but the damage and demoralisation caused to our secret services by disinformation. The second case came from French intelligence. In the Algerian war they had managed to 'turn' agents to make the Algerian High Command believe that some of their top people were traitors, which was quite untrue. His question was whether the use of such disinformation in intelligence operations is just and proper, and is it useful?

Sir Michael agreed that this was a legitimate question that needed to be studied, but he was unable to comment further.

Brian Latell, formerly of the CIA and now a professor at Georgetown University, urged Sir Michael to expand on his remarks about just espionage, perhaps, if he preferred, by saying what he thought was particularly *un*ethical.

Sir Michael replied that what he had said represented the current state of his thinking, that there was a problem and that further thought was needed.

James Woolsey added that the best formulation he had heard was from a former friend in the clandestine service who, on Woolsey's first overseas trip as DCI, came over to him in the plane and said: "'You're new in this job. Would you like to know what we're like?" And I said, "Yes." And he said, "Well, you know, the CIA gives people all these psychological tests, and you know they produce these standpipes of ratings. At the top is generally 'good' and at the bottom is 'bad'. Well, if you give those others who have spent our careers in the clandestine service and come up to the top of it these types of tests, you'll be generally pleased. On each of these – personal integrity, truthfulness, devotion to duty, intelligence and so forth – maybe we're not at the 99 plus percentile, but we're up there at 97–98, and that's pretty good." Then he said, "I don't remember what this other standpipe is called, this other graph, but at the top is essentially St Francis of Assisi and at the bottom is a sociopath, and when you go along the standpipes and you come to that one, there's just a little dip. It's not a big dip, it's a little dip."'

In the light of the information revolution, a British academic asked Sir Michael how he expected new types of intelligence to affect the covert intelligence process, what effect such intelligence will have on the needs of the consumers, and whether the particular preferences of individual leaders and their like or dislike of intelligence would continue to play a part.

Sir Michael expected that in Britain at least interest in intelligence by Prime Ministers would continue to be a matter of personal taste and choice. But the shift from the inter-state confrontation of the Cold War to the many other kinds of actors that have emerged and that have already been mentioned here, such as terrorists, drug barons and financial criminals, means that consumers of intelligence will want more product that addresses these areas.

Ambassador Kettis added that it was national interest, rather than the personality of a leader, that determined what kind of intelligence operations were needed.

Admiral Martini remarked that in Italy the intelligence services were not held in very high regard. His first Prime Minister was Mr Craxi, who greatly admired Mrs Thatcher. When Craxi returned from meetings with Mrs Thatcher, he would always ask why his intelligence service did not provide him with the sort of file that SIS always provided for Mrs Thatcher.

Sir Michael suggested that the differences were not so much between individual leaders as between different countries in their disposition to take intelligence seriously. It was quite high in the UK, but he thought less so in, say, Germany. And that, he thought, may be in some sense a factor not just of history but of whether the other components alongside the collection capability – interpretation, dissemination and evaluation – were integrated as a whole.

A British journalist reverted to the question of just espionage, and detected a fundamental difference of perception between what Sir Michael had said and what James Woolsey had said in his after-dinner speech. On another issue, that of political correctness and the outing of Stasi agents, who does it serve? The participant was struck by Tsarev's contribution where he detected an undertow of pride in the way he reminded the conference of how Philby and Co. had got all this stuff to Moscow Centre. The speaker questioned whether it was the people in Moscow who are cheered up by all this being brought out into the open. On disinformation, Kosovo gave an example of obvious media manipulation, of media being briefed constantly about the atrocities by the Serbs. It seems the International Tribunal in The Hague is going to have to arraign some Muslim in order to create a sense of balance, and they will again try to use the media to back this up.

The general discussion was concluded by a member of SIS, who made a comment on three topics. First, on the question of determining targets, he pointed to the JIC as an example of an efficient way of ordering risks and priorities. He noted, however, the importance of serendipity, 'You drop the bait and hope for a bite.' Second, on the question of SIGINT versus HUMINT, he believed that they complement each other. On the morality of intelligence he offered two maxims: honesty inside the service, however much deception might be practised outside it, and never descend to the other side's methods.

[At an earlier stage in the general discussion, Sir Marrack Goulding commented that Ambassador Kettis's remarks were of special interest, as he was the only speaker at the conference who is a national of a country that was neutral in the East-West confrontation, and it was hoped that he might lift the veil a little more on co-operation between the intelligence agencies of NATO and Sweden, either historically or as a projection into the future. Sir Marrack cited the example of Soviet naval activities in the North Atlantic as having been of common interest to NATO and Sweden. Ambassador Kettis has responded by expanding his replies to Sir Marrack's and others' questions in the following addendum.]

I. Referring to the breakthrough made by Swedish intelligence during the Second World War, this success created expectations that it would be possible also in the future to obtain valuable information through maintaining a substantial intelligence service. At an early stage negotiations about a Nordic Defence Alliance broke down resulting in Denmark, Iceland and Norway joining NATO and Sweden and Finland becoming neutral. This outcome combined with the realities of the Cold War led Swedish leaders to invest even more in their own intelligence as help from outside was not an option any longer. In this situation technical intelligence methods, in reality signals intelligence, had the definite advantage of being carried out from our own territory, from international airspace and from international waters. The collection was geared towards the north-western Soviet Union, in particular the Baltic area. (The historical record shows there were sadly unsuccessful missions sending Balts into their native areas. Most of them were caught by the Soviets.)

For a neutral country co-operation with other countries

with similar interests was of course most important. The nature of this co-operation has been described in surprising detail in *Had there been a war . . . Preparations for the reception of military assistance 1949–1969 Report of the Commission on Neutrality Policy 1994* (SOU 1994:11, pp. 129–35). Co-operation involved communications intelligence in support of analysis of deployments, readiness, exercises; and technical signals intelligence (ELINT) concerned radar and positioning systems, and helped identify ships, aircraft and military activities. The partners were Denmark, Norway, UK, US and other friendly nations. Involved on the Swedish side were the Defence Staff, the secret intelligence service, at different times called the T-office, B-bureau, IB, SSI and now KSI, and the National Defence Radio Institute (FRA – a name that has never been changed). The nature of the co-operation was bilateral and in principle it continued as long as both partners wanted. There were no agreements, especially not in writing or about what to do in case of a war with the Soviet Union. Discussions were recorded and formed the basis for continued activities. However, it is fair to say that there was a tacit expectation or understanding that the exchange could continue even in a war crisis or war situation if both sides wanted to do so. At least that is the way I felt about our relationship. The military reality was that the only conceivable aggressor was the Warsaw Pact, and why would Sweden discontinue an exchange that was so clearly in our advantage if we became involved in a conflict?

It is worth pointing out that the Swedish Government and the Parliament were firmly behind the foreign intelligence co-operation in principle. Knowledge about details was limited to very few persons, even in the Government: the Prime Minister an overall picture, the Defence Minister in more detail, and from time to time also the Foreign Minister. However, the Government was extremely sensitive to any leaks about what was really going on. The knowledge was therefore kept within a core group of perhaps not more than a dozen individuals. There were two reasons for this super-secret attitude: intelligence co-operation generally had a seventy-five-year statute of limitation and, more importantly, it would not fit well with the neutrality policy propaganda if something like this came out.

The Report mentions some interesting details about half-done planning in the 1940s for a FRA group to travel to England in case of a war with the Soviet Union to supervise continued SIGINT operations and eventually move the units over to England. A rumour about the same time had the FRA management evacuating to the US in the event of war. These plans gradually lost their relevance and later during the Cold War they were forgotten.

The 1999 Report underlines the importance of foreign co-operation in the intelligence field and recommends a wider scope for co-operation to handle the broad range of threats today and international peace operations. The Report, however, does not go into particulars concerning countries, but leaves that to the imagination of the intelligent reader. It is fair to surmise though that the networks generally speaking will grow rather than be disrupted.

I would like to add to the discussion about HUMINT versus technical collection. It depends on what you want to obtain and what you can achieve. If you want to know what military forces are planning or actually doing, there is no substitute for technical means. Modern weapons are inundated with IT, sometimes they are IT itself. But IT is of course everywhere in modern life: if you want to know what is happening, you have no choice but to look into the data streams. Intentions and decisions will in all likelihood not show up early enough on IT. As in the old times, they have to be searched for with more human methods. When you target terrorists, I believe it is prudent to use both HUMINT and technical intelligence. After all everybody is using radio and satellites nowadays, when couriers take too long to despatch or are exposed to interception. Whatever choice you make about how to mix HUMINT and TECHINT, the ground rules have to be observed: without a long-term approach and good friends, you will achieve little.

II. A British writer on intelligence asked Ambassador Kettis if he could comment on another great SIGINT success, the VENONA. A large amount of VENONA traffic that has been declassified in the United States was on the Moscow-Stockholm channel, and he wondered if it was intercepted in the same way as the *Geheimschreiber* material had been. Ambassador Kettis confirmed that a lot of VENONA material, not known as such at the time, was collected by the FRA, not destroyed but stored in a basement. From there it could be retrieved and handed over to the US, and probably the British, in exchange for decrypts of relevance to Sweden.

III. On the debate about a leader's personal attitude towards the importance of intelligence, Ambassador Kettis's view was that national interest, rather than the personality of the leader at the time, was the determining factor for what kind of intelligence operations were needed. But undoubtedly personalities play an important role and can stimulate or limit the interest for intelligence. Therefore it is vital to have a central organ in government that can follow the production of intelligence to evaluate which programmes give the best result as compared to the needs. That enhances healthy competition between intelligence agencies and makes it necessary for them to react properly to the perceived threat.

IV. On the question of the impact of the information revolution, Ambassador Kettis agreed that it undoubtedly added a great deal to the picture, but it was not possible to

say it provided everything. He cited the example of Kosovo,
where the coverage in the media and daily briefings from
NATO in Brussels and other sources were impressive in quan-
titative terms. Yet if all this was added together, one did not
have a clear or accurate picture of what was happening, which
became evident after the fighting was over. The real information about the events in Kosovo was actually very limited. He
recalled that one of the very few journalists who had managed
to get into Kosovo and to report from inside had sent outstanding reports. The other sources were either extremely partisan,
like the Kosovo bureau in Geneva and official Yugoslav information. The NATO briefings were also very selective. All in
all, the CNN war seems to be a phenomenon of the past. The
real picture had to be pieced together by intelligence services
with a wide range of devices.

Notes to Ambassador Kettis's paper

1. *Underrättelsetjänsten – en översyn. Betänkande av underrät-
telsekommittén. Statens offentliga utredningar* (SOU 1999:37,
Försvarsdepartementet) – The Intelligence Service – a review.
Investigation by the Intelligence Committee (Government
Public Investigations SOU 1999:37. Defence Ministry. ISBN
91–7610–956–9. ISSN 0375–250X, 361 pages).
2. *Rapport från försvarsberedningen, Förändrad omvärld –
omdanat försvar Ds 1999:2 (Regeringskansliet.
Försvarsdepartementet)* – Report from the Defence
Commission, A Changing World – A Reformed Defence
(Government Office. Defence Ministry), p. 51.
3. *Regeringens proposition 1998/99:74, Förändrad omvärld –
omdanat försvar* – Government Bill 1998/9:74, A Changing
World – A Reformed Defence, p. 28.
4. Bill Kovach and Tom Rosenstiel, *Warp Speed: America in the*

Age of Mixed Media (The Century Foundation/Twentieth Century Fund: The Century Foundation Press, NY, 1999), pp. 7–9, 17.

THREE

ASSESSMENT AND ANALYSIS: BUILDING AN ACCURATE PICTURE

Sir Rodric Braithwaite

Sir Rodric Braithwaite was British Ambassador in Moscow from 1988 to 1992, the years when the Cold War ended and the Soviet Union collapsed. Before then he served as a member of the British foreign service in Poland, the Soviet Union, Italy, Brussels (European Community) and Washington. Throughout his career he dealt extensively with East-West relations, including the preparations for the Conference on Co-operation and Security in Europe and for the negotiations on Mutual and Balanced Force Reductions. On leaving Moscow, he worked for eighteen months as Foreign Policy Adviser to the Prime Minister and Chairman of the Joint Intelligence Committee. He is currently Senior Adviser on Russia to Deutsche Bank, member of the Board of UralMash Zavody, and Chairman of the Moscow School of Political Studies.

Introduction

All of us, whether individuals or organisations, need as much reliable information as we can absorb and use. We could not operate in its absence.

It is difficult enough to acquire and act on relevant

information even when the information is in the public
domain. Witnesses report inaccurately. Prejudice, politics,
incompetence get in the way of sensible interpretation. And
even when the actors possess all the accurate information they
need, they may still for a whole lot of subjective or extraneous
reasons do something quite different.

If all that is true of actors working on overt information, it
is even more true of the acquisition, interpretation and
exploitation of secret information. This is because working in
secret imposes all sorts of specific pressures and constraints.

First, the information may be tainted at source. The agent
who produces it may be unobservant, frightened, corrupt, or
working for the other side. Documents – produced even by
the most sophisticated technical means – may be irrelevant,
untimely, or even forged.

Second, the information may be misinterpreted. This may
not only be because it is unclear. The assessors suffer from
prejudices, or are subject to pressures, which consciously or
unconsciously introduce bias. A notorious example is the
regular overestimation by the American intelligence agencies
and the Pentagon of Soviet military strength, which led in the
1950s to the gross overestimates of Soviet bomber strength
which Eisenhower called 'nothing more than imaginative
creations of irresponsibility'. Third, raw or processed intelligence may fail to reach the actors in time, because the flow
of information has been restricted by the 'need to know', or
as a result of institutional rivalry.

The unsatisfactory nature of much analysis based on intelligence led George Shultz to say that,

> . . . As a general proposition, the basic State Department
> reporting, using open sources, and observation, and
> talking to people, gives you the basic picture. Sometimes
> you can be even misled by what you pick up in some

clandestine way. Because there is a feeling that if you got it by some secret means, it must be very important. And it may be that it's not anywhere near as important as things that are just obviously there.

George Shultz's view is the common prejudice of many professional diplomats. But whether these people like it or not, one irreducible fact remains. Governments, soldiers, corporations and all sorts of villains need information about their opponents – and sometimes about their friends – which their opponents are determined to keep secret. This is a fact of life which will not go away. In practice liberals who would like the secret world to be abolished are wasting their time.

Raw Materials

Governments, soldiers and others want secret intelligence for two broad reasons. They want the facts about their opponents' organisation, equipment and means of communication. This is what Richard K. Betts of Columbia University – one of the most sensible writers on these matters – calls FACTUAL-TECHNICAL WARNING.

And they want to know as much as they can about their opponents' plans, intentions and motivations. Richard Betts calls this CONTINGENT-POLITICAL WARNING. These two different kinds of information raise different problems of acquisition and interpretation.

In theory, facts are solid and concrete. If you are sufficiently ingenious and determined, you should to be able to break through your opponent's defences and acquire the solid information you need as a basis for your own planning. In the military sphere, this means orders of battle, military and communications technology, and weapons characteristics. In the economic field, it is things like the size of another country's gold reserves. And in the commercial field, companies are always trying to filch one another's new inventions.

Even in this area, it is possible of course to get the facts wrong, or to misinterpret or distort them. This is what happened over the 'bomber gap'.

But it is much harder to establish our opponent's intentions. Intelligence agencies occasionally get hold of mouth-watering documentary evidence – a military order, the briefing papers of your negotiating partner, internal policy documents. But that is only a shaky guide to what is going on in your opponent's mind. Dictators, generals, admirals and politicians may reject advice, change their minds, or misunderstand their instructions.

It is hard enough to get into the heads even of one's own family. The problem is much worse if one is trying to judge the intentions of a man whose mind functions according to entirely different principles. A Western analyst, brought up in a comparatively rational liberal atmosphere, can do little more than make a well-informed and well-judged guess. That is why Western governments have been no better at getting inside the minds of Stalin and Hitler, Saddam Hussein or Milošević than the intelligent outside observer.

Methods

The reliability and usefulness of secret intelligence depends to some extent on the way it is gathered. Nowadays this means either spies, or technical means.

Up until the First World War, the spies predominated. The methods employed have varied little for hundreds, if not thousands, of years: bribery, corruption, blackmail and old-fashioned seduction. The technology of dead-letter boxes, brush contacts and secret writing has also changed little, even if it is pursued with greater sophistication and more elegant gadgets. Today's spy uses a miniature camera rather than a sketchbook, and communicates by microbursts rather than invisible ink. But in substance he operates little differently from the two men that Joshua sent into Canaan to spy out the city of Jericho.

But the First World War saw a qualitative leap with the invention of radio direction-finding, communications intelligence and aerial reconnaissance. The Second World War saw a further great leap forward, of which the ENIGMA operation remains the most brilliant example. During the Cold War, the Americans and the Russians deployed a great deal of money and highly sophisticated brain power on the development of gadgets that were able to reach right into the heart of their opponents' military and technological machine. The most important was probably the reconnaissance satellite. Not only did the satellite make arms control agreements possible, it fatally eroded centuries of Russian secrecy and made a major contribution to the still unfinished wave of openness which overwhelmed the Soviet Union.

Some think that this means that the old-fashioned spy has become redundant. Others think we need HUMINT to give us the human insights that technology ignores.

That is all a great oversimplification. Information provided by an agent is indeed more likely to be intrinsically unreliable than information provided by technology. The agent is subject to the pressures of fear, vanity, greed, sloppy thinking and crooked vision. You should not necessarily believe him when he claims to be reporting the intimate thoughts of the dictator. 'Political' information of the kind so often peddled by agents can be very soft indeed. *The Quiet American* may be a satire, but like all good satires it is rooted in reality.

But from time to time the agent can deliver the jackpot. In the decades of strenuous underwater competition between the Americans and the Soviets, the United States spent billions of dollars on the most complex technical devices for evaluating, tracking and countering Soviet submarines. By spending a small part of that sum on purchasing the Walker family, the Soviets seem to have found out very nearly as much about the American submarine effort.

And of course, one thing an agent can do is direct you to the Chinese embassy in Belgrade.

How is the stuff analysed?

But it is by no means enough for clever agents or clever gadgets to collect information and transmit it to their principals. The stuff has to be properly analysed and evaluated, and presented to the actors in a comprehensible form.

Governments set up machinery of varying size and complexity for the purpose, what Richard Betts calls the INTELLI-GENCE BROKERS.

The most important requirement for the intelligence brokers is that they should be dispassionate. They should be divorced from the pressures both of intelligence-gathering and of operational decision-making. An example of what can go wrong if you don't do that occurred in the summer of 1916, when an impatient British admiral waylaid a piece of signals intelligence. He misread it to mean that the German High Seas Fleet was still in harbour when it was already thundering across the North Sea. As a result, Admiral Jellicoe arrived at Jutland too late to secure a decisive victory. In this country, the task is done by the Joint Intelligence Committee. Percy Cradock, probably the Committee's most distinguished Chairman, recently described the Committee's workings in an elegant book, *In Pursuit of British Interests: Reflections on the Foreign Policy of Margaret Thatcher and John Major* (1997). The Committee brings together the heads of the three intelligence agencies and senior representatives of the Foreign Office, the Treasury and the Ministry of Defence. It was originally set up in 1936 by the Chiefs of Staff. Its membership was later broadened and the chair was taken by a Foreign Office Deputy Secretary. After the Falklands War, the JIC was judged by Lord Franks to have failed in its alleged duty of predicting the future. For years it was chaired by an outsider, whose lack of departmental connections was supposed to leave him with an unbiased mind. But the logic behind Lord Franks's solutions was flawed, and at the end of 1993 the Chairmanship passed to a serving official once again. As far as I know, the system works at least as effectively as it did before.

The JIC does not deal in factual technical issues. Its unglamorous task is to discuss, approve and disseminate brief analyses of foreign events and foreign intentions. Its products draw on open information as well as on secret intelligence. They are based on drafts prepared by the Assessments Staff, a small body of about forty officials on secondment from the military, the agencies and the Whitehall bureaucracy who have access to the raw intelligence. The JIC works by consensus. Ministers occasionally grumble that its assessments are boring, or that they say things that Ministers would prefer not to hear. The first is hardly a criticism, while the second is a positive accolade.

By contrast, the American system favours big battalions, a vigorous dialectic and a multiplicity of paper: A teams and B teams of rival analysts, devil's advocates, anything but the bland British system of understated consensus. To the British eye, the American system is ponderous, confusing, open to departmental and political pressures, and unlikely to lead to a sober judgement. The Americans retort that the Toytown system operated by the British is merely a complacent and convenient device for eliding the uncomfortable.

The Russians appear never to have attempted to create an independent mechanism for assessment, even before the Revolution. The Russian intelligence agencies regarded

themselves – not their political superiors – as the ultimate
guardians of the state. There was no attempt to create an independent machinery for assessment. Secret information, spun
as the secret policemen thought best, was fed direct to the
political leadership, of whom the chief of intelligence was in
any case usually a key member. Of course the Russians had
huge successes. They intercepted the telegrams of the British
ambassador at the end of the nineteenth century. They scored
many coups against the West during the Cold War. But even
the intelligence muddle which preceded Pearl Harbor pales
into insignificance before Stalin's refusal to believe the
evidence that he was about to be attacked by Hitler. And the
ultimate fiasco of the Russian secret police was the abortive
coup of August 1991, which destroyed the very system that
the KGB leadership was trying to preserve.

How is it used?

But even if you get solid information, and draw the right
conclusions from it, that is by no means the end of the story.
You have to get the information to the people who can make
operational use of it. And at that point you get into all sorts
of trouble, because it turns out that some of the people who
need the information are not entitled to see it; or that you
cannot use the information because that would reveal your
sources to your opponent.

And even if you are able to give the right information to
the right people at the right time, they still have to take the
right action. There was plenty of relevant intelligence swilling
around before Pearl Harbor, but the Americans were still
caught bending. There was intelligence about German tank
concentrations just before the airborne forces took off for
Arnhem, but by then it would have been difficult, and unat-
tractive, to abort the operation.

Conclusion

Public attitudes to intelligence matters, and above all to so-called intelligence failure, often borders on the hysterical. So I conclude with two points.

A lot of what the press calls 'intelligence reports' are no more than analytical documents, produced by one or other intelligence agency. They may or may not draw on secret information. But their production is subject to all the prejudices, pressures and potential failures of judgement which attend the production of similar documents in other organisations. The insights of intelligence analysts are not intrinsically superior to those of academics, serious journalists, or diplomats. Four or five years ago the CIA hit the headlines with an analytical paper that gave a high possibility to war between Russia and the Ukraine within six months. I do not know whether there was any secret intelligence underlying that report, but the war has still not occurred. That was not an intelligence failure, though it was clearly a misjudgement by the analysts concerned.

Above all it is wrong to pillory intelligence agencies for failing to predict the future. Most of us knew well in advance that the Shah's regime was shaky, and that sooner or later the Soviet system would collapse, but we did not know whether this would happen in a generation, a decade, a year, or a month. All even the best analysts can do is to make well-informed guesses about the most likely future course of events. The CIA did warn the President a few days in advance that something like a coup might occur in Moscow in the middle of August 1991. That warning was based on sound judgement rather than secret information. But inevitably the analysts will get things wrong from time to time. For as the US Congress has sagely observed, 'Policy-makers and private citizens who expect intelligence to foresee all of sudden shifts are attributing to it qualities not yet shared by the deity with mere mortals.'

DISCUSSION

Dmitri Trenin

Dmitri Trenin has been Deputy Director of the Carnegie Moscow Center since July 1997, and was a programme associate from 1994 to 1997. He is co-director of Carnegie's foreign and security policy project. Graduating from the Military Institute of the Soviet Defence Ministry in 1977, his military service included assignments with the military assistance group in Iraq (1975–6), the external relations department of the Soviet High Command in Germany (1978–83), the USSR delegation to the nuclear and space talks in Geneva (1985–91), and teaching English and area studies at the current Defence University in Moscow. In 1993 he was the first non-NATO officer selected as a senior research fellow by the NATO Defence College in Rome. He resigned from the Russian army in October 1993 as a lieutenant-colonel. His publications include (in English) Linking Transatlantic and Eurasian Security: Prospects for Peace Operations *(1993),* Baltic Chance: The Baltic States, Russia and the West in the Emerging Greater Europe *(1997),* Russia's China Problem *(1998) and* Between Geopolitics and Globalisation: The Changing Shape and Nature of Russia's Borders *(forthcoming). He is a member of the International Institute for Strategic Studies in London and the Russian Association of International Studies. He serves on the editorial boards of* International Politics *(Kluwer Law Publications) and* Pro et Contra *(a Russian policy journal).*

Sir Rodric's brilliant paper is also a highly provocative one. In one of its earlier versions it opened and ended with Clausewitz, or rather the great theorist's sceptical assessment of the value of secret *military intelligence*, which is dismissed as an oxymoron. Here, one can't help recalling Stalin's favourite wartime phrase: 'What would Marshal Zhukov have to say to that?' Indeed, the pre-dawn haze on 22 June 1941 was so thick that the scale of Germany's actual preparation for war remained a mystery to Soviet commanders until it was too late. Soviet intelligence reported on the eve of the war that the Germans kept 50 per cent of their forces in the West, whereas the real figure was about 30 per cent. In the long weeks that followed, the smoke of battle was so intense that the Soviet High Command often only had the vaguest idea of where enemy or even friendly forces were, in what condition they were, and what they were doing.

In early September 1999, a Moscow newspaper called the fighting in Dagestan an 'unknown war' – unknown, above all, to the Russian High Command, who, after a tactical success in late August – when Prime Minister Putin prematurely declared victory – had lost track of the adversary's moves. The Russian generals seemed genuinely to believe the military intelligence reports of a 'thousand' enemy dead. The small number of bodies discovered by the Russians after the Chechen retreat was conveniently explained by a story of 1,500 donkeys used by the insurgents to carry their dead across the frontier. The simple fact was never seriously considered that it is impossible to keep 1,000 deaths secret in a small place like present-day Chechnya, with a total population barely above a half-million, and only a quarter of a million men.

Yet, it is precisely on the battlefield that the value of secret intelligence is at its unsurpassed highest. Like Clausewitz, Zhukov in his *Memoirs and Reflections* had little to say about the value of military intelligence. He did, however, give a generally positive spin to his remarks, claiming general satisfaction with the information the *Stavka* received during the war. On the computerised battlefield, one cannot move or fire without knowing, in real time, what the enemy is doing, where and how. And there is precious little specific information about your enemy that is openly available. Modern military commanders have at their disposal tools which no Clausewitz, or Zhukov for that

matter, could have imagined – and yet it may never be known
how many Yugoslav army tanks were actually destroyed in the
ten weeks of NATO's bombings – 140, as SHAPE claimed, or
a mere 13 as was reported by the merciless press. This is not an
indictment of Allied military intelligence. Technical capabilities
are usually exaggerated, and such counter-measures as camou-
flage and dispersal are often underrated. However, despite all its
failures and inadequacies, military intelligence has largely
contributed to a first-ever military victory without a single Allied
life being lost. If there is a problem with military intelligence, it
is that, as Sir Rodric points out, it is often inadequate and/or
confusing when you need it most.

The picture changes when we look at political intelligence,
and thus leave the realm of the tactical and go strategic. What
is so essential to the general is generally of marginal importance
to the statesman – except in absolutely rare cases, such as the
transfer of US atomic secrets to the Soviet Union in the 1940s.
What the secret services can and do provide is often redundant,
as it is based on the same open sources as the analysis performed
by the diplomats. Moreover, a militarised bureaucracy is even
less prone to fresh thinking than its civilian counterpart. A closed
organisation cannot engage in free exchange with independent
analysts and presents its findings to a very limited audience; this
also automatically limits potential criticism.

More seriously, some members of the secret services develop
a vision that only accepts the 'secret world' as the true one,
dismissing the much more complex reality as merely a cover.
Conspiracy theories, never in short supply, make the imagined
world much more logical than life itself and consequently easier
to explain. The statesmen who preferred to live on a daily fare
of intelligence briefings only erred when they thought that the
secret services were 'uncovering the truth' for them. In fact, the
most they could expect to get was an important and unique
element of the general picture but not the picture itself.

The rise of political intelligence during the Cold War to a position of unprecedented eminence had a lot to do with the total nature of the confrontation. In the course of a forty-year-long preparation for a Third World War, nothing seemed too extravagant, or too unimportant, not to be attempted. As a result, the services became giant vacuum cleaners. What they sucked in often overwhelmed the physical and intellectual abilities of those who had to assess and interpret the collected material. Interpreting was not always intellectually honest. The war machines and intelligence communities of both sides had an understandable institutional interest in exaggerating the adversary's strength, readiness, etc. On the other hand, even among the most knowledgeable and well-briefed people there existed precious little understanding of the way the other system worked. Soviet leaders were genuinely surprised by the implications of the Watergate scandal; Western leaders by the sudden demise of the Soviet Union. Even as late as mid-1991, the CIA was still predicting the Soviet Union's disintegration within the next five years. The irony seems to be that, in a confrontation between two states one of which represents a 'closed' society, *both* sides entertain distorted views of each other. The totalitarian or authoritarian adversary, in addition, also has a distorted view of itself. The abortive Moscow *putsch* of August 1991, inspired among a few others by Vladimir Kryuchkov, then head of the KGB, testified to the critical lack of understanding of his country by the very person who was in theory its best-informed bureaucrat.

The Cold War environment with its cosy certainties bred intellectual sloth. The political masters were rarely stimulating the secret services with insightful questions. The political leadership also rarely bothered to put their services to the five demanding tests so aptly sketched by Sir Rodric. Large sums of money were thoughtlessly wasted, but the same argument applies to the Gargantuan Cold War machines as a whole. Another problem is the propensity to consciously exaggerate the adversary's strength

in an effort to increase defence and intelligence funding. Since
the end of the Second World War, both Soviet and Western security services have fully exploited their virtual monopoly to these
ends when informing their own leaders. Sir Rodric referred in
his paper to the so-called 'bomber gap', but other examples are
numerous. He also correctly points out the lack of an independent authority, in the USSR, to assess intelligence information. The attempt by Stalin in 1947 to create for this purpose
an Information Committee, under the chairmanship of a senior
diplomat, was short-lived and has never been revived.

What is needed now is to place the intelligence services in a
new political, economic and information context, which won't
be easy. The professional conservatism of the intelligence
community is a well-known fact. After a half-century of intense
confrontation the power of inertia is enormous. And no matter
how clear-thinking the political masters may be, they will hardly
be able to formulate the new tasks of their intelligence services
with such attractive clarity as their predecessors were able to at
the outset of the Cold War.

Intelligence, however, is only as useful as political leaders
permit it to be. In his memoirs Zhukov discusses how in early
1941 Stalin repeatedly dismissed intelligence reports about
impending war because he thought his 'reading' of Hitler was
far superior to that of the services. Of course, Stalin was a dictator. However, Fritz Ermath's recent piece in *The National Interest*
points to situations when elected leaders pursue policy initia-
tives which, once set in place, become highly resistant to non-
conforming data from intelligence services. Ermath refers to this
as 'politicisation' of intelligence – the warping of intelligence
analysis to fit political agendas. This is hardly surprising. After
all, intelligence services are a separate, yet inseparable, part of
the government bureaucracy, sharing most of the latter's characteristics. So, Zhukov's praise of the intelligence services' contribution must be put in a proper context.

Conclusions

1. Despite all the advances of the information revolution, secret intelligence remains a useful and necessary tool for political decision-making. The end of Cold War confrontation requires a fresh look at the concept, and probably its complete over-haul, but hardly its abolition.

2. Secret intelligence is a vital, but mainly tactical instrument, an auxiliary means to understanding the environment in which a statesman acts. Its value is at its highest when specific and carefully formulated questions are involved. Conversely, it is at its lowest when fundamental issues are raised. This is a crucial difference that policy-makers must bear in mind to be able to ask their secret intelligence services the right questions, at the same time as they avoid looking at the world through their spymasters' eyes.

3. Instead of giving them a global mission, statesmen could do better by exploiting the secret services' comparative advantages. This could be done by concentrating the scarce resources in the field of tactical intelligence. There is no substitute for that on the battlefield. As to political intelligence, it is at its strongest where opaque actors are concerned, such as authoritarian regimes, terrorist organisations, rebel groups, organised crime networks, drugs/arms traffickers, etc.

4. There is an obvious need to provide constant and competent political guidance to the services, to raise their accountability and redirect them to new tasks. Like the armed forces who have outlived the strategic environment for which they were created, the intelligence services need to be assigned a wholly new role which would serve the nations' – and not the services' – interests, while allowing the intelligence community to maintain their professional self-esteem.

5. There is a growing need for government secret analysts to come into the open and for governments to let their men

compete with outsiders, such as independent think-tanks, the
more analytical sections of the media, etc. This would ideally
result in reducing redundancy and emphasising the services'
undeniable comparative advantages in the areas where they
can, at least theoretically, outperform the others.

R. James Woolsey

Sir Rodric's excellent and fascinating presentation leads me
to suggest really only four footnotes and one quibble. But I
want to begin by saying that his opening plea, that we recognise and have sympathy with him for his amateurism, recalls
to me my father's favourite line when sitting down at a poker
table. My father was a shrewd trial lawyer and a very fine
poker player, but particularly when playing against individuals from out of town, wealthy lawyers from New York and the
like, he was given to emphasising his Oklahoma twang and
beginning the evening by saying in a wide-eyed and rather
simple tone, 'Well, ah don't reahlly know how ta play, but
ah'd shure like ta learn.'

Sir Rodric says that intelligence may be, 1) tainted, 2) misinterpreted, 3) late and 4) ignored, and all of those are true.

Risking sounding like an American infatuated with technology, let me admit that I am an American often infatuated
by technology, and point out that sometimes, for misinter-
pretation and lateness especially, there are technological fixes.
The main reason, of course, for the bomber-gap fears and the
missile-gap fears of the 1950s was that we really didn't know
that much about what the Soviet military was doing, but the
man who unfortunately went to his grave as the father of the
Bay of Pigs, Richard Bissell, a senior official in the CIA, fixed
that. Because Bissell was also the father of the U-2.

Bissell had been able to save some $20 million in a

separate account from various other expenditures, as sort of a slush fund, and he took it and went to Kelly Johnson at the Skunk Works at Lockheed, and said, 'This is all I've got; I need a brand new aeroplane that will be able to overfly the Soviet Union above the level of its air defences.' Kelly looked at it a little bit and said, 'Well, it's going to take a new engine, a new camera and a new airframe.' Bissell said, 'This is what we've got,' and Kelly said, 'Let's see what we can do.' Now, $20 million in the American Defense Department acquisition system, even then, would generally buy you at most a modest set of view-graphs. Kelly and his handful of craftsmen and engineers at the Skunk Works, however, in eighty-eight days had a prototype, in eight months had a first flight, and in eighteen months, with a new camera from Polaroid and new engines, were flying operational missions over the Soviet Union. And they gave Bissell back around $2 million.

The day the U-2 was shot down, the Corona satellites were far along in development, also due to CIA technological innovation, and the day Gary Powers was traded for Colonel Abel the first Corona mission flew. So although there were some interruptions and there were some problems, for misinterpretations and lateness sometimes a Kelly Johnson and a Richard Bissell, and technology, can solve the problem.

Now about being ignored, Brian Latell and I know a little something about that. As National Intelligence Officer for Latin America, Brian did a very fine intelligence estimate of Haiti, right at the end of the Bush administration, before I came into office. But because six months later, in the summer of 1993, there was a leak from Capitol Hill to the effect that it contained some critical comments about President Aristide, he got more press attention than he really wanted. He and I spent twenty-nine hours together, sitting before various Congressional enquiries about whether or not he was in fact being too negative with respect to President Aristide. I think his assessment has, over time, proved to be right on the money, but the point is that policy-makers, both in Congress and in the Executive Branch, often want to be told what they want to hear, not what you objectively think as an analyst. And in my judgement, the worst characteristic that the head of an intelligence service, or for that matter a professional analyst, can have is wanting too much to be liked by the policy- makers. Brian and I never really had that problem.

Tainted, yes, it can be tainted. Not just human sources, but certainly *Our Man in Havana* remains, on this point, the finest spy novel of all time. It is also true of SIGINT and imagery that they can be tainted. Underground construction, such as what the Soviets and now the Russians do at Yamanta Mountain, can be hidden. Or SIGINT can be wrong: people can be lying to one another in encrypted communications that you break, and then you believe that the substance is accurate because you decrypted the message. Tainted sources are possible in all of these ways, it's not just humans.

Footnote number 2, diplomatic scepticism and George Shultz. The problem to my mind is not diplomats as individuals, or anything of the kind. I've been in that world, too, and I think the American State Department and the British Foreign Office contain many remarkably able and objective individuals. The problem is an institutional one. The problem is that Foreign Ministries and the US Department of State have this propensity for 'clientitis', of wanting to say nice things about their clients (and sour things about their opponents) in whatever region they are dealing with. This is one of the most important reasons for those in the secret intelligence services and intelligence officers to be in a very important position in making many assessments. It really is not a uniquely American State Department disease. I think it's common in a number of Foreign Ministries and Foreign

Offices, and it is one of the main reasons for the existence of intelligence services and intelligence analysts.

A third footnote: reconnaissance satellites and their erosion of the secrecy that undergirds totalitarian and secret systems, such as the Soviet Union. About this, I guess I would say, 'You ain't seen nothing yet.' If you saw the news this morning on television, Ikonos, a 1-metre resolution commercial satellite, a joint venture of two American and one Japanese company, was launched successfully from Vandenberg yesterday. Before too long 1-metre resolution imagery will be available within hours on the Internet for thousands of dollars to news organisations, and the old stuff that is boring and in the archives, which is where it goes after five days, will be available for hundreds of dollars to people who are interested in using it to plan agriculture, or for all sorts of purposes.

Now, there are complex issues associated with this. The United States Government retains some capacity for shutting off these commercial satellites in the event of wartime and the like – at least the American ones. But as a general proposition, this is much, much worse news for autocratic and totalitarian societies than it is for open ones. We are used to dealing with the problems of people knowing largely what we are doing. Mr Kim Jong II and Mr Saddam Hussein, and for that matter Jiang Zemin, are not really used to that yet, and they are about to experience seeing some things on CNN that they would just as soon not see there.

Footnote 4: contrasts between information provided by agents and those provided by technology. The main point, I think, is that now increasingly we have not just complementary information provided by spies and by technical collection, but rather complementary collection. Increasingly it is the case for us, and it will be for many intelligence services over time, that whether you are talking about signals intercepts or reconnaissance satellites, spies tip off technical collection and technical collection tips off spies. And we will see more of that in the future.

My one quibble is with Sir Rodric's delicious sentence that the American system favours big battalions of vigorous dialectic and a multiplicity of paper, A teams and B teams of rival analysts, devil's advocates, anything but the bland British system of understated consensus. Apparently, we are thought to generate too much heat on our side of the Atlantic.

I remember thirty-five years ago, when I was an undergraduate just down the street here at St John's – I came from Oklahoma with summer temperatures regularly over 100 degrees and we didn't think too much about it – we had several days of what I considered to be perfectly lovely late spring, early summer weather in June, and one of the tabloids ran a headline, '79 Degrees Again Tomorrow: No Relief in Sight'.

Now I will never quarrel with the British propensity for understatement. It is one of the most delightful features of the transatlantic dialogue. But just a word about bland consensus, British or otherwise. It doesn't, in my experience, take any particular effort to get bureaucrats to reach a bland consensus. It's kind of what comes naturally. That's sort of like saying you have to work hard and exert some effort to get Washington lawyers to argue with one another, or to say that if a group of male and female undergraduates are away on some college overnight trip, you need to exert effort to get them to get, let's say, romantic with one another. These things are what people do naturally, and so the hard job is keeping bland and deceptive consensuses (consensi?) from coming about.

The problem also is that bland consensuses may be a result of mirror-imaging, which is a particular disease that I think all intelligence services are prey to. In my judgement and experience, it takes a good deal of pestering and nudging of the bureaucracy to get analysts to be clear and to inform their bosses with what they write, rather than just agreeing with one another on bland language.

Joe Nye was my first Director of the National Intelligence Council; Christine Williams who is here was the second. In the very first estimate that Joe and I oversaw in early 1993, I reviewed an assessment on narcotics trafficking. It was extremely bland and had been wholly agreed upon by all agencies involved, and it was absolutely worthless. It had, for example, predicted an increase in the price of cocaine, but it wasn't clear whether or not that was because demand was going up or supply was going down. After sending it back five times to be rewritten, we finally got something in which the reasons for the disagreements between the various agencies were clear, and the document became a rather decent teaching mechanism to help decision-makers, new ones in a new administration, understand things like how money-laundering works and the like.

Mirror-imaging deriving from consensus, on the other hand, can produce not just worthless paper, but real policy failures. My favourite current example is the 1995 National Intelligence estimate on the ballistic missile threat to the United States. This was put out not by the CIA alone but by the NIC, which includes all of the intelligence community, after (I am compelled to point out) I had returned to private law practice. It answered the question, 'If there is negligible or no international trade in ballistic missile technology and weapons of mass destruction, and if we look only at the lower forty-eight states, ignoring Alaska and Hawaii, how long would it take North Korea and Iraq and Iran by their own devices to design, produce and test to American standards an ICBM that could reach the lower forty-eight states?' The answer came out fifteen years. It was probably the right answer to that question, it was just an idiotic question. But it was a question that had presented the possibility of consensus for the bureaucracy.

It's taken a couple of years, the Rumsfeld Commission, and a new and much finer intelligence analysis of ballistic missile threats to the United States, to move the intelligence community around to a rather more divisive, but far more useful, assessment.

Apparently our Russian friends developed a bland consensus that persists, perhaps even to this day, that some silly verbiage by a junior British Colonel Blimp in the late 1940s was a better indicator of British intentions to attack the USSR in 1957 in order to preserve the British Empire, than a) the dismantling of that Empire in the late 1940s and early 1950s, b) the 1956 attack on Suez, which alienated us, their presumed principal ally, in this planned 1957 attack on the Soviet Union, and c) the huge drawdown in the UK military forces in the late 1940s and early 1950s. Now if that bland bureaucratic consensus can survive, even apparently until today, I'd say it's a rather major statement about the survivability of even the oddest of bureaucratic consensuses.

GENERAL DISCUSSION

Sir Rodric opened the discussion with a comment on James Woolsey's paper, specifically on the question of consensus. He had not intended to give the impression that he was advocating bland consensus, but had suggested it rather as a cultural phenomenon. He agreed that intelligence analysts had to be capable of challenging wider governmental complacency and consensus, but felt it was incumbent on them to come to a single view of what they think the situation is, rather than present their bosses with a range of competing views, thus putting the onus on people who may not be in the best position to make the judgement.

On the question of conspiracy theory, he remarked that it was a substitute for religion in a secular age, replacing the will of God as the unseen and therefore incomprehensible cause. That was plainly unsatisfactory. But it is also unsatisfactory, and indeed frightening, to believe that everything that happens in the world happens by accident. People therefore invent conspiracy arguments – the CIA, KGB or the Jewish Masonic conspiracy – and everything slips back into place again. This is true of open societies, but even more so in closed societies.

Turning to Dmitri Trenin's point about how the Soviet leaders perceived the world, he referred to the memoirs of, for example, Gorbachev or Kryuchkov, that show that both the producers and consumers sincerely believed that their view, not only of the outside world but also of what was going on in their own country, was somehow superior to everybody else's. And the West also believed that the KGB knew what was happening in the Soviet Union. The West believed it because the KGB believed it, and no doubt members of the KGB told their Western counterparts what the facts were, namely, that only the KGB understood what was happening in the country because only they had a network, there being no free press, etc. They were, he concluded, living in a dream world, and that was the danger of a situation where the agencies, particularly in a closed society, also assume responsibility for policy.

A British academic stressed the importance of the part played by the mind-set of the analysts, especially if they are specialists in a particular region because of their language training. He cited as an example the Far Eastern Department of the Foreign Office, whose attention was so focused on Japan in 1939 that for six weeks they diverted the attention of the economic planners from planning a blockade of Germany. On the Soviet side, as recently published archival research has shown, the most extraordinary example is seen in Stalin's surprise in June 1941. Since the visit to Ankara by Anthony

Eden in January 1941, both Stalin and Molotov were terrified by the thought of a reactivation of the Anglo-Turkish alliance, with – inconceivably – a British naval invasion into the Black Sea and the re-staging of the Crimean War. The situation now is that the intelligence services are concentrating their attention on capabilities and ignoring intention as essentially unknowable. Historically it was often the other way round. For example, Britain in the 1930s was petrified with fear of a German air attack at a time when the Germans had no aircraft capable of reaching Britain from a German base. Such examples demonstrated the danger of the institutionalisation of anxieties.

James Woolsey accepted that this was a good point, but pointed out that technology, particularly intelligence from reconnaissance satellites, has made it easier to concentrate on capabilities, about which there are fewer mysteries than there are about intentions, and they therefore had been a more attractive option for bureaucracies, whether Western or Soviet. He added that in the case of very ideological parties, the best guide to their intentions was what they told their own people. For example, the best guide to Hitler's intentions was *Mein Kampf*, and the best guide to what the Soviets had been trying to do in the world was in their public statements. In a more recent case, *Economist* magazine, simply by reading what the VJP was publishing a week or two before the Indian nuclear tests, had said that the Indians might test a nuclear weapon, whereas Chanceries around the world were listening to the Indian Government's lies instead. So, while intentions are important, often intentions for ideological parties and governments that are ruled by them are out in the open. He agreed that the institutionalisation of anxieties was an obstacle to sound intelligence, and had had this in mind when speaking about consensus in his presentation.

Referring to Sir Rodric's point about the need for intelligence services to produce a judgement, he regarded a single-point design of the future as a likely recipe for an intelligence failure. He regarded as more valuable a judgement that both suggested a particular outcome and also indicated the possibility of a different alternative, giving the reasons for both arguments. Sir Rodric agreed that capabilities were easier to establish than intentions, since they deal with concrete facts – 'counting beans' – but noted that the facts themselves can be influenced by institutional bias, not least of the people who want more 'beans' of their own. The former US Defense Secretary Caspar Weinburger used to produce a glossy booklet about the Soviet threat, based on brilliant photographs of shining weapons, and always just around budget time. Sir Rodric accepted that this practice was not only understandable, since it was the defence establishment that was blamed if there were not enough resources when the need arose, but that over-insurance was built into any system.

He recounted an anecdote about the difference between capabilities and intentions. During a debate in the early 1970s about mutual and balanced force reductions in Europe, he was arguing against the scepticism of the British military, when a recently returned RAF officer from Germany said that the Russians now had an air-portable force that was capable of flying into Frankfurt airport, setting up a perimeter and seeing off the miserable forces that we would send against them. 'He said, "What do you think about that?" and I said, "Well, they are not going to do that," and he said, "How do you know?" and I said, "Of course, I don't know, but they are not going to do it." And actually they didn't.' While it was both natural and not reprehensible to over-insure against one's worst fears, Sir Rodric urged the need to introduce a balancing factor into policy-making. The admirals and generals need to be told, for example, that their wish for three full-size aircraft carriers is understandable but that the economy cannot afford them, and that, in any case, the intelligence judgement is that a particular threat is very unlikely. This may be wrong, and the judgements made about the Falklands show how wrong one can be, but since it is not possible to control the future, one is going to be wrong from time to time. 'That's life.'

A British Military Intelligence officer took up the discussion on looking at one future or multiple futures, and argued that the more one tried to pick one future, the more likely one was to be wrong. On the other hand, at a certain point the idea of multiple futures is too confusing for the policy-makers. While it had worked reasonably well for force development, he wondered whether the presentation of multiple scenarios was a useful way to build a dialogue at the senior bureaucratic, if not the political, level, and asked how it could be done.

A former member of the Assessment Staff, now a member of the UK delegation to NATO, commenting on the discussion about 'bland consensus', remarked that, while this may apply at the exalted level of the JIC, at the lower CIG (Current Intelligence Group) level things were quite different. There, difficult arguments took place to reach some kind of agreement as to what all the information meant; nothing was out of bounds, including technical intelligence which one could challenge. Argument continued until everyone felt reasonably comfortable, and it was the end product that went up for further discussion. He regarded this as an important process. He asked whether that process, both at the CIG level and at the higher levels, was not in itself more important than the product, i.e. a formal JIC paper, because it allows the policy-makers to internalise the intelligence, so that when they are writing their telegrams of instructions they do not quote the intelligence but are aware of it and it can influence what they write. It allows the agencies to have some feel for the current policy preoccupations, and this in turn may help them to focus their own understanding.

Sir Rodric replied that this described the process exactly. In his view, one of the most useful things the assessment machinery did was to develop through the dialectic a common view of the meaning of information collected, which was then circulated.

He recalled that there had been many bloody battles, and that he had seen one of his functions as Chairman of the JIC as challenging assessments, asking such questions as, 'Do you really mean it when you say that the Chinese Army is about to invade Hong Kong? Are you sure that's what you mean?' On other occasions he would defend an opinion, as for example when the agencies argued that all sides in Bosnia were villains and not to be believed, and that the latest ceasefire was not going to hold. The policy-makers found such a judgement most unpleasant.

He also agreed with James Woolsey that what finally went up to the policy-makers should not be bland to the point of meaninglessness. Although the JIC did not always achieve it, the ideal was a common view of what was most likely to happen and what was the extreme. He cautioned that although scenarios were desirable, they should not exceed two. As Henry Kissinger had said, 'If you have three scenarios, it's because the bureaucrats want their bosses to choose the middle one.'

James Woolsey declared that he did not want to be understood as opposing a sound consensus that was developed by analysts and that sometimes made possible that rarest of all events, an intelligence success. 'Since policy-makers run things,' he said, 'as almost everyone in this room knows, 99.9 per cent of the time we have policy successes and intelligence failures. We very rarely have intelligence successes and policy failures.' As a very good example of the latter he cited Austrian intelligence, which in 1912 or 1913 came up with a judgement sent up to Count von Berchtold, the Austro-Hungarian Foreign Minister, who was a great consumer of intelligence. Count von Berchtold received an assessment from Austrian intelligence which said that, 'due to the current tensions in Europe and the relationships between the Great Powers, we badly fear that there may be the risk of general war in Europe, and if that should occur the opportunity would probably arise through the weakness of the Russian state for a revolution in Russia which we

fear may come under the sway of the Bolsheviks.' Count von
Berchtold wrote in the margins of this fine piece of intelligence
analysis, 'and who, pray tell, is going to lead this revolution? This
idiot Bronstein [Trotsky] who spends all day playing chess at
the Café Central?'

A Canadian intelligence officer drew attention to the changed
requirements of national security that now have to include organised criminal activities, immigration matters, terrorism, all of
them foreign to intelligence agencies or that used to be shared
with law enforcement, whose goal was criminal prosecution. He
asked what intelligence agencies are able to do to meet these
new requirements.

James Woolsey replied that the mind-sets of the law enforcement and intelligence agencies, at least in the USA, were
markedly different. An intelligence officer, he said, generally
wants to recruit a source, lie low, and continue to work quietly
with his source and not let anyone know about it, occasionally
feeding an item of information up the line that might be useful
to the Head of State, hoping that nobody else would know, and
to keep going like that for as long as possible. Law enforcement
authorities, on the other hand, are lawyers and are therefore
focused on cases. Their view is that absolutely everything that
might remotely be relevant to a prosecution should be gathered,
studied thoroughly, digested and used as necessary, and if an
objection is raised that using part of it may endanger a source
or a method, it is to be ignored. All the facts are gathered, the
villain is prosecuted and sent to jail, and the files are bundled
up and sent down to the basement of the court house, and the
next case is begun. These approaches, he said, represented very
different mind-sets.

In his experience, he continued, the best way to get these two
institutions working together is to have at least enough of a treaty
between the intelligence services and the law enforcement entities that they understand that on such things as, say, narcotics

work, which in the United States often involves Latin America, teams of intelligence officers and law enforcement officers are formed to work together. They need to be told that it is important that they work together, and that it is important for them to realise that they come from different backgrounds with different emphases. In the US system, he went on, this works best overseas where there is a strong ambassador who is willing and able to crack heads together and make them work together, even when sometimes they don't want to. In his experience this sort of arrangement works well, and the problem comes not from the professionals in the field, but rather more often from bureaucratic elbowing for turf in Washington. But a handshake between the senior law enforcement staff and their counterparts in the intelligence communities will usually produce good results, though it needs a lot of effort. 'It really is the governmental analogue of "Men are from Mars and Women are from Venus." You've just got to have different perspectives on the whole thing.'

FOUR

INTELLIGENCE AND THE POLICY PROCESS: WHO DRIVES WHOM?

Brian Latell

*B*rian Latell has been an Adjunct Professor at Georgetown *University, Washington DC, for the last twenty-two years teaching courses on Latin America and Cuba, including a full semester option on the Cuban Missile Crisis. He has written and lectured on Cuba under Fidel Castro, contemporary Mexico and US foreign intelligence issues. In 1998 he co-edited* Eye in the Sky: The Story of the Corona Spy Satellites, *published by the Smithsonian Press. He served as National Intelligence Officer for Latin America at the National Intelligence Council between 1990 and 1994. From 1994 to 1998 he was Director of the Center for the Study of Intelligence at the CIA and chaired the Editorial Board of* Studies in Intelligence, *the journal of the intelligence profession. He retired from government service in 1998. He is the recipient of the CIA's Distinguished Intelligence Medal, the Helene M. Boatner Award and Georgetown University's Silver Vicennial Medal.*

In his farewell remarks to his staff at CIA Headquarters, a former Chairman of the National Intelligence Council employed an analogy freighted with meaning relevant to the dynamics between American foreign policy-making officials[1] and their intelligence counterparts. He noted that although he was leaving the intelligence service with great regret, he looked forward to his onward assignment because there he would be in a driver's seat.

He would soon assume a senior policy-making position. There he would levy requirements on his former intelligence colleagues, judge their work from the perspective of a sub-cabinet position, and be courted by representatives of the intelligence community expecting he would be more likely than most policy officials to appreciate what intelligence could do to support his requirements. He would move from a primarily passive and supporting role as a provider of intelligence analysis and become instead an activist, a policy architect and builder.

At the staff meeting, his audience – mostly National Intelligence Officers (NIOs) – themselves all senior and seasoned veterans of intelligence-policy interactions, appreciated and seemed unanimously to concur. Given a comparable opportunity, nearly every one of these producers of national intelligence estimates – the highest level intelligence assessments – would no doubt also have switched from being 'back seat drivers' to drivers of policy.

In fact, dozens of NIOs have done just that since 1973, when DCI William Colby abolished the Office of National Estimates (ONE) and established the NIO structure in its stead. NIOs, both career intelligence officers and others inducted into those positions from the military, other government agencies, academia and business, have moved on to senior policy positions at State, Defense, the White House and elsewhere. Robert Gates, a former NIO for the USSR (also a former Chairman of the National Intelligence Council), became Deputy National Security Adviser under President Bush, and later Director of Central Intelligence. General Paul Gorman, a former NIO for General Purpose Forces, was promoted to four-star rank and to the leadership of a unified military command. Others have served as ambassadors, senior Pentagon policy officials and NSC senior directors.

The frequency and ease with which NIOs and Chairmen of the NIC have moved from the metaphorical back seat to the driver's seat of policy-making is notable for several reasons. Perhaps of greatest relevance to questions of policy-maker–intelligence relations is the fact that their emigration to policy jobs appears to be highly *uncharacteristic* of the career paths of senior officers virtually everywhere else in the American intelligence community.[2] For example, senior CIA officers whose careers have been concentrated in one of the Agency's four directorates (and have not served tours in the NIC) have rarely moved to policy positions. It appears, moreover, that officials of such other entities of the intelligence community as the Defense Intelligence Agency, the Bureau of Intelligence and Research, the National Security Agency, or the National Reconnaissance Office, have infrequently transferred to policy-making positions.

Why then has one small component of the intelligence community[3] so disproportionately contributed senior members of its staff to policy-making? The answer seems to reside in the unique role of NIC Chairmen and NIOs as brokers between the intelligence and policy communities. That role is based on at least the following five factors: 1) their demonstrated and often widely recognised expertise as regional or functional specialists; 2) the activist temperament and organisational-bureaucratic skills of individuals typically selected to serve in these positions; 3) their unique responsibility for preparing the co-ordinated analysis of all components in the intelligence community; 4) their responsibility to produce national intelligence estimates, the most formal and authoritative analytic documents produced by American foreign intelligence; and 5) the recognition in policy councils, at least since the early 1980s, that NIOs who later assumed policy-making positions readily and effectively adapted to the demands of their new positions.

The Demise of the Office of National Estimates

Thus, DCI Colby's vision in 1973 of creating a more activist and specialised cadre of intelligence policy-brokers has been vindicated. In fact, by the time Colby intervened, the need to improve policy support had been evident for some time. Years before, the ONE had been a top innovator in the field of strategic intelligence, and the national intelligence-estimates style that was perfected beginning in the 1950s fitted well the policy-making styles of the Truman and Eisenhower administrations. But in 1961 the once distinguished estimates office had begun to decline as policy-makers in the new Kennedy administration broke with the more structured, even familial, intimacies that had existed between top policy and intelligence officials.[4] National intelligence estimates, and the Board of National Estimates that moulded them, had been created after all by Eisenhower's former Chief of Staff Walter Bedell Smith. He had endeavoured to make certain that his innovations succeeded in providing policy-makers with better intelligence support.

But John Kennedy and the rousing young men of his New Frontier initially were enamoured not of the temperate, scholarly (and generally older) intelligence analysts but rather of the swashbuckling leaders of the CIA's operational directorate, whose missions included covert operations.[5] There were close social ties between Kennedy administration luminaries and top operations officers, but apparently few such relationships with top analysts. Soon after John Kennedy's inauguration, the seductive power[6] of the clandestine service shaped his administration's entire view of intelligence, and continued to do so despite a brief disenthralment following the Bay of Pigs calamity in April 1961.[7]

The decline of the ONE was accelerated by the Cuban Missile Crisis and what proved to be the most unfortunate national intelligence estimate ever produced. On 19 September 1962, before any U-2 imagery or other conclusive evidence was available, the Board of National Estimates, under the leadership of its redoubtable Chairman Sherman Kent, issued a laboured special estimate that concluded that Nikita Khrushchev would be unlikely to despatch strategic nuclear missiles to Cuba. The timing could not have been worse. The estimate appeared less than a month before the Soviet SS-4 ballistic missiles were discovered in Cuba.

The Board of National Estimates argued in the estimate (Special National Intelligence Estimate 85-3-62), *The Military Build Up in Cuba*, that the installation of strategic weapons in Cuba by the Kremlin would 'be incompatible with Soviet policy as we presently estimate it. It would indicate a far greater willingness to increase the level of risk in US-Soviet relations than the USSR has displayed thus far, and this would have important policy implications in other areas.'[8]

This was no mere error of prognostication. Kent and the Board of National Estimates made other errors that in retrospect seem inexplicable. Most notably, they were recklessly cavalier in ignoring the concerns that the relatively new DCI, John McCone, had repeatedly been expressing in the intelligence and policy communities since that summer. He had told the President and his most senior foreign policy advisers that he believed that Khrushchev *would* place strategic missiles in Cuba. He had no evidence to support his hunch other than the installation of a number of Soviet surface-to-air missile sites on the island that he concluded were to provide a defensive shield for a strategic capability.

McCone, who had become DCI after Allen Dulles's departure in November 1961, was travelling in Europe on his honeymoon when the estimate was completed. But he was in regular communication with the CIA, providing comments on the draft and urging a tougher line, which in the end the Board of National Estimates ignored. McCone was poorly served by Deputy DCI Marshall Carter, who could have insisted that the DCI's objections be incorporated. But the responsibility to have done so was squarely on the shoulders of Kent and the Board of National Estimates, who, for whatever reasons, decided not only that McCone was wrong but that it was unnecessary to acknowledge his views in any fashion in the estimate. Since the advent of the NIO structure, such disregard for the views of a DCI has been unthinkable. To a considerable extent that is because of the much closer relations that have existed since 1973 between successive DCIs and their NIOs.

The Missile Crisis estimate fiasco provides other important lessons relevant to how American intelligence and policy officials interact. Kent and the Board did McCone and the Kennedy administration a substantial disservice when they minimised alternative analysis in the estimate and failed to more than superficially examine Soviet and Cuban rationales for the worst case scenario, the one that would soon come to pass. The estimators did briefly evaluate the 'contribution which Cuban bases might make to the Soviet strategic posture', but then merely observed that 'this contingency must be examined carefully, even though it would run counter to current Soviet policy'.[9] Had they in fact examined the possibility carefully, they might have included analysis or speculation about how vulnerable Khrushchev believed Castro's regime was in 1962 while it was still under unrelenting covert assault by the Kennedy administration.

Finally, the estimators failed egregiously to place the estimate in its unique political context by recognising the extraordinary sensitivity of Cuba issues in the Kennedy White House. This was no mystery to McCone. Despite his own misgivings about the advisability of new covert actions against Cuba, he endeavoured to satisfy the demands of the President and Attorney General Robert Kennedy to topple Castro.[10] And, mindful that Allen Dulles, and his Deputy Director for Plans Richard Bissell, were both political casualties of the Bay of Pigs, he was appropriately neuralgic about keeping the President and other policy-makers fully apprised of developments there.

The Kennedys' obsession with Castro required that the CIA devote substantial resources to intelligence collection and analysis on Cuba, and McCone made certain that coverage was comprehensive.[11] Kent and the Board of National Estimates should have been more sensitive to the political exigencies that affected Cuba policy, and if they had been, they might have produced an estimate more nuanced in the range of possible explanations for the huge and sudden Soviet military build-up on the island. In Kent's puritanical view of the proper role of estimators, however, acknowledgement of the political environment in which an estimate was produced was anathema.

Worse yet, when it was all said and done, Kent and others in the ONE proudly but foolishly insisted even long after the Missile Crisis that the estimate had not really reflected poorly on their endeavours.[12] Despite their protestations, the fiasco caused the Board to retreat and become more cautious in its analysis. Access to Kennedy administration officials was impaired and the policy relevance of many ensuing estimates eroded further.

Veteran estimates officer and Congressional intelligence staffer Harold Ford includes the adverse impact of the Missile Crisis estimate among eleven principal reasons for the demise of the ONE.[13] The changing policy-making style of administrations beginning with Kennedy's New Frontier is at the top of Ford's list. Second is the conclusion that the 'ONE's senior officers became progressively more separated from the principal policy-making consumers'.[14] He amplifies this, pointing out that by 1961 national intelligence estimates had tended to 'become simply bureaucratic staff inputs that did not carry the added intangible weight among consumers of personal confidence in the particular authors of those estimates'.[15]

Kent's Philosophy of Intelligence-Policy Separation

One critically important factor was what Ford describes as 'an explicit governing philosophy' in the ONE that dictated analysts not to get too close to policy-makers.

Dr Sherman Kent was the chief proponent of this guidance, holding that 'too much mixing it up in policy-making circles would cause intelligence officers to become policy advocates, and hence lose their credibility as objective judges of world trends. There was merit in such caution, but ONE officers overdid it.'[16]

It is difficult in retrospect to assess the rationale for this point of view, which so clearly contributed to the decline of estimates and the Board. Part of the answer lies no doubt in Kent's passionate conviction that intelligence analysis is a distinct profession, and in his desire to help develop methodologies and cultures of intelligence analysis into a virtual new academic discipline.[17] In support of this view Kent argued that intelligence 'has developed a recognised methodology; it has developed a vocabulary; it has developed a body of theory and doctrine; it has elaborated refined techniques'.[18] He pressed this theme in an article published in the first issue of the journal *Studies in Intelligence*, which he founded and then nurtured into what has become the most prestigious publication of the American foreign intelligence profession.

But as a former Yale history professor, Kent was steeped in a non-experimental and non-comparative academic discipline and was criticised for relegating, or not paying enough attention to, social science theory.[19] For example, his fairly copious writings on intelligence contain scarcely any mention of economic forces, variables, or uncertainties.[20] On balance then, Kent's donnish conceit that intelligence analysis would become a new academic discipline proved vastly less attainable than his pioneering endeavours to legitimise foreign intelligence work as a distinct profession.

Finally, any analysis of Kent's philosophy demanding the strict separation of intelligence analysts from policy-makers must acknowledge the suspicion with which he viewed at least some policy officials. This likely had its roots in his appreciation of how in the Truman administration a number of policy-makers knew little about their areas of responsibility. Kent's error, however, was in persisting in his critical assessment of policy-makers even into the 1960s. In one essay,[21] for example, he argued, in effect, that the Board of National Estimates might actually convey conclusions in particular estimates that included more sophisticated or encompassing thoughts about 'national interests' than would otherwise occur to policy-makers. In contrast, by his reckoning, the keen and intellectually gifted members of what he more than once referred to as 'the brotherhood of the NIE' would typically illuminate and enhance policy deliberations, even in situations when the policy-makers were not consciously aware that they were being influenced.

Not surprisingly, the detachment, increasing caution and isolation of Kent and his office caused estimates to fall into further irrelevance during the Johnson and Nixon administrations. Other factors weighed heavily in this evolution, including notably the resistance of both Presidents and their top National Security Advisers to the pessimistic judgements of the intelligence community with regard to the war in Vietnam.[22]

The conspiratorial secrecy that characterised much foreign policy decision-making during the Nixon administration, as well as the President's belief that CIA analytic offices were 'staffed by Ivy League liberals' who had 'always opposed him politically',[23] began immediately to isolate the Agency from policy-makers. Furthermore, Nixon relied on National Security Adviser Henry Kissinger, who may have shared Nixon's bias 'to exclude the CIA from the formulation of policy'[24] and who, in any event, generally preferred his own analysis and that produced by his large White House staff to the Agency's efforts.

Furthermore, during the half-dozen years or so preceding the demise of the ONE, the once exceptional quality of its personnel had deteriorated and its Board members continued mainly to be generalists and Atlanticists in an era when Third World and other regional studies had become highly influential. It had become its own worst enemy. And it antagonised many elsewhere in the intelligence community through what were perceived by many as arrogant and patrician practices increasingly out of place in the activist, confrontational era of the late 1960s and early 1970s. Kent and the Board became increasingly vulnerable targets for competing producers of intelligence analysis.

From Policy Separation to Excessive Activism

DCI William Colby was aware of the shortcomings of the estimates' efforts and was under pressure from the Nixon White House. He was also influenced by James Schlesinger, who briefly preceded him as DCI. Both were committed to creating a new, more vigorous and activist system for supporting policy-makers that would: replicate the early successes of the DCI's Special Assistant for Vietnam Affairs (SAVA) George Carver, who was the single CIA representative at policy meetings with competence to speak on operational as well as analytic issues; minimise the redundancy and rivalries in the CIA's interactions with policy officials that are virtually inevitable because of the Agency's differing missions, cultures, decentralised structure, and strict separation between analysts and operators; on given issues, authorise a single, senior officer to represent the DCI in his capacity as head of the entire intelligence community; as individual members of the Board of National Estimates had previously, preside over the production of national intelligence estimates and other co-ordinated intelligence community analysis, including the presentation of dissenting and alternative views when appropriate; promote closer contacts with academic and other non-government specialists; encourage more focused, disciplined and creative analysis along regional and functional lines based on the specialised portfolios each NIO has held;[25] and provide leadership in identifying collection gaps.

The NIO concept has succeeded in all of these respects while undergoing relatively little alteration in missions, structure and operating dynamics over more than a quarter of a century – a long time in American foreign intelligence history. A major reorganisation (1980) and a significant refocusing (1992–4)[26] have occurred, but in each case without fundamentally altering Colby's original concept.

In 1980, in large part because of the failure of the NIO system to produce any estimate at all before the downfall of the Shah of Iran,[27] the Carter administration demanded better analytic support. DCI Stansfield Turner ordered the creation of the National Intelligence Council as a result. Senior leadership was provided for the first time over what had been a loose confederation of NIOs all reporting directly to the DCI. Now they reported to him through the Chairman (and Vice Chairman) of the Council, who presumably would exercise sufficiently strong leadership to compel an NIO to produce an estimate when policy needs clearly called for one. Duplication of NIO efforts would be better avoided, greater collegiality promoted and staffing decisions better co-ordinated. In addition, with the creation of the NIC, a small, elite estimates drafting staff was organised in recognition of the serious difficulties NIOs had encountered in finding qualified and available drafters. Soon the new staff was drafting about a third of the estimates produced.

These enhancements of the NIO system brought positive results, and when William Casey was unfurled upon the intelligence community by the new Reagan administration in early 1981, he kept the estimates system he inherited intact. His commitment to a strong and prestigious NIC Chairman was evident in the choice for that position of former RAND president Henry Rowen, and in the selection of increasingly activist senior officers for NIO portfolios.

The Dangers of Casey's Activism

As a member of Reagan's Cabinet and an unabashed policy
advocate and activist, Casey pursued an anti-Communist agenda
with impatience and zeal. He sought out NIOs of similar views
and inclinations and then aggressively used them to provide
cutting-edge analysis to policy-makers to advance the administration's policies, including in particular its expanding covert
action programmes.[28] But some of Casey's new NIOs and other
NIC personnel were so untrained as intelligence officers, and so
conspicuously committed to Reagan administration policy
agendas, that complaints of politicisation soon proliferated.

Certain NIOs, it was alleged in the intelligence community
and Congress, had crossed the line and had become policy advocates, bending and shaping the analysis they presented to fit the
policies they preferred.[29] Some seemed to cross the line to
become drivers of policy. As former DCI Robert Gates reveals
in his memoirs, Casey 'was wise enough not to place any of these
people in the strongholds of the CIA career service, such as the
Directorate of Intelligence. Rather he assigned them to the
National Intelligence Council . . . . '[30] Gates's point seems to
be that because it was small – less than a year old when Casey
arrived – and because the estimates production function had
traditionally been host to non-CIA officers, it would be relatively
easy for Casey to transform the NIC. It bears emphasising, moreover, that Casey clearly was enthusiastic about how Bill Colby's
original concept for the NIO missions so neatly suited his own
purposes.

Meanwhile, Sherman Kent's dicta that 'intelligence is not the
formulator of objectives . . . drafter of policy . . . maker of plans
. . . carrier out of operations'[31] were being defied more flagrantly
than ever before. The problems that Casey's activism caused were
unprecedented in most respects,[32] yet they made the NIC vulnerable to becoming irrelevant just as the Board of National
Estimates had been in its waning days. In that event, it would

really not matter if policy-makers were ignoring estimates because they were too cautious, flaccid, unfocused, or plain wrong; or (as in the Casey era) because estimates were viewed as biased, policy prescriptive, or ideological.

And it became clear, too, that there were possibilities even worse than policy officials simply ignoring intelligence estimates. On occasion estimates and the estimators were the victims of vicious leaks to the media and were accused of producing biased analysis, or of pandering to, or being co-opted by, particular Reagan administration officials. Such public criticism of estimates and estimators was more common during the Casey era than at any other time before or since. These and other open wounds were demoralising for professionals unaccustomed to reading exaggerated and often false accounts of their sensitive work in the press. And as a result, working relations among analysts throughout the intelligence community were strained, and in some quarters severely damaged, as suspicions and accusations of policy-pandering multiplied.

The animosities, tensions and public recrimination generated by the Casey-era activism persisted for a number of years. One of the worst legacies has been the much greater propensity of analysts to charge colleagues with politicisation, a trend that in turn has caused senior managers to institute various mechanisms to adjudicate such allegations. Charges of politicisation burst into the open again during the Senate hearings in 1991 on Robert Gates's nomination by President Bush to be DCI, and they festered through his term as DCI.

Lessons Learned from the ONE and Casey-Era Experiences

The latter-day ONE and the Casey-era NIC lost the confidence of many senior policy officials, and the legitimacy of the process and intelligence products in each instance had to be restored.

How then can estimators profit from the experiences of their predecessors? How can national intelligence estimates and the NIOs who produce them best serve their policy counterparts? How close should they get, and how much about policy disputes and options should they know?

Probably most importantly, the record demonstrates clearly that the dangers lurk in the extremes. But navigating steadfastly in the middle to avoid the opposing shoals of politicisation and irrelevance is no easy task. As DCIs Schlesinger and Colby recognised in the early 1970s, some measures of activism, salesmanship and marketing skills are necessary if NIOs are to succeed in providing valuable policy support. At a minimum, therefore, NIOs must regularly be in communication with their policy counterparts at the National Security Council, the State and Defense Departments, and other agencies and departments. One key responsibility of NIC Chairmen and Vice Chairmen is to help ensure that such minimum levels of contact with the policy community are in fact being sustained.

But under the best of circumstances, maintaining productive and apolitical relations with policy-makers is difficult. Some officials are unreceptive to intelligence analysis, perhaps because they believe they or their staffs can do it better. They may have been poorly served by intelligence in the past, or may work portfolios where intelligence capabilities are unable to provide a flow of critically relevant information. As one perceptive former NIO has observed, some policy-makers 'have a strong vested interest in the success of their policies and will be disproportionately receptive to intelligence that "supports" these policies'.[33] Some new recruits to senior policy jobs, particularly political appointees with no previous government experience, have unrealistic expectations with regard to intelligence. Occasionally they have entered government service with strong biases against intelligence missions and personnel. Some seek to shop around the intelligence community for support, in effect taking advantage of the relative weakness of the DCI's charter as head of the entire community. All of these are difficult hurdles to surmount.

Few policy-makers remain in the same positions for more than three years or so, and with new Presidential administrations there is wholesale turnover. Yesterday's close intelligence-policy relations may evaporate in a blink, and typically the often tedious work of building a relationship of trust with a newly installed policy-maker can be time-consuming. Maintaining trust across departmental borders can be complicated when policy disputes, for example, pit State and Defense against each other, possibly with an NIO dodging to keep intelligence analysis neutral while at the same time endeavouring to provide comprehensive and balanced analytic support to both parties.

The quality, relevance, timeliness and therefore utility of national intelligence estimates varies widely. A significant number have always failed to provide policy-makers with much more insight or warning. Individual estimates can be no better than the intelligence information that is available combined with the analytic and drafting skills of the estimators. Furthermore, NIOs are often expected to produce estimates even when they have no particular comparative advantage through access to intelligence sources with unique information. Sophisticated policy-makers will understand that every estimate cannot be groundbreaking or provide unexpected insights. But if an NIO only produces such low threshold estimates, his or her product will increasingly be devalued as irrelevant to policy needs.

More daunting is the issue of NIO and NIC relations with the CIA's operations directorate. Even in the founding days of the NIO system, when DCI Colby wanted NIOs to broadly represent him in policy councils, the 'need to know' principle typically shielded operational activities from the purview of even the most senior analytic officers. In practice, therefore, NIOs rarely should be expected to substitute for senior operations officers. And consumers often look to senior DO (Directorate of Operations) officers for support rather than to NIOs.

But as evident during the Casey era, covert action – especially large, semi-acknowledged activities like the 1980s' Contra war in Nicaragua – raises truly daunting dilemmas for NIOs and analysts. Even if analysts were broadly apprised of the capabilities and activities of covertly sponsored political actors in a country, how can they feel confident they are not being politicised by their counterparts in the CIA's operations directorate? How can they fairly assess the fortunes of rival forces and trends in a country if the US administration, acting through the CIA's operations directorate, is doing much to shape events? And who after all are the drivers of a covert action programme? If it is a large one with strong administration and Congressional support, have CIA operations officers been transformed in effect into policy-makers? Certainly the lines were blurred during the Casey era.

Inevitably in such circumstances, analysts are vulnerable to charges of politicisation. If, on the one hand, they report favourably about the prospects of US-sponsored groups, they may be criticised in Congress and by executive branch officials who object to the covert action. But on the other hand, they run the risk of antagonising Agency colleagues, even the top leadership, if they seem to be critical of a favourite covert action programme. There are no easy solutions to such dilemmas. And unfortunately the most obvious strategy is one of avoidance or denial; although that in turn is likely to result in NIOs and analysts producing analytic mush.

Alternatively, analysts may simply be unwitting of CIA sponsorship of a covert action which resolves one dilemma but causes others, perhaps worse. In the case of the Bay of Pigs, the estimators were completely cut off from knowledge of the operation. Had they been briefed on the covert plan, almost certainly they would have strongly questioned some of its key, erroneous assumptions.

Thus, there is simply no avoiding the reality that the 'seductive power' of the CIA's operations directorate will continue to complicate intelligence-policy relations and analytic support. The most effective NIOs are those who have come from the DO, or have collaborated closely with their operational counterparts while eschewing any temptation to compete with them for access to policy-makers. NIOs from other career paths are well advised to learn as much as possible about clandestine collection priorities, activities, methods and problems as well as the unique bureaucratic culture of the operations directorate and perhaps even of a particular regional division. The most successful NIOs have found many areas in which they and their operational counterparts have worked closely together to the benefit of policy support. On balance, therefore, it is incumbent on NIC officers to take advantage of the 'seductive power' of the operations directorate in policy support activities.

Given the multiplicity of negative historical lessons, institutional hurdles and other problems that inhibit the production of cutting-edge national intelligence estimates, it seems remarkable that NIOs over the years have enjoyed the success they have. Most have succeeded in providing their policy counterparts with valuable analytic insights and warnings, and have been respected members of national security teams addressing regional and functional issues. As indicated above, the success of NIOs in these endeavours has been evident in the large number of them who have moved on to senior policy positions where they have typically been successful.

In the end there are only a few key measures of success for NIOs and senior NIC managers. Have they scrupulously and consistently avoided the temptations of politicisation? Have a good percentage of their estimates made truly significant and timely contributions to policy deliberations? Have they warned policy-makers of impending surprises? Do they fairly and comprehensively account for the spectrum of legitimate views and evidence? Do they think boldly and in the future tense, assessing alternative possibilities when they might have a great impact on US interests? Have they made the difficult transition from current or historical analysis to estimative thinking?

It is really a fundamental proposition and Sherman Kent got it right: 'in intelligence as in other callings, estimating is what you do when you do not know'.[34]

DISCUSSION

Lieutenant-General Vadim Kirpichenko

Lieutenant-General Vadim Kirpichenko served in Soviet airborne forces during the Second World War, and from 1947 to 1952 trained as an Arabist at the Moscow Institute of Oriental Studies. He entered the intelligence service in 1952, remaining in it until the present, first in the KGB until 1991 and then in the Russian Foreign Intelligence Service. He was deputy chief of KGB station in Egypt from 1954 to 1960 and chief from 1970 to 1974. He was chief of KGB station in Tunisia from 1962 to 1964 and chief of the African Department in Moscow from 1967 to 1970. From 1974 to 1979 he was deputy director of the intelligence service and chief of 'S' department (illegals), and from 1979 to 1991 he was first deputy director of the intelligence service. Since 1991 he has been a general consultant of the Russian Foreign Intelligence Service. He was made a lieutenant-general in 1980. His books include From the Archives of an Intelligence Officer *(1993) and* The Intelligence Service: Persons and Personalities *(1998, both in Russian). He is assistant chief editor of a six-volume* History of Russian Foreign Intelligence *(in Russian), of which four volumes have been published so far.*

The dramatic changes taking place in the international environment are mirrored in the activities of intelligence services.

In particular, in a number of countries public opinion is growing in force and demanding that the activities of the secret services should be conducted in strict conformity with the law regulating them and under greater Parliamentary control.

A law on foreign intelligence was adopted for the first time in Russia in 1992, and since then all our practical activities are entirely consistent with its provisions.

1. Foreign Intelligence under the KGB

During the Soviet period, foreign intelligence was one of the tools of the ideological struggle on the international scene. Its activity was not conducted on the basis of law, but in accordance with the directives of the Central Committee of the Communist Party of the Soviet Union and instructions of the heads of the KGB. Numerous recommendations on intelligence work also flowed directly from various departments of the Central Committee. This situation created conditions for the use of the intelligence service for purposes that were alien to its proper functions.

2. Disbandment of the KGB and Formation of Intelligence as a Separate and Independent Service

In the autumn of 1991 the KGB was disbanded and foreign intelligence became a separate organisation, tasked to deal with external activity only.

The activities of the secret services are now co-ordinated by means of regular working meetings of their chiefs. A number of agreements has been concluded, various protocols of interaction have been signed, and senior intelligence officers maintain regular contacts with various state agencies.

To a certain extent the activities of the secret services are also co-ordinated by the Security Council, which consists of national security and law enforcement ministers and other high-ranking state officials. The Security Council is under the direct control of the President of Russia. Nevertheless, the co-ordinating function of the Security Council is of a rather generalised nature, because the practical activities of the secret services are controlled by the President personally, and because the Law is sufficiently explicit on the aims of Russian foreign intelligence and how it must achieve them.

The transformation of the Foreign Intelligence Service (FIS) into an independent institution has both positive and negative aspects. It is obvious that within the KGB, intelligence was more easily able to interact with other KGB services at different levels. Now, however, personal contacts between the officers of the intelligence and counter-intelligence services have decreased. Positive factors nevertheless appear to be much more numerous: decisions on all aspects of operational activities are taken more expeditiously, and, most importantly, the intelligence service now reports directly to the President, Prime Minister and various other state bodies, omitting intermediate authorities. Now nobody can alter intelligence information in order to gain opportunistic advantage.

3. Federal Law on Foreign Intelligence

As mentioned above, up to 1992 there was no law on intelligence in Russia. Intelligence activities were carried out on the basis of directives issued by the Central Committee of the CPSU, instructions from heads of the KGB and the orders of the intelligence chief. In practice, an operative was compelled to carry out any order, even of the most unexpected kind. In the new phase of Russia's evolution and, in particular, following the disbandment of the KGB, the acute need emerged for a law on the intelligence service that would also place it under the control of the legislative and executive authorities. Since late 1991 special Russian Parliamentary commissions, jointly with political and military foreign intelligence officers, began drafting this new law. Those responsible for formulating the law set about studying the laws on intelligence of other countries, and found to their surprise that, in the overwhelming majority of states, there were no open laws on intelligence, which of course left their services open to abuse and infringement. We found more or less full legislation on the activities of the intelligence service only in the USA.

The first law on intelligence was adopted by the Russian Federation Parliament on 8 July 1992.

In December 1995 the Russian Federation Parliament adopted a revised law on foreign intelligence with more precise wording of some provisions of the law. Now the officers of our service know precisely what they may do, what they must do and what is prohibited to them. At present all intelligence activities are organised in strict compliance with this law.

The main provisions of the law are as follows:

a) The Russian intelligence service acquires sources of information only on the basis of their voluntary consent; intelligence activities cannot be carried out to achieve inhumane aims and should not inflict damage on the life and health of persons or the environment. Intelligence activities are under the control of the supreme organs of the legislative and executive power of the Russian Federation.

b) The intelligence service is barred from actions that may be considered as interference with the internal affairs of other states. Now we do not transfer money and weapons to anybody, or support any political parties or formations in foreign territories. The intelligence service's functions are limited to the collection of information on problems directly related to the security of our state.

c) The intelligence service is not allowed to use drugs or exert any form of pressure on a person, e.g. blackmail, compromising material, intimidation.

d) The law prohibits intelligence officers from taking part in the activities of political parties and organisations. The decision to 'de-partyise' the intelligence service, i.e. to prohibit membership of a political party, was greeted by its officers with equanimity, because the intelligence service itself was saved by this process. It is quite clear that if intelligence officers were members of Russia's different political parties, in a state of acute confrontation, any serious work within the framework of the FIS would be out of question.

e) Parliamentary committees and commissions maintain permanent contacts with the FIS of the Russian Federation and through these contacts they exert parliamentary control over its activities.

4. Main Directions of FIS Activities

As a result of the positive changes that have taken place in the world, the threat of a world nuclear missile war is now minimal. Nevertheless, the potential threat of military attack has not yet been entirely eliminated: acute local conflicts continue to break out, including on the boundaries of the CIS. Furthermore, the possibility of creating fundamentally new types of weapons of mass destruction still exists.

According to the law on foreign intelligence the main directions of the FIS activities are as follows:

(i) production of political information on matters which are most important for Russia's security;

(ii) assistance of intelligence forces to governmental institutions in pursuing the foreign policy of the Russian state;

(iii) scientific and technological intelligence, above all in the interests of state defence;

(iv) defence of the Russian economy;

(v) ecological security;

(vi) security problems of the intelligence service;

(vii) co-operation with the special services of other states.

In recent years co-operation with the special services of foreign states has acquired special importance, and this direction of intelligence activities is worthy of a more detailed account. FIS contacts within the framework of the CIS, and those beyond it, should be distinguished in this context.

5. FIS Contacts with Intelligence Services of the Commonwealth of Independent States

Following the collapse of the USSR and the formation of the Commonwealth of Independent States, the question of how to build relations between the special services of the new states arose. It should be noted that the Baltic States (Latvia, Lithuania, Estonia) did not join the CIS and are considered as independent foreign states, not connected with Russia by any special relationships in the sphere of special services. As for the other former republics of the Soviet Union that are now members of the CIS, they have close working relations with the intelligence and counter-intelligence agencies of Russia.

The CIS countries have concluded a collective agreement on co-operation in the field of intelligence. In addition, the Russian FIS has bilateral agreements with the CIS countries, whose intelligence services have committed themselves not to carry out human intelligence against each other. There are appropriate laws and directives to this end.

6. Partnership Connections with Foreign Countries

The FIS of Russia has business contacts and partnership

connections with a dozen special services in different countries, including those of the majority of NATO members.
These contacts are bilateral and confidential, and are based
on the mutual interest of the co-operating parties. This interaction should not be aimed against the interests of a third
country. Typical issues of this interaction are: the exchange of
information on problems of non-proliferation of weapons of
mass destruction, imminent crisis situations, current crises
(the Middle East, Yugoslavia, CIS borders), problems of
mutual security, information on terrorism, nationalist extrem-
ism, the 'narcomafia' and organised crime, and other issues
of the criminal sphere. We regularly exchange experts with a
number of special services; exchange visits by heads of the
intelligence services take place on a regular basis.

We proceed from the fact that, as long as states exist and
have national interests, intelligence agencies will also exist as
an integral part of the state apparatus. Intelligence activities
in a post-confrontation period, however, should be conducted
by civilised methods, without 'arm-twisting', threats, blackmail and intimidation. Normalisation of the international situation, the transition from a policy of confrontation to one of
co-operation, oblige the special services to revise their
doctrines and modes of operation. The intelligence and
counter-intelligence bodies are beginning to see the need for
laws regulating their activities. If these tendencies develop
further, the intelligence services, whose activities often complicated relations between states in the past, can become effective instruments of international stability.

7. Glasnost *in the SVR*

The development of democratic processes in Russia has
promoted greater openness – called in Russian '*glasnost*' – in
the activities of all the country's state institutions, including
intelligence. The law 'On Foreign Intelligence' provides for *glas-*

nost in our service, too. The intelligence service is required, within reasonable limits, to inform the Russian and foreign public of its activity. In accordance with the law, a special service, called the Public and Mass Media Relations Bureau, has been set up within the SVR. Russian and foreign journalists request current information from this Bureau every day, while scientists, historians and writers ask for help in their research.

Senior intelligence officials regularly make reports to the public and the press, as well as on the TV and radio.

Some intelligence veterans have published political studies and their memoirs. The FIS has made four documentary films for Russian TV about its work in different periods of history. Four volumes of a six-volume declassified history of Russian intelligence have been published; the fourth is on 'Intelligence in the years of World War II'. I am the head of the team of authors, and SVIR Director, V.I. Trubnikov, is Editor-in-Chief.

The FIS accepts invitations from foreign scientific and public organisations, and gives talks on questions of intelligence to international conferences, seminars and university audiences.

General Shlomo Gazit

Major-General (Res.) Shlomo Gazit retired from the Israeli Defence Force in 1981. He began his military career with the Palmach, and in 1953 became executive officer to Chief of Staff Moshe Dayan. Liaison officer to the French military command in planning and operations of the Sinai War of October 1956, he became Assistant Military Attaché in France immediately after the war. From 1964 through the Six Day War of June 1967, he headed the Research and Estimate Department of the IDF Military Intelligence Branch, and established the office of Co-ordinator of Government Operations in the Administered Territories. In 1974,

following the Yom Kippur War, he was appointed Head of IDF
Military Intelligence. He was responsible in 1976 for intelligence
in planning the Entebbe rescue operation, and in 1977–8 he took
part in negotiating peace with the Egyptians. In 1985–6 he headed
a small team that opened the first clandestine political talks with
PLO officials, and in 1995–6 served as the Prime Minister's adviser
on Palestinian Affairs and special delegate to PLO Chairman
Arafat. His publications include The Carrot and the Stick, *dealing*
with the first two years of Israeli policy in the West Bank, and
Trapped Fools *– Thirty Years of Israel's Policy in Judea,*
Samaria and the Gaza Strip, *(both in Hebrew).*

The title of this conference is 'Intelligence in a Changing World'.
I have to admit that I am not really competent to discuss the
changes in our world; my problem is to analyse and to see if my
part of this world, namely, the Middle East, is indeed also undergoing these changes. Or, perhaps, is it in our case just *'plus ça*
change, plus c'est la même chose', namely we are facing very little
change. And if there is a change, is it a change for the better or
for the worse? I don't have an answer to these questions and
personally, I must say, these are questions that have been intriguing me very, very much. Literally the future of Israel in the next
decade or generation will be very much dependent on these
crucial questions. Is the Middle East changing, and if the answer
is yes – in what direction?

Admiral Martini spoke earlier about the fact that he was an
exception in this audience; he was not representing one of the
big powers, but he was representing a relatively small regional
power. Well, I am an exception even more than he is; I am not
representing even a small regional power, I am representing a
tiny little country: the size of Israel is altogether something like
20,000 square kilometres, and our population is very small, some
six million people. On the other hand we are facing enormous
problems.

From our point of view, the question of who is in the driver's seat and who is in the back seat does not exist. Also, we are using a different terminology from the one that has been discussed here, and especially different from what Brian [Latell] was talking about here earlier this afternoon, about what goes on between policy-making officials and NIOs. Intelligence officers in Israel are part of the policy-makers. However, intelligence officers are not decision-makers. The decision-makers in the case of Israel are only the politicians, namely, the political functionaries of our system, those who have been directly elected by the people. There is no difference, in our case, between officers serving with intelligence and those serving in any other policy-making function within the Israeli establishment. Furthermore, it has been a tradition in Israel, from our very first days as a state fifty years ago, that intelligence officers are considered to be the right-hand men of the decision-maker. This has been true for all levels and ranks, beginning with the military and going up to the highest political level. Nevertheless, they serve as the right-hand man, but never as decision-makers.

Allow me to tell you a small anecdote, even if I am not so sure if it is very relevant to our discussion. It is, however, a nice anecdote. In 1977, about a month after the dramatic visit of President Sadat to Israel, I left together with our Minister of Defence at the time, General Ezer Weizman, for a clandestine meeting in Egypt to begin negotiations with the Egyptians. It was meant to be a clandestine trip, and yet it was disclosed by the Egyptians a few hours later, of course. We arrived at Cairo airport and as we stepped out of the plane I saw in front of us some faces that I knew from our intelligence files, but had never had the opportunity of meeting in person. At the centre stood General Gamasi, the Egyptian Minister of War. We all went to a helicopter, an Egyptian military helicopter that took us to Ismailia to meet President Sadat. Now, what do you do when you have your first encounter with your former enemy and you

have to spend some thirty minutes together? It was quite embarrassing.

So, what did we talk about? We started by asking how old
President Sadat was and how old Mr Begin was, and then
Weizman asked Gamasi, 'How old are you?', and Gamasi
answered, 'Fifty-eight'. And we kept on flying. Some ten, fifteen
minutes later Gamasi said, all of a sudden, 'General Weizman,
I must correct myself.' He tapped me on my shoulder and said,
'I don't want this man here to tell you that I am a liar.' I got
frightened already. 'I am not yet fifty-eight years old.'

Obviously I had no idea how old Gamasi was at the time, but
the first thing I did on my arrival back in Israel was to look up
his file. The date was 26 December and Gamasi's birthday
was 7 January, so legally he was not yet fifty-eight. Anyway, on
7 January we sent him a cable of congratulations. So, as I said,
I'm not sure how this story relates to the problems of intelligence being involved in the decision-making process, but I believe
that it is a nice story.

I am going to talk mainly about the intricate relationship
between the decision-maker and the intelligence officer in the
Israeli case. I hope that there is a close similarity between our
problems and that the lessons of our experience may serve others.
I would like, however, to begin with the emphasis on the major
differences between the Israeli system and the systems you are
familiar with.

From the very first days following the establishment of the
State of Israel fifty-two years ago, Israel has been in a permanent state of emergency. Or, if you like, you may even call it in
a permanent state of war. From this point of view the main tasks
of Israeli intelligence were, are and probably will be in the fore-
seeable future:

1. to deal with the threat of a possible enemy military surprise
   attack;
2. to provide the armed forces with all the necessary intelligence

for the conduct of war. While Israeli intelligence has had many problems in analysing the possible so-called strategic developments in the area, we have always been successful in providing the necessary intelligence for the conduct of war and combat;

3. the third element, relatively new, is to closely monitor the possibility of a political opening in the countries surrounding Israel;

4. and last, but unfortunately not least, Israeli intelligence has to deal with the threat of terrorist attacks against Israelis and Israeli, as well as Jewish, targets all over the world.

In his remarks yesterday evening, Christopher Andrew discussed the different roles of intelligence in a totalitarian and in a democratic regime. He claimed that intelligence was a crucial, vital element in a totalitarian regime, while it was not so in a democracy. This comparison is no doubt true. I must, however, make one slight correction. A democracy at war operates very much like a totalitarian country, and from that point of view, intelligence is crucial in every democracy when it comes to the conduct of a major war, and especially a war for existence.

Because of this background, as well as because of historical changes and developments in Israel, we have to mention two organisational characteristics of Israeli intelligence. First, in the case of Israel, Military Intelligence is in charge of the National Intelligence Estimate. Quite unusually, and even in spite of the fact that we are already in the midst of the peace-making process, Military Intelligence is still in charge of our National Estimate.

The second characteristic is an organisational decision. Following the 1973 Yom Kippur War, it was decided not to rely any longer on a single analytical service. As of 1974, Military Intelligence lost its monopoly; Israel today depends on three independent intelligence services that are charged with analytical intelligence research. These are Military Intelligence, Mossad and the Foreign Ministry.

The difference and the relationship in Israel between the decision-maker and intelligence cannot be compared to the difference between the driver and the man in the back seat. The difference in our system is unfortunately very simple: who will 'pay' if there is a catastrophe, if there is a blunder? Because of the special character of our democratic political system, the people in charge of intelligence always pay, and pay heavily, and never have our politicians had to share responsibility and pay the price.

In the last fifty years of Israel's short history, no fewer than nine heads of intelligence services have been fired. None of our politicians has ever been removed because of those very same blunders.

Now, allow me to deal with some aspects of the interrelationship between the decision-maker and the heads of our intelligence services.

1. First, the procedure and tradition of the nomination or the appointment of a head of service. Obviously it is always the political system that appoints the head of an intelligence service. Surprisingly, however, we have never yet had a political appointment, and I thank God that this is the case. All appointments, without exception, in our three major intelligence services (Military Intelligence Service, Mossad and the Internal Security Service, i.e. Shin Bet), have always been clear professional decisions. This is the case when it comes to the nomination of the head of service. When it comes to any appointment at a lower level, the political system is not involved at all; it is exclusively a professional decision.

2. A problem we often encounter is the lack of intimate knowledge between the two parties. Intelligence knows very little about the political system, about its problems and about the way it formulates its decisions, and the political system, with some rare exceptions, knows almost nothing about the intelligence agencies and their capabilities. This is a very serious

problem. There have been exceptions, of course; for instance, Ehud Barak today, or Yitzhak Rabin in the past, both of them decision-makers who rose through the ranks of the military system and knew the intelligence community very well, and had long experience with intelligence. The norm, however, allows a politician to be elected without any former security and intelligence background, nor any intimate knowledge of the things that are done. Such novice politicians may suddenly find themselves in charge of complex intelligence activities, and they are responsible for making the decisions, for better and for worse.

We believe it is our role, the role of the heads of the intelligence services, to educate the political leaders and to teach them what intelligence is, what the capabilities of the services are, how best to exploit the instrument they have in their hands, and last but not least what the sensitivities of intelligence operations are and how to protect vulnerable intelligence sources.

The best way to do this is by forcing them to spend some time as visitors and trainees of the intelligence services, their various units and their *modus operandi*. It's never easy to do so. These people are normally very busy and don't have time to spare as students on an intelligence course. They don't have the months, the weeks, or even the days. Still, I would like to mention two alternatives.

One is to bring the decision-maker over for a number of visits, a few hours each, every few months. This is quite feasible.

The second and no less important way is for intelligence to 'plant a mole' in the decision-maker's office, as an aide serving in the decision-maker's vicinity. Once he is there, it will be his role to whisper into the decision-maker's ear, 'Listen, I suggest you do not make this move before you consult your intelligence services. I know that those guys can help you a lot by giving you their analysis or their advice.' At the same time, he may also suggest, 'Do not trust those guys when they tell you this or that.'

Having such a 'mole' at the decision-maker's side will no doubt improve the relationship.

3. There are several problems that are part of the inter-depend-ency between the two systems – that of the decision-maker and that of the head of intelligence. I will only mention two or three points here.

First of all, it is clearly the decision-maker who sets the prior-ities for intelligence work. One priority is obvious, namely, the intelligence service's budget, the allocation of national resources, and whoever is in charge of intelligence will do whatever he can with the resources he is allocated. These national resources are part of the Government's plan of how to divide resources and responsibilities between education and the health service, secu-rity and intelligence.

The other priority is far more complex. The decision-maker is always responsible for the EEI, the Essential Elements of Intelligence. That is to say, he should be responsible, but in prac-tice he almost never exercises this responsibility. In most cases the decision-maker simply does not understand the problems involved in producing the EEI. In most cases he doesn't even know what you want from him, this in part because he is an outsider to the system. Thus, the head of service in charge of the national estimate and in charge of co-ordinating the collection effort has to bring his suggested plan for the EEI to the deci-sion-maker, and force him to listen to your proposal, as well as to add his signature to your list of proposed national intelligence priorities. One should always remember that this priority list serves as the basis for the national intelligence collection effort.

4. The responsibility of intelligence is no less important when it comes to the most delicate and sensitive responsibility of protecting one's intelligence sources. Politicians almost without exception are far from trustworthy when it comes to the protec-tion of intelligence sources. Not that they have bad intentions. You won't find one who does not want to protect sensitive

sources, but they have their political career to look after. Thus, when in a tight corner, when in the midst of a tough argument with a political rival, they may speak out without control and restraint and say things that should not have been said in public. In some cases they simply do not remember if they have learned something from a 'Top Secret' intelligence document or from the morning paper, and almost always they do not know or understand the sensitivities and fragility of the intelligence sources concerned.

Your problem is what intelligence data will you tell or show your Prime Minister, your Minister of Defence, your Foreign Minister? There are no guidelines, there is no binding advice that I can give here and say, 'this should be done' or 'this should not be done'. My suggestion is that, unless it is totally, vitally necessary, don't tell your decision-maker the intimate details, don't show him the original document. Give him the edited information, but don't tell him anything about the 'source'.

This brings me to another problem that is even more delicate. And that is the problem of 'Black Intelligence'. Once in a while, we may receive a piece of intelligence, a very intimate piece of intelligence, which tells us what Syrian President Assad thinks of Prime Minister Barak, be it good or bad. Or what Yassir Arafat thinks of Foreign Minister David Levy. I'm mentioning the names of present-day Israeli politicians, but my professional memory goes back to Israeli politicians who served in those positions twenty-five years. What do you do in such a case? Should you tell or show the story to your Prime Minister, your Minister of Defence, your Minister of Foreign Affairs, or should you do your best to conceal the document from them? Here again, my personal advice is, don't tell and don't show them such intimate and extremely delicate intelligence. This is the kind of intelligence data that your decision-maker will find it extremely difficult to keep secret. He cannot remain neutral with such a story, and you can never know when, where and how he will mention it, brag or complain about that piece of intelligence. In such a case, the risks to your sources are very serious. It's not an easy decision. Furthermore, you will never be, unfortunately, the only person to have seen or heard that data. There are always a number of collection officers, as well as NIO officers, who share the information. They have seen or heard what Assad or Arafat think of your Prime Minister or of your Foreign Minister, and all of them, without exception, will have to keep these sensitive stories to themselves.

5. One of the most complex issues of the relationship between the decision-maker and the head of his intelligence service deals with the character of the intelligence report he presents to his decision-maker. Should he present an edited intelligence analysis, or should he provide the raw intelligence data? This question has been an on-going controversy in Israel, especially since the Yom Kippur War of October 1973. I assume that this is a problem not only in Israel. It is very easy and even convenient for intelligence to say, 'Here is the bulk of the raw intelligence data, this is what we have collected, this is all we know. Now it is your business, it is your responsibility to make the analysis and to reach conclusions.' My personal opinion in regard to this controversy is very clear – the role and the responsibility of intelligence is always to provide an analytical estimate and not the raw material. The decision-maker has neither the tools, the staff nor the time and expertise to make his own analysis.

The head of our military SIGINT unit claimed, after the Yom Kippur War, that his unit had intercepted some 300 messages that should have given us the necessary early warning. When he showed these messages to our Chief of Staff at the time, Lieutenant-General El'azar, the latter said that had he seen them before the war he would have immediately called up the reserves. What General El'azar did not know, or understand, at the time was that these 300 messages were 'voices' hidden among some

300,000 'noises'. The file with the 300 relevant messages was the clear work of intelligence analysts.

6. My next point deals with the need of intelligence closely to monitor developments across the border in order to find and to identify possible political changes or moves towards a political solution and towards peace. In the past this was not the standard responsibility of Israeli intelligence. It had never been asked for by our political leaderships and it had not been part of our national EEI and intelligence priorities. In 1975 I introduced this as a standard and routine question in our EEI and a clear task of our collection efforts. We made a point of including in every annual intelligence analysis that we presented to the decision-makers a clear reference to this intriguing question, and we tried very hard to report the changes – the positive or negative ups and downs of the past twelve months, from this point of view.

7. And my last point deals with the delicate problem of the need for checks and balances among the main personalities involved in the process of decision-making. There always is an interplay between the characters of the political decision-makers, the military decision-makers and their head of the intelligence service. You can devise the best possible theoretical organisation or system, but there will always be a serious problem because of the individual personalities involved. If you take those three personalities, the President or Prime Minister, the Minister of Defence, the Chief of Staff, and their Head of Intelligence, in one combination of those three or four persons the decision they make will take one direction, while at exactly the same point but with a different combination of three or four personalities, it may move in the opposite direction. The decisive factor depends on whether there were checks and balances in the personalities of those persons. Obviously, the four functionaries are never elected, appointed or nominated with this point of view as the main consideration. Unfortunately, we know the people involved, and

we know the possible dangers, were they all to pull or push in the same direction, and the possible benefits, were they to pull or push in opposite directions.

8. We have an interesting and beautiful analysis, published some twenty years ago by a former member of Israeli intelligence, Aluf Hareven, entitled 'Disturbed Hierarchy'. Hareven compares two cases: the first is the story of intelligence and Israeli decision-makers in 1954. The combination of Prime Minister Moshe Sharett, Minister of Defence Pinhas Lavon, Chief of Staff Moshe Dayan and Head of Intelligence Binyamin Gibli, constituted a tragic mixture of personalities. Israeli intelligence had recommended at the time the initiation of clandestine operations in Egypt, what we later called 'The Affair'. Israeli intelligence had organised a small group of young Egyptian Jews as a potential underground and 'fifth column' to be employed in sabotage acts in case of a future Egyptian-Israeli war. In this specific case these youngsters had been ordered to sabotage targets in Cairo and Alexandria in an attempt to prevent, or at least delay, the evacuation of British forces from the Suez Canal. Hareven compares the character of the Israeli individuals involved in 1954 with the character of the individuals involved in the set-up leading to the catastrophe of the Yom Kippur War in October 1973, that is, the Prime Minister Golda Meir, Minister of Defence Moshe Dayan, IDF Chief of Staff David (Dado) El'azar and Head of Intelligence Eli Ze'ira. In both cases there were no real checks and balances between the persons involved.

9. I began this presentation with an explanation of the unique case of Israel being in a permanent state of emergency and war. This reality is responsible for certain decisions, for the attitude and for the relations between intelligence and the decision-maker. There is, however, one more point that needs mentioning: Israel has never had a National Security Council, or anything like it. From this point of view, intelligence and the defence establish-

ment in Israel play an enormously important role, because there is nobody to present an alternative to any policy suggestion, or to any proposal originating in that system.

10. Israel has no serious problems in its relations with other foreign services, whether in the West or in the Arab countries with which we do have close intelligence relations. Life isn't easy and whoever deals with intelligence knows it. We all know the famous saying, 'Intelligence is the second oldest profession in the world, only with fewer morals.' From this point of view I was rather perplexed by the discussion this morning, when speakers were talking about 'just espionage'. Anyone who wants to be 'just' had better become a priest or a rabbi. They shouldn't join the intelligence services!

GENERAL DISCUSSION

The discussion was opened by a former British Military Intelligence officer who asked for a US and Russian view of the appointing by President Yeltsin of career intelligence officers, in succession, Primakov, Stepashin and Putin, as Prime Ministers, adding that this approach seemed to avoid too great a difference between the decision-makers and the intelligence world.

General Kirpichenko replied that for Russian foreign intelligence it was an advantage not to be involved in domestic policy: 'We are outsiders.' The intelligence service has no idea who the next Prime Minister or the next President is likely to be. He described the last Prime Minister, Primakov – a friend for fifty-two years – as a man who wanted to co-operate with politicians of all parties. But it was hard to predict who the next one was going to be. 'Maybe while we are speaking at this minute, we have a new Prime Minister.' He concluded that, while it had been true that former heads of the KGB had certainly been policy-makers, the present Director of the Russian Foreign

Intelligence Service (SVR) had stated: 'We are not policy-makers at all now.' Brian Latell felt that there was nothing in principle against someone who had been a senior intelligence officer becoming a political figure, and cited George Bush as the best example in American politics.

A retired senior MI6 officer asked Brian Latell how effective Penkovsky's revelations had been at the time of the Cuban Missile Crisis, adding that it was difficult to understand how the Board of National Estimates could have ignored them, and also asked what the Russians felt about this at the time.

Brian Latell replied that Penkovsky's oral reporting and all the documentary reporting in the two series were crucial to US intelligence, especially after the U-2 discovered the sites in Cuba. With Penkovsky's material, particularly the SS-4 manuals for the sites that the imagery analysts were observing in Cuba, they were able definitively to tell President Kennedy in the very first meeting of the Executive Committee on 16 October that 'these are SS-4 installations'. They did not say they may be, probably are, or there is a very good chance that they are; they could say definitively, and it was unlikely that they would have been able to do that without Penkovsky's material.

General Kirpichenko added that, although Penkovsky had caused the Soviet Union serious damage, he believed the West had exaggerated his importance.

On the issue of oversight and public accountability, General Gazit was asked whether he had intended to give the impression that the decision-makers in Israel controlled intelligence only on terms determined by the intelligence community itself.

General Gazit replied that what he had wanted to stress was that the state of emergency in Israel in a sense forces the decisions, forces the attitude, and forces the role between the two. He took this opportunity to repeat that Israel does not have anything like a National Security Council, although it is possible Prime Minister Barak is about to establish one. This has meant that intelligence and defence have played an enormously important role, as there was nobody to present an alternative to any proposal coming from that system.

In response to a question from a US academic concerning Congressional oversight of US intelligence, Brian Latell pointed out that in his paper he does not address the members of the US Congress as decision-makers or policy-makers, but in reality a very large percentage of them have become policy-makers. As DCI, James Woolsey used to refer to the entire Congress as 'the Board of Directors for Foreign Intelligence', and that was very accurate. US intelligence had almost no Congressional oversight until the mid-1970s, and since then there has been steadily increasing and intensifying Congressional oversight, so, yes, the CIA answers to many in Congress, as well as in the Executive Branch, and it increasingly creates interesting triangulation of paradoxes: who are you directly supporting and who are you helping or hurting, especially if the White House and the majority in Congress are from different parties.

A question was raised about relations between the Russian foreign intelligence service and those of other countries. General Kirpichenko replied that the SVR was prepared to co-operate, especially on the question of corruption. He conceded that relations with the CIA or Mossad were not completely open, but Russian foreign intelligence was trying to co-operate honestly, and there had been positive development in relations with the CIA, the British SIS and the Israeli services. On the other hand, he pointed out, it was impossible for any intelligence service to be completely open.

Notes to Brian Latell's paper

1. Throughout this paper 'policy-maker' is meant to refer only to senior Executive Branch officials involved in foreign policy and national security decision-making.

2. The author is not aware of any empirical data on the emigration of senior intelligence officials to top policy-making positions. Thus, this discussion is impressionistic though based on the author's more than fifteen years of service in the National Intelligence Council and more than thirty-six years in all as a foreign intelligence officer.

3. Through all three of its institutional forms over the last fifty years, the DCI's estimates-producing staffs have probably never at any one time had more than fifty to seventy-five professional staff members. The ONE (1950–73) never exceeded about forty-five professionals, usually about a dozen Board members and some twenty-five to thirty staff members. It was succeeded by a smaller, decentralised structure of National Intelligence Officers (1973–80) which had no drafting staff. The National Intelligence Council emerged in 1980, adding a Chairman and Vice Chairmen and restoring a small drafting staff, the Analytic Group. Through most of the ensuing years it has also included about a dozen NIOs, their deputies, and other supporting and evaluation personnel.

4. In the fifty-one years since the creation of the CIA, there has never been such an intimate policy-intelligence relationship as the one that existed during the Eisenhower administration when Allen Dulles was DCI and his brother John Foster Dulles was Secretary of State. Both enjoyed the confidence of the President and his senior staff.

5. See Evan Thomas, *The Very Best Men*, p. 237, for a revealing treatment of the macho camaraderie at a dinner at Washington's exclusive Alibi Club soon after Kennedy's inauguration when Dulles 'invited the top men of the new administration to meet the upper echelon of the CIA'. For commentary on President Kennedy's keen interest in clandestine agent reporting, see Jerrold Schecter and Peter Deriabin, *The Spy Who Saved the World* (1995).

6. The term was employed poignantly by Kennedy speech-

writer and White House adviser Richard Goodwin in
Remembering America: A Voice from the 60s (1988), pp. 169–70.
He wrote that he was 'overwhelmed . . . impressed, even
excited' after he was briefed in the White House about CIA
clandestine operations. 'The veil had been lifted on the
alchemical magic of the clandestine, its power to transform
the most innocent-seeming reality into an instrument of
freedom's struggle.'
7. The allure of the CIA's clandestine service has worked
much the same way on virtually every Cold War administration, only differing in intensity. The unique missions and capabilities of the Operations Directorate – collection through
agent recruitment, covert action, wielding influence in quarters of foreign governments rarely accessible to US diplomats
– has provided unparallelled advantages to CIA operations
officers in relations with policy-makers.
8. *Foreign Relations of the United States,* vol. X, 1961–2 Cuba,
p. 1078.
9. *Ibid.,* p. 1079.
10. See Christopher Andrew, *For the President's Eyes Only,* p.
271.
11. The author recalls cutting his teeth as an intelligence
analyst in 1964 by writing briefs on developments in Cuba for
a daily summary exclusively on that country that was
produced for McCone and the policy officials he regularly
briefed. Within a year or so, the rigours of producing that
Cuba Daily Summary were relaxed when McCone consented
to converting it into a *Cuba Weekly Summary.*
12. In 'A Crucial Estimate Relived', in *Studies in Intelligence,*
vol. 36, no. 5, 1992 unclassified edition (originally published
in *Studies in Intelligence,* Spring 1964), Sherman Kent labori-
ously endeavoured to exonerate himself and the ONE. He
argued, for example, that 'even in hindsight it is extremely
difficult for many of us to follow (the Kremlin leadership's)

inner logic or to blame ourselves for not having thought in parallel with them'.

13. Harold P. Ford, *Estimative Intelligence: The Purposes and Problems of National Intelligence Estimating* (University Press of America, 1993), pp. 97–105.

14. Ford was a veteran of the ONE and friend of Sherman Kent. See Harold P. Ford, ' A Tribute to Sherman Kent', in *Studies in Intelligence*, Fall 1980, included in Donald P. Steury, *Sherman Kent and the Board of National Estimates: Collected Essays* (Center for the Study of Intelligence, 1994). Ford also served in the National Intelligence Council in the 1980s as Vice Chairman, Acting Chairman, and founder and director of its Analytic Group. More than any other intelligence officer, he has experience in all of the stages in the history of national estimating.

15. Ford, *Estimative Intelligence*, p. 98.

16. *Ibid.*

17. See Steury, *op. cit.*, p. xiii.

18. Sherman Kent, 'The Need for an Intelligence Literature', in *Studies in Intelligence*, September 1955 (included in Steury).

19. Jack Davis, 'The Kent-Kendall Debate', in *Studies in Intelligence*, vol. 36, no. 5, 1992 unclassified edition.

20. See for example, Sherman Kent, *Strategic Intelligence for American World Policy* (1966).

21. Sherman Kent, 'Estimates and Influence', included in Steury, originally published in *Studies in Intelligence*, Summer 1968.

22. See Harold P. Ford, *CIA and the Vietnam Policymakers: Three Episodes, 1962–1968* (Center for the Study of Intelligence, 1998).

23. Henry Kissinger, *White House Years* (1982), p. 11.

24. *Ibid.*

25. The portfolios have varied little since 1973 with the total number of NIOs ranging between a dozen and sixteen. In

recent years, in addition, the Directors of such DCI offices as
the Non-Proliferation Center and the Crime and Counter-
Narcotics Center have functioned much as NIOs.
26. The constructive changes in the NIC implemented under
the chairmanship of Joseph Nye are not treated in this paper.
For a full examination of what was accomplished, see Joseph
S. Nye, Jr, 'Peering into the Future', in *Foreign Affairs*,
July–August 1994.
27. This was probably the most egregious failure in the history
of national intelligence estimating in the category of a squan-
dered opportunity to produce an estimate on a critically
important issue. See Ford, *Estimative Intelligence*, pp. 122–3,
for a discussion of the unsuccessful effort to produce an estimate. He indicates that 'in the end, the Intelligence
Community never did tell the policy-makers how to think
about the tumultuous revolution then in progress in Iran'.
28. See Robert M. Gates, *From the Shadows* (1996), for eluci-
dation of numerous Reagan and Casey era covert actions.
29. The Latin America portfolio seemed especially susceptible
to politicisation charges and distorted accounts by journalists
and others. See, for example, Bob Woodward, *Veil: The Secret
Wars of the CIA, 1981–1987* (1994).
30. Gates, *op. cit.*, pp. 207–8.
31. Quoted in Jack Davis, *op. cit.*, p. 93.
32. See, for example, George Shultz, *Triumph and Turmoil: My
Years as Secretary of State* (Charles Scribner & Sons, NY,
1993), pp. 691, 849, 851.
33. Hans Heymann, 'Intelligence-Policy Relationships', in
Alfred C. Maurer, Marion D. Tunstall and James M. Keagle
(eds), *Intelligence: Policy and Process* (Westview Press, 1985),
p. 323.
34. Sherman Kent, 'Estimates and Influence', in Steury, *op.
cit.*, p. 35.

FIVE

INTELLIGENCE AND
INTERNATIONAL AGENCIES

Sir David Hannay

Sir David Hannay entered the British Diplomatic Service in 1959 and served, inter alia, *in Tehran, Kabul, Washington and the United Nations. He took part in negotiations with the EC in 1970–2 and from 1985 to 1990 was the UK Permanent Representative to the European Communities in Brussels. His final posting was as British Permanent Representative to the UN. During his forty years' diplomatic career, he was a constant consumer and user of intelligence, convinced of the valuable contribution that intelligence can make to the conduct of international diplomacy. He retired in 1995.*

As a small health warning, could I say that, although I have consumed quite a lot of intelligence in my life, I haven't ever produced any, and secondly, that I only did this introduction under slight protest, since there is in the room, in the form of the Warden of St Antony's, somebody who is a great deal better equipped than I am to address this subject.

You could, and I don't mean any disrespect by this, have held this seminar at almost any time in recent decades with the title we have, 'Intelligence Services in a Changing World', and at any time in recent decades you would have had practically every one of the chapter headings of the sessions, except this one. This one you would not have had, because people would have thought it really quite absurd to be talking about intelligence and international agencies. Most would have dismissed it either as completely impractical, because of the leakiness of international agencies, because of the fact that Soviet Bloc countries were naturally members of these agencies, and that, therefore, any exchange of information was unthinkable, but secondly also because most of the international agencies in question would have hung large strings of garlic around their necks, crossed themselves and done various other forms of fending-off on the grounds that this would have affected their impartiality. People in those days regarded international agencies as a target or a cover, but not as a customer.

There were perhaps one or two exceptions. NATO obviously was an exception. From the very beginning the integrated military command made sophisticated intelligence-sharing an absolute must. Perhaps there was one other exception in the Warsaw Pact, though I hope my Russian friends here will forgive me for saying that I sometimes doubt whether they passed on a great deal of intelligence to the other members of the Warsaw Pact, apart from that which they wished to give them. But this exception apart, for forty years that was the rule; international agencies were outside this matter we are talking about.

Now all that has changed in the last few years, but so far it has only changed in a rather ill-thought out, haphazard way. Why has it changed and why is it haphazard? Well, one basic reason for the change, of course, has been the end of the Cold War. Once East-West confrontation in Europe and all the proxy confrontations around the world, mainly the developing world, which had been one of the main obstacles to some degree of intelligence provision to international agencies, once that faded, of course things changed.

Then many of the problems that the international community now faces are, to a great extent, general and global in nature, not specific and geographic to the extent that they were. So, when you are talking about drugs, terrorism, international crime, ethnic wars that destabilise whole regions, proliferation of weapons of mass destruction, the enforcement of economic sanctions and all these things, these are general problems which require some kind of more general response than nations, individual nations, can bring.

At the same time, in a second development, the battle against these threats tends more and more to be confided collectively to international groupings or agencies, as individual countries, even superpowers, recognise that they can't achieve their desired policy objectives on their own. So, the international dimension looms larger, even if it certainly doesn't entirely replace the national effort and the meeting of national requirements in the intelligence field.

And this inevitably brings with it a paradox. How can we expect international agencies to be effective, often to be effective at disciplining or handling national governments, aberrant national governments, if they are so much less well informed than the national governments they are trying to corral or handle?

Now, it is worth looking in a little bit more detail at what international agency tasks I am talking about when I say that the demand for international agencies to take on tasks that require intelligence has gone up so exponentially.

First of all conflict prevention. A lot of the information needed, of course, comes from straightforward diplomatic reporting or from the media, and one mustn't get obsessed with the need for intelligence in this area. But a lot doesn't, and if we are going to have an effective world organisation in the UN, effective regional organisations in the Organisation for Security and Co-operation in Europe, or the Organisation of African Unity, or such like, which are going to be effective in the field of conflict prevention, they do need access to some intelligence, particularly as the countries in which you are trying to prevent the conflict are only too likely either to be manipulating information that gets out about them – if they are in an international dispute they certainly will – or they will be trying to suppress it completely, if it is about internal conflicts that are bubbling up within them. You can see examples of these phenomena in the period before the break-up of the former Yugoslavia, in Rwanda before the killing started, in Iraq before they crossed the frontier into Kuwait.

Secondly, you have peace-keeping. I think it's fairly obvious that if you are sending peace-keepers whose lives are on the line into a difficult mission – not, I should make clear, an enforcement mission, but a peace-keeping mission – even then you have to provide them with intelligence if you are to get the job done, and if your conscience is not to reproach you for the fact that you've sent them there and then didn't tell them what might happen to them. Examples of that would be found in Namibia and in Cambodia and to some extent in Bosnia.

Thirdly, there is peace enforcement, not usually now of course entrusted to the United Nations, but nevertheless conducted very frequently collectively. There is a lot of talk of coalitions of the willing, but, if you have a coalition of the willing, how does it get its intelligence? Well, if the coalition of the willing is based straight on NATO, then the answer is fairly obvious, but if it goes wider than that – and currently we are seeing that in East Timor – how then does it get its intelligence, its military and its political intelligence? East Timor and Kosovo are good recent examples.

Fourthly, peace-making, which I am using here in the sense of negotiating a peace settlement, not in the sense of enforcing peace. In those terms, either the United Nations or some other regional mediator is very often put into play to try to bring about a peace settlement. That person, or group of people, desperately need political intelligence, because otherwise they simply don't have the means to negotiate effectively with the two or more parties whom they are trying to bring to the table and trying to get to compromise.

Fifthly, you have economic sanctions, and I am talking here only about general mandatory sanctions under the United Nations, not unilateral national sanctions, ones where the international community has given them the force of law and where, therefore, they are being imposed for certain policy objectives. You need to be able to use intelligence to deal with breaches of these sanctions and to catch up with third countries, not the immediate object of the sanctions, who may be co-operating in those breaches. And here we've had very elaborate operations required in the context of Iraq, in the context of the Federal Republic of Yugoslavia, in the context of Unita and the diamonds that provide so much of its livelihood.

Sixthly, you have the proliferation of weapons of mass destruction. The legal framework to prevent the proliferation of weapons of mass destruction is very nearly complete now. Nuclear and chemical is complete, biological nearly so, and then there are some quite elaborate regimes that deal with missiles. What's missing now is enforcement, and enforcement requires intelligence because nobody who is breaking their obligations under any of these treaties is going to go around telling everyone that. In fact, they are probably going to pay more attention to concealing that than to anything else, including their own military security. So, if we are to make a reality of steps to avoid weapons proliferation, we are going to have to arm the international organisations which have been set up to deal with nuclear proliferation, with chemical warfare proliferation, biological warfare proliferation, with an ability to recognise when there are breaches of it and also, but that is not the purpose of this talk, with a back-up from the Security Council if the offender refuses to come to order. Now, we have had plenty of examples of people breaking their treaty obligations under proliferation treaties, Iraq is one, North Korea is another, South Africa was a very notable one, although it came back into line with the huge political shift there and still represents the only country that has ever willingly given up nuclear weapons, had the IAEA in and been given a clean bill of health. Let's hope there will be one or two more.

Then, seventh, there are other weapons control regimes that exist, whether it is the interdiction on land mines or whether it's arms embargoes instituted under Chapter 7 by the United Nations, which have been notable in their complete inefficacy, partly because there is no proper supply of intelligence about how the arms are getting in, and little attempt made to provide it. That is not the only reason they haven't been effective, but it is one of the main reasons, so that is another category.

Eighth, there is the whole area of drugs, international crime and terrorism. The intelligence needs are quite obvious, although I would make the point here that most of the international action against drugs, crime and terrorism is not handled by international agencies directly in an operational sense, and so one shouldn't exaggerate the amount of intelligence-sharing there would have to be on that. Most of it will be sharing between nation states who are working together within a broad framework of international rules, but are not trying to do it through international agencies.

And ninthly, and you will be pleased to hear lastly, there is the whole issue of bringing people to justice before international tribunals, the attempt to break the doctrine of impunity, which took shape in the form of the tribunal on the former Yugoslavia, the one on Rwanda and now, hopefully, the International Criminal Court. It is perfectly clear that bringing people to justice for crimes against humanity requires the co-operation of intelligence agencies, who often will be the only people who can give the leads, or who have knowledge to give the leads, to bring some of these people to court. But naturally enough that raises many problems which I will mention in the next section.

Now, this is a huge list; it is easy to flinch from it, to say it's all too difficult. But just remember that if the agencies handling

these issues are not given access to intelligence, they are fighting *our* battles with *their* hands tied behind their backs.

The response has been very haphazard so far and why is that?
Well, at first, for some time, a lot of effort was wasted on what
I think was a complete red herring: could the UN be given its
own dedicated source of technical intelligence? Could it have a
satellite, a system of satellites, and so on? Answer, no it could-
n't, firstly because the member states weren't prepared to finance
it; secondly, because they weren't prepared to put something up
in the sky that was peering into their own backyards; and thirdly,
because the United Nations wouldn't have known what to do
with all the material it got from it because it doesn't have the
staff actually to process it, and so on. So, I think that was a red
herring, and I hope that we won't hare off in that direction again.
But that means you are driven back in a very difficult direction,
which is that intelligence will have to be provided to international agencies by national intelligence assets and governments,
and that raises plenty of problems.

If the only sensible route is that route, what are these problems? There is the problem of security in the first place. Leakiness
is endemic in international agencies, we all know that. The only
way in the Commission in Brussels to ensure that a document
was not in the newspapers the next day was not to classify it. If
you classified it, it was immediately published. If you didn't, it
might get lost amongst the other million pages that the organisation produced that day and take some time to find. Moreover,
international agency practitioners, the officials who work in these
international agencies, are not at all used to handling and using
intelligence material; they have no experience of it. Some of them
recoil from it in horror, but even the ones who want to use it
haven't got any experience of doing so.

Secondly, there is the question of bias: how do you ensure
that intelligence material that comes from national sources isn't
slanted or used manipulatively? There have been many

accusations, in my view most of them unfair and unsound, that UNSCOM, the UN Special Commission that dealt with Iraq, was influenced in this way. How do you deal with that? Is it possible to conceive of some kind of oversight board at an international level that would at least filter out blatant attempts to slant intelligence?

Thirdly, there is the issue of politics. Look again at UNSCOM, where, the minute it became clear – I thought it took rather a long time for the obvious to become clear – that a large amount of the information getting to UNSCOM was coming from the Israelis, all the Arab countries cried foul. But that was a pretty silly thing to do, since the people most likely to have the best intelligence on Iraq were, of course, the Israelis, because it was against the Israelis that most of the weapons the Iraqis were developing were designed to be used. So, it was naïve to complain about this, but the world is a naïve place sometimes.

Fourthly, the agencies, the intelligence agencies, do risk in passing on material a loss of cover, deniability and all these things, and that is particularly so if the information they pass on ends up in front of a court of law, i.e. one of the tribunals. But that in a way is something that people have faced already in the context of material about the IRA, for example, where the agencies have had to be dragged kicking and screaming to a position where they are prepared to allow it to appear in a court of law, because otherwise you couldn't get any convictions.

All this seems to me to point towards the need to get away from a haphazard approach and to adopt a careful and systematic approach to this problem. You need to assess the needs of each international agency and each set of problems, because the responses are completely different. They all have their own different characteristics. For example, conflict prevention probably requires nothing more than a kind of JIC-type of political analysis paper, which gives people the best possible knowledge of what is happening in country A or B that is at risk. Obviously if you are dealing with weapons of mass destruction, you need highly technical, highly precise indications of where nuclear parts or weapons are being produced, where chemicals are going to and from, what the chemicals are, and all that sort of thing. It is very technical, completely different in nature from what you require for conflict prevention. For peace-keeping and peace-enforcement, you are in the straight-forward military intelligence field. So, again you want something completely different. I believe therefore that this subject will only be properly dealt with when it is broken down into its component parts, and each one is looked at carefully and analytically, not in a sort of broad-brush, 'My God, we can't give intelligence to these people', sort of way.

One final point. The biggest immediate challenge on the provision of intelligence to international agencies is sitting fair and square in the court of the Europeans. They have set up something called a Common Foreign and Security Policy and have appointed Javier Solana to run it; and the old excuses about why things didn't go terribly well in CFSP aren't going to wash much longer. But let's face it, if he is to be effective and his staff are to be effective – and he has been given a pretty modest staff – they are going to have to have a lot of national intelligence provided to them, otherwise they will not be able to operate. Well, I will be interested to see just how and how much they get. It is, of course, a slightly *sui generis* case because the EU is turning itself into something more like NATO in this respect – an integrated approach to common, foreign and security policy – than some of the other organisations. But even so, this problem of intelligence-sharing will come up and it will be interesting to see how it is dealt with.

DISCUSSION

John Roper

John Roper is an Honorary Professor at the University of Birmingham and a Visiting Professor at the College of Europe in Bruges, as well as a member of the Council of the Royal Institute of International Affairs, London. He was, from April 1990 until September 1995, the first director of the Institute for Security Studies of the Western European Union (WEU) in Paris, and a member of the International Commission on the Balkans in 1995–6. After teaching Economics at the University of Manchester in the 1960s, when he also served as a part-time adviser to the British Government's Department of Economic Affairs, he was a Member of Parliament (1970–83), an Opposition spokesman on defence (1979–81), and Chief Whip of the Social Democratic Party from 1981 to 1983. While an MP, he was a member for seven years of the House of Commons committee dealing with defence and of the Parliamentary Assemblies of the Council of Europe and of the WEU. From 1983 to 1990 he was a senior member of staff of the Royal Institute of International Affairs, where he edited the Institute's journal International Affairs *from 1983 to 1988 and was responsible for its International Security Programme. A founder member of the European Strategy Group, he is the author and editor of a number of published works on the problems of British and European defence and Western security.*

I must begin with a caveat. I am not only a layman but, particularly after what we heard from our Israeli colleague, I am something even worse: I have been in Parliament, so, on one interpretation of his views, I am certainly disqualified to speak on this subject. My only qualification is that ten years ago I had the great pleasure of taking Michael Herman's book through Chatham House when I was acting Director of Studies, and I happen to believe that that was something very useful, as his book is a most important contribution to the public debate on this subject.

I have been asked to take up some of the issues arising from the development of European co-operation, and to pick up the final paragraph of David Hannay's paper as to what this might imply for the future.

Christopher Andrew last night said that not in his lifetime would the UK be transferring decrypts of the kind that are exchanged with the United States to another European nation. I am not an actuary, but would suggest that this is an assertion we will only be able to assess in another forty years. But what is I think quite clear is that we are not likely to be looking at a supra-national European intelligence agency in the near future. I suspect the decrypts, particularly of the kind that Christopher Andrew was referring to, are probably rather close to nuclear weapons as being the most difficult things to bring into a common policy.

But, in spite of that, we have to ask, is the best the enemy of the good? Is it necessarily the case that, because we do not have the ability, either in terms of hardware or indeed of a shared intelligence culture, to do everything, does it mean we shouldn't attempt to do anything? I will be arguing that we should at least see what it is we might be able to do usefully in terms of exchanges among Europeans.

Before coming to the European Union – and indeed I think it is perhaps important to put it into the wider context – I would like to make a comment on something that Sir David Hannay said at the beginning of his remarks about NATO. How good and how effective in practice has sharing, or integrated, intelligence been within NATO? Sometimes I suspect in the United Kingdom we equate NATO with the bilateral relationship that this country enjoys in transatlantic links, which has been one of the so-called *specialités* of the special relationship. But certainly within NATO more widely my impression, talking to people from elsewhere, is that some have been more equal than others. And, on the one hand, of course, the European members of NATO, according to recent estimates, only make about 20 per cent of the contributions to Allied security assessments. On the other hand, there is in a number of European countries greater or less resentment of the position of a quasi-monopoly of raw intelligence material of the United States, and this has led from time to time for demands for European national technical means. The classic dilemma of this occurred for NATO in the situation in October 1994, when our ships were operating in the Adriatic in 'Operation Sharp Guard', and when, as a result of a decision in the United States Congress, the issue arose as to whether the United States was going to withdraw its co-operation particularly in the intelligence area. The problem was resolved, but this demonstrated to many the risk of relying on any single member state within the Alliance.

This continuing difference which exists in intelligence cultures within NATO, and the consequential limitations on NATO, I found best summarised in a paper that Michael Herman wrote in 1995, when he pointed out that it was national intelligence services' concerns over document security that obliged NATO to abandon any idea of creating an integrated intelligence body within the Alliance.

Turning to the European Union, as Sir David Hannay has said, we now have at the level of institutional development some evidence of a move to common assessment. The policy planning and early-warning unit, which will now be set up following the Treaty of Amsterdam coming into force, will have, as he said, a relatively limited number of people, not more than thirty, but the most important problem is what will the inputs to it be from member states? It is difficult to say. Certainly the experience of the WEU, which created an intelligence centre some time ago, has not been particularly encouraging. The last time I saw a public analysis of what it received, it was suggested that only half of the ten member states ever provided it with any significant information and that almost all of it came from three of them, France, Germany and Italy.

We have, however, had over the last twelve months what has been described by some people as the Franco-British political revolution in the area of common defence policy, set out initially by the Declaration of St Malo last December, which in its declaration included the assertion, 'the European Union must be given a capacity for analysis of situation, sources of intelligence and a capacity for relevant strategic planning without unnecessary duplication'. For those who have a taste for the creative ambiguities of diplomatic drafting, 'relevant' before strategic and 'unnecessary' before duplication suggest that there may have been more than one view in the discussion.

What then is necessary, or what could be necessary, duplication? An interesting question. There is the European wish to have alternative sources already referred to. A parallel and quite interesting example is that the European Commission is taking forward a proposal to establish a European Global Positioning System (GPS) to provide security for our aircraft and shipping services, in the event that the US GPS were removed. So, issues are being raised in that area, too.

The Franco-British initiative was carried forward in the Cologne Declaration of the European Union, in which they went on to say, in the European Union's first reference to intelligence, as far as I know, that the European Common Security and Defence Policy 'requires the maintenance of a sustained defence effort, the implementation of the necessary adaptations, and notably the reinforcement of our capabilities in the field of intelligence, strategic transport, command and control'. This was agreed to by fifteen heads of state in government, including the four non-Alliance countries, Ireland, Sweden, Finland and Austria. So far it is only a declaration, but it is an interesting fact that intelligence is now on the European Union's agenda.

Of course, there have already been some examples of how

co-operation among Europeans may sometimes paradoxically have
benefits, even in the areas we are discussing. There is the experience of the WEU Satellite Centre in Kosovo. They are using primarily open and semi-open sources, which they have obtained from
satellite material from Russia and commercial sources; they have
been able to produce a CD-rom of maps and other materials
covering Kosovo, and because the material has not been of high-
grade origin, it has been able to be distributed in Kosovo to units
down to company level, whereas material coming from NATO
cannot be taken out of Brigade Headquarters, apparently because
it blends material of higher degrees of classification. So, paradoxically, sometimes working with open or semi-open material, e.g.
the Iconos satellite referred to this morning, is a further addition,
and may mean that one can do something useful.

Another grey area in which Europe has already moved was the
work of the European Community Monitoring Mission within
former Yugoslavia, and although this was not explicitly an intelligence activity, it became what one might describe as a grey area.

There is one other point that we have just been discussing,
and that Chris Andrew has referred to, on intelligence in the
European Union. The existing work of the European Union,
other than the Common Foreign and Security Policy, already
requires a good deal of intelligence, and would, if it was being
dealt with at a national level, include material obtained, I suspect,
by covert methods.

There is also the question of economic intelligence. It is the
European Union that represents all its fifteen member states in
international trade negotiations. Therefore, Commissioner Lamy,
who will be representing the Union at Seattle and thereafter,
will presumably wish to have information about his partners'
negotiating positions. In other situations this would, I assume,
be an intelligence requirement. How is this handled at the level
of the European Union? Similarly, the European Union increasingly takes common positions within the IMF on loans, partic-

ularly the eleven who have adopted the Euro as a common currency. When making a decision on further loans, is an analysis of Russia something that requires intelligence or not?

Reference has already been made to the areas of drugs and thugs, but of course the European Union, within the justice and home affairs pillar, has already taken this quite a long way into a common position. And the Schengen countries, including Norway and Iceland who, as a result of the Nordic Passport Union, are participating in the Schengen activities, are already exchanging quite a lot of information in certain areas about people whom they do or do not wish to have admitted into the European Union area.

So, we can see that we are moving into the intelligence area within the existing pattern of work of the European Union, and one could give further examples.

Clearly the question of the assessment of candidates for admission to the European Union would, if one was thinking of getting so close to a country on a bilateral basis, require inputs from one's intelligence sources. Is that also taken into account at a European level when we are making decisions?

There are two questions that one should ask. I have been trying over the last few days to try and work out how much Europe collectively spends on these sorts of activities. I thought one could get up to about $8 billion. I find when I think about it harder, and when I ask questions, it's not terribly easy to get it very much above $5 or $6 billion. That is a very small proportion of what the United States spends, but we only get a fraction of the material and there is obviously a great deal of duplication. But, in spite of what I've said so far about the European Union, we also need to ask ourselves whether fifteen is always the right number?

There is, as I have suggested, a problem of differences in national intelligence cultures that is greater among some countries than it is among others. There have always been, and will continue to be, clubs within the intelligence community. Is this an area in which one may be able to make more progress among a limited number initially and then subsequently extend this? This at least seems to be something worth considering.

Michael Herman has said somewhere that 'states guide each other towards common perceptions through intelligence, exchanges and dialogues. Mutual education also promotes common action, just as having a common basis of intelligence knowledge promotes agreed decision.' Common intelligence in my view is a prerequisite for common analysis, which in turn is a prerequisite for common action. Therefore, if Europe is going to have a common foreign and security policy, it has got to move to having some greater degree of intelligence-sharing.

Perhaps I can conclude with a comment made to me by a colleague from RAND a few years ago. He said, 'The trouble with you Europeans is that not only do you not have the same knee-jerk reaction to a problem, you do not even have the same knees.' Maybe after what we've heard today, some of us will need to have new artificial knees. On the other hand, perhaps thinking about developing more commonality in our approach both to collection, but also more importantly to assessment, would lead to more common knees.

Andrew Rathmell

Dr Andrew Rathmell has been Executive Director of the International Centre for Security Analysis, Department of War Studies, King's College, London, since 1996 when he set up ICSA, where he is responsible for the management and development of research and training, focusing on applied intelligence studies, including Information Warfare. He lectures on 'War and Peace in the Middle East' and 'Intelligence', and runs a seminar on 'Intelligence and International Security'. Recent publications include: Mind Warriors at the Ready in the World

Today *(November 1998);* Assessing the IW Threat from Sub-State Groups, *in* CyberWar 2 *(AFCEA, 1998); 'The Privatisation of Intelligence', in* Cambridge Review of International Affairs; *'Brotherly Enemies: The Rise and Fall of the Syrian-Egyptian Intelligence Axis, 1954–1967', in* Intelligence & National Security *(Spring 1998); 'Strategic IW: Responding to the Threat', in* CDS Defence Yearbook *1998 (Brassey's, 1998); 'Information Warfare: Implications for Arms Control', in* Bulletin of Arms Control *(April 1998); 'Cyber-terrorism: The Shape of Future Conflict?', in* RUSI Journal *(October 1997);* The Changing Military Balance in the Gulf *(Royal United Services Institute, 1996), 'Syria's Intelligence Services: Origins and Developments', in* The Journal of Conflict Studies (Fall 1996); Secret War in the Middle East *(I.B. Tauris, London, 1995). He is editor of* Gulf States Newsletter *and* Jane's Sentinel, The Gulf States, *and is a specialist correspondent for* Jane's Intelligence Review.

Sir David Hannay's paper performs a very useful service in outlining the case for a more systematic approach to the use of intelligence in the international arena and also in elucidating the problems with wider sharing of national intelligence in support of international agencies and international policies. I cannot disagree with much in his paper but will instead reinforce his argument and take it a couple of steps further.

I want to make one contextual argument, focus on two areas in which intelligence-sharing and collaboration are particularly called for, and then make the case that a combination of technology and market forces are making easier the sort of sharing and collaboration for which Sir David calls.

Absent Centres and Fluid Boundaries

The arcane discussions of post-modern theorists may seem light years removed from the day-to-day requirements of intelligence agencies working at the sharp end of real problems. Nonetheless, some of the analytical concepts developed by post-modern theorists to describe emerging society usefully encapsulate changing intelligence requirements.

Two of the post-modernist concepts that usefully characterise contemporary intelligence are:

1. Absent Centres: Intelligence must embrace the fluid set of mutating identities that are being thrust upon it. There is no longer a single answer to the question of who are intelligence's customers; these will be in constant flux, as indeed will be the organisations and individuals who make up the intelligence community.

2. Fluid Borders: The Cold War model of a closely knit and exclusionary intelligence community must be discarded. Horizontal knowledge networks need to be embraced, even at the expense of vertical integration. Knowledge must be sought where it resides, whether by topic (on obscure geographic regions, on Cyberia, on cults, etc.), or by source (non-governmental organisations, corporations, other governments or other departments).

Joined-up Government

One specific example of the need for the intelligence community to serve different masters, collaborate more widely and answer new information requirements, was mentioned by Sir David – drugs and crime. By now there is nothing new in the observation that, since the end of the Cold War, transnational crime issues have moved up the national and international policy agendas. Likewise, they have moved up the agenda of national intelligence agencies, which traditionally disdained dealing with such 'low politics' threats.

However, despite all the efforts that have been made to co-ordinate the work of national and law enforcement intelligence agencies in the UK and abroad, the requirements for, and potentials of, joined-up government in an intelligence sense have not been fully recognised. This applies at a national level and even more at an international level.

At a national level, the divide (culturally and institutionally) between traditional elements of the international community and other parts of government that hold data on citizens (police and law enforcement, tax authorities, regulatory agencies, etc.) remains wide. Yet, at least in terms of their focus on organised crime, drugs and terrorism, the information requirements of these agencies are similar, as are the problems of information-gathering and information-management in the context of a rapidly changing technological and legal environment.

Given that collaboration and sharing between national agencies remains limited, it is not surprising that such collaboration across national boundaries remains even more limited and so the international community fails to exploit the wealth of information already available.

The failure to achieve 'joined-up government' in this specific intelligence field indicates both the requirements for, and the potentialities of, greater collaboration and sharing in what is still a relatively new field for intelligence agencies.

Intelligence in Cyberspace

The emerging problems of Critical Infrastructure Protection and of policing cyberspace highlight some of the challenges for international intelligence collaboration. As yet only the USA has taken very seriously the threat posed to its Critical National Infrastructures by electronic attack. Although this threat is probably exaggerated at present, there is little doubt that, as more governments and economies become reliant on Networked Information Systems, their vulnerability to attack from criminals, terrorists or hostile states will increase.

One of the pressing problems in implementing protective policies is the requirement for intelligence on attacks. At present, the state of the art in detection technologies and intelligence mechanisms is unable to fulfil this requirement. Even as nations work to improve their capabilities, though, the transnational nature of information networks such as the Internet will make it impossible for any one nation to be electronically self-sufficient. Whether states treat such attacks as criminal activities or national security threats, they will need to put in place collaborative mechanisms for joint investigations and sharing of information on attacks and attackers.

Given the lack of warning time inherent in electronic attacks, this sharing will come to resemble the sort of sharing required in an operational combat zone – it will have to be real time and allow the instantaneous integration of intelligence with operations to enable victims of attacks to react appropriately.

The challenge of protecting information infrastructures, therefore, poses the problem of international intelligence co-operation in its most extreme form. The global nature of cyberspace means that co-operation needs to be as broad as possible; states will have to risk sharing sensitive data on their vulnerabilities; and co-operation will have to be in real time.

Transparency and Technology

Having outlined further challenges for collaboration between intelligence agencies, it is useful now to highlight one respect in which the emerging global environment will make it easier for the intelligence community to meet some of the challenges outlined in Sir David's paper. Put simply, a combination of technological and commercial developments are making the globe much more transparent than ever before – the wide availability of these capabilities should make it easier for agencies to collaborate since they can meet many of their requirements without access to sensitive sources and methods.

There has been a great deal of hype surrounding the role that open-source information (OSINF) can play in the intelligence process. In practice, though, many intelligence agencies have been slow to make full use of cost-effective and widely available OSINF.

OSINF now has a much greater role to play in intelligence (whether for defence, foreign affairs or law enforcement) since a combination of technological developments (electronic data-bases, the Internet) and commercial developments (the diffusion of technologies such as high resolution satellite imagery into the civil sector) is greatly increasing global transparency.

The OSINF 'revolution' means that intelligence agencies can fulfil many (though by no means all) of their tasks using unclas-sified sources and methods. This particularly applies to some of the political-military tasks outlined in Sir David's paper (conflict-prevention, peace support, sanctions and weapons of mass destruction proliferation).

Although for national purposes OSINF will continue to be only one input into the all-source analytical process, in an inter-national context it becomes much easier to share intelligence derived from such sources and methods. Whether it is a ques-tion of sharing the raw data or semi-finished analytical product underpinned from OSINF, the Western intelligence community should find it much easier to share this information both with international agencies and with non-traditional allies, such as Partnership for Peace nations. Moreover, international agencies themselves are more able to develop their own intelligence capa-bilities and so become less reliant on handouts of sensitive intel-ligence. The IAEA (International Atomic Energy Authority) is already going down this route by exploiting OSINF, including commercial satellite imagery. It will be interesting to see the extent to which evolving EU/WEU strategic intelligence mech-anisms can make effective use of OSINF.

GENERAL DISCUSSION

Sir Marrack Goulding had two observations and a question. The first observation was that, in view of the plethora of information available overtly or semi-overtly – from the media, from UN missions, from non-governmental organisations and academics – the UN Secretariat does not need covert intelligence in conflict-prevention and peace-making. But he agreed with Sir David that covert intelligence was of importance in the peace-keeping field in two areas. Firstly, that of 'tactical battlefield information', e.g. 'Is it true that the Iranians are about to flood part of the no-man's land between them and Iraq?' This became a major issue that nearly destroyed the ceasefire in the latter part of 1988. The technology that can answer such questions is available, for instance, in the form of the Iconos satellite and commercial satellite imagery. The question is whether the UN is in a position to buy and use it?

Sir Marrack cited Southern Lebanon as an example of the other area in which peace-keepers need information. The UN is supposed to be confirming Israel's withdrawal. In trying to persuade the Israeli leaders to withdraw and let the UN, working with local forces, ensure security, he had felt handicapped because the Israelis had so much very detailed, necessarily covert, information about the different armed groups and what they were doing and where their supplies were coming in, that it was very easy for the Israelis to out-manoeuvre him in discussion.

Sir Marrack's second observation concerned the usability of covert information provided by member states, which he illustrated with a particular case. The Security Council was concerned about alleged combat in a remote part of the Horn of Africa and pressed the Secretary-General for information. There was no UN official in the area, not even one UNICEF local worker, who might have provided information. Instead, an approach was made to several delegations, one of which was thought most likely to have information, which indeed turned out to be the case. But the information was given on condition that it not be used. When the Security Council was informed that the Secretary-General's office had been unable to obtain any information, the permanent member which had given covert information led the attack on the Secretary-General for inadequacy in failing in his duty to provide information.

Sir Marrack's question concerned Sir David's call for a systematic approach responding to the different types of requirement. He asked if Sir David, as the former representative of a permanent member of the Security Council, could comment on how the UNSCOM operation had worked as an intelligence operation.

Sir David doubted whether the member countries will ever authorise the United Nations itself to lay out the large sums of money needed, and thought that some of it will have to come from countries that are interested in stability and in responding to a threat to international peace and security in a particular area. On the other hand, he predicted that the European Union would allow the Policy Planning and Early Warning Unit some access to that sort of material before too long.

Sir David remarked that he was not sure that it is true that the United Nations knows enough in the field of conflict-prevention and peace-making. A common problem in all international agencies, he said, is that third countries are able to manipulate them by controlling the flow of their dealings with them and playing on the fact that these international agencies do not normally have really serious missions in the country in question who are sending back a steady flow of reporting. The clear advantage that such agencies may gain from access to a wider range of information would be as a protection against the manipulation that is endemic in all dealings between nation states and international agencies.

As for the duplicity of a permanent member in the case cited by Sir Marrack, Sir David described it as just another example of the damage such behaviour inflicts on the system, as well as to the credibility of the permanent member and the morale of the Secretariat. 'I think they have just got to get serious and realise that if international agencies and organisations are to look after some of our concerns and interests for us, they have got to be treated in a grown-up way.' On the question of UNSCOM, Sir David described it as 'a superb operating machine for a very long time'. It managed with great discretion to set up a series of technically sophisticated activities, despite the fact that it was the object of incessant intelligence attack by the Iraqis. The fact that it survived for about seven years, without a serious problem arising, was a remarkable tribute, both to the countries that provided the intelligence and to UNSCOM, particularly under Rolf Ekeus. What subsequently happened showed the vulnerability of the exercise. Sir David concluded that this was the most sophisticated example of the United Nations getting to terms with a serial breaker of international obligations on the proliferation of weapons of mass destruction.

An academic participant asked Sir David in his EU, rather than his UN, capacity about the role of intelligence in policy-making amongst allies, a topic that had been raised by Sir Michael Quinlan in an earlier session. He noted that several references had been made to the effect that it was important not only to spy on our enemies and potential enemies, but also to spy on our friends. To say, as Sir David had, that 'manipulation is endemic in all dealings between nation states' does not say 'manipulation endemic in all dealings between states which may have hostile aims'. Did Sir David think that this might not be a successful way of making policy in the European Union, and that we might conceivably alienate more people than we do if we follow this line?

Sir David explained that what he had said had nothing to do with manipulation between member states, but that nation states that were in difficulties with an international organisation, or breaking the rules or liable to fall within the ambit of the Security Council, were highly manipulative in their dealings with international agencies, and were aided in their manipulative activities by the fact that the international agencies did not have large, well-staffed embassies in the country concerned, which could act as a control mechanism to see whether what they were saying about themselves bore any relation to reality at all. Where a country had very full press coverage, this presented less of a problem, but if it was a country where there was virtually no press interest, then that was where a JIC-type analysis, available through large nation states to the UN, for example, could be very valuable as a check against that.

The question of money-laundering was raised, and the need for some sort of international financial intelligence and co-operation to deal with it. Recent events, such as the international agreement on the restitution of Jewish gold, suggested that countries and banking organisations were now willing to allow access to their records and to publish information to a degree which would have been unthinkable even ten years ago. Against the background of this development, Sir David was asked if he thought that UN agencies should be provided with some assessment staff so that, whether it is public information or private information, they can collect and put it together and brief their people properly. And was it a logical development from his argument that this agency would be empowered to issue contracts for the collection of intelligence to national intelligence agencies or possibly even to private ones, where particular areas were of importance to their work?

Sir David agreed that more co-operation in the financial area was needed in order to pursue these crimes more effectively. It was encouraging that in recent years even Switzerland had changed its long-held attitudes and was now co-operating much more actively than hitherto. On the question of assessment staff,

Sir David was cautious about the possibility of duplication. He also noted that the task of assessing a paper from, say, the JIC, would require qualified specialists in the UN, though not a large staff. As for an international organisation contracting and paying specialist agencies for this purpose, Sir David thought this was not a desirable approach. Instead, he would expect the member states that were best placed and best informed to give a political assessment to the UN on a particular issue as a matter of course. In fact, this is what happened during his time at the UN, not that the Secretary-General asked very often. He hoped that this would become common practice.

Sir David was then pressed on the problem of the reliability of intelligence coming from member states for international organisations, such as the United Nations. Confessing that he had no simple solution, Sir David thought it worth pursuing the idea of 'a board of wise persons' who could keep an eye on the flow of material and who would, because of their experience, probably notice if some really egregious things came along. Multiple sources would also offer some broad protection against the blatant slanting of information. Finally, countries that got caught doing it probably would not be asked a second time, so a certain amount of self-discipline would be built into the system.

On the question of co-operation for intelligence, Sir David was asked about organisations other than NATO, for instance, the Organisation of African Unity (OAU) or the Southern African Development Committee (SADC). The SADC is now in agreement with the United States to get imagery from the United States for their peace-keeping operations, but an organisation such as the OAU has very little technical intelligence capability at all.

Sir David replied that the whole thrust of British, French and American policy towards Africa is to increase indigenous African capacity to handle conflict-prevention, peace-keeping, and so on, a policy which he endorsed as sensible and enlightened, though it cannot be carried out cost-free or with little effort. If this policy works, he added, intelligence is going to be involved at some stage. Several countries, including Britain, the United States and, possibly, France, have been trying to build up, for example, the OAU's Conflict Prevention Unit and a Situation Room in Addis Ababa, and this means providing them with equipment through which they could receive intelligence, without it immediately being seen by the object of the intelligence.

An academic participant – who in the course of the discussion coined the term 'HACKINT' (computer-hacking intelligence) – asked Andrew Rathmell to clarify his position on open-source intelligence, and suggested that an open intelligence issue might belong more properly in the domain of organisations like the BBC's foreign broadcast monitoring service. His second comment was to point to the huge volume of 'rubbish, misinformation, disinformation, lies, confusion and delusion' that can be downloaded from the Internet under the search-term 'Intelligence', information that has been dubbed NOSINT, i.e. network-based open-source intelligence, and he argued that this cast doubt on the reliability and quality of information that can be collected from many of the new information technology open sources.

Andrew Rathmell replied that open-source information has always gone into all-source intelligence systems, and would continue to do so, even though he did not think that it could solve all problems. He summarised the argument, namely, that there is more available now which previously required expensive, clandestine national technical means, or traditional Cold War intelligence mechanisms, to collect; that there is more available now commercially through open sources than there was; and that some of the intelligence requirements laid out by Sir David Hannay for international agencies, or indeed nation states, can be met through open sources, commercially available sources, more readily now. He argued that for technological and commercial reasons it is easier to acquire certain sorts of information – commercial satellite imagery being the epitome of this – whereas it used to be accessible only to a select number of nations that had invested in it or could exploit special relationships. That sort of capability is increasingly available commercially to international agencies. It is only one source, he concluded, but in so far as it can fulfil many of the information requirements of international agencies, it can aid the ability of the international agencies to do their own assessment and not to rely on classified material. He described this sort of technology as a marginal addition rather than a revolution.

A member of the UK delegation to NATO asked Sir David and John Roper to say what their advice would be to Javier Solana, who was soon to take up his appointment as the new head of the WEU – 'Mr Common Foreign and Security Policy'.

John Roper, replying first, noted that both the Washington Summit Communiqué and the Cologne European Union Declaration called for more constructive transparency between the European Union and NATO. He noted that the cultures of those two institutions were very different, and that the amount of information exchanged between them had been small, as their staffs tended to report back to their respective capitals rather than to each other. Javier Solana knows both cultures and would therefore respond more readily to the need to negotiate between the European Union and NATO the sort of agreements which have been agreed between the WEU and NATO about exchanges of information. Answering the question more directly, he thought that it would be important for Solana and for the Council to make the decisions which are suggested in the German Presidency Report to the Cologne Council about the transfer of assets, such as the Satellite Centre, in order to make that sort of information accessible to the planning staff in the European Union relatively soon. Finally, it will be most important for

Solana and for the Council Secretariat where he is going to be based, and also for Chris Patten in his role as the Commissioner responsible for external relations, to try to change the culture of the Commission, so that it is able to start tackling these things seriously and bring about effective collaboration and communication between the two organisations.

Sir David Hannay expressed some embarrassment because he had already given his advice in an open letter to Javier Solana which was published in *Prospect*, mainly along the same lines as John Roper. He thought the important thing was to build up Solana's position and his office gradually, to work at it in a systematic sort of way, not to think that it can all be done in five minutes flat, or that he can write down on a piece of paper exactly what he needs. The Committee that Solana was going to be given – if the member states ever stop squabbling amongst themselves as to how it is to be headed up, and who is to be present on it, and how the noses of the permanent representatives and the political directors are not to be put more out of joint than necessary – will, Sir David believed, get around to doing that quite soon, and it will be absolutely crucial, because Solana must have a day-by-day dialogue with the member states through that Committee. They must talk to him through this Committee, which he will preside over, and he must talk to them about his requirements, and when he has a requirement in a particular situation, the member states ought to respond very actively. There will, moreover, have to be a systematic approach to the provision of intelligence, and it is hoped that work is in hand of a serious kind about how to make available intelligence to Solana and his staff, and how that can be available also to Chris Patten and a certain number of his staff, so that an intelligence-user culture is established in this new institution from the very beginning.

SIX

INTELLIGENCE AND WEAPONS PROLIFERATION IN A CHANGING WORLD

Paul Schulte

*P*aul *Schulte joined the Ministry of Defence in 1973, working in central budgeting, naval procurement and international equipment collaboration. A secondment to the Northern Ireland Office covered security policy, industrial development, human rights and family law. Returning to the MOD, he was involved in Non-Nuclear Arms Control (where he invented the important verification method of 'Managed Access'), Middle East Defence Commitments, Land Systems Procurement, Armed Forces Medical Planning and Gulf War Syndrome allegations. He wrote and presented the widely publicised Assessment Report on the MOD's Homosexuality Policy and attended the Royal College of Defence Studies in 1996. He is now the MOD's Director of Proliferation and Arms Control (PACS), and UK Commissioner on the UN Special Commission for Iraq (UNSCOM). He was a member of the Security Council's Special Panel on Iraqi Disarmament in early 1999. He practised as an Honorary Group Therapist at Guy's Hospital between 1983 and 1996.*

Introduction

My basic proposition is that intelligence and proliferation are, and will stay, profoundly linked. Proliferation implies the spread, or further development, of weaponry which others regard as dangerous, destabilising, often immoral and sometimes unquestionably illegal. *Horizontal* proliferation, the geographical spread of new capabilities, receives most publicity; but *vertical* proliferation, the continuing enhancement of those capabilities (which used to be a term applied mainly to the superpowers) is of increasing importance in the developing world as well.

Proliferation is significant because it brings about a modification of power relations and a change in the degree of military threat felt by the proliferants' potential adversaries. But part of the international context is a frequently encountered feeling in the self-proclaimed non-aligned states that such changes may often be *no bad thing* and that non-proliferation rhetoric is simply the self-interested hypocrisy of the powerful, and by no means sincerely intended to avoid destabilising, economically ruinous and self-defeating arms-racing. That reaction is important and not confined to proliferant states themselves.

A further unavoidable feature of this field is that the best resourced, most experienced and effective intelligence organisations do tend to be in countries which have already achieved the capabilities which proliferators seek, even if they have often themselves then publicly foresworn some options, like chemical and biological weapons, for moral reasons and because they can look after themselves without them.

Proliferation is normally planned and implemented in secret. When the process is complete, there may be a deliberately spectacular demonstration (as with the Indian and Pakistani nuclear tests in 1998). But, until then, proliferant states and their suppliers usually put great effort into frustrating any outside knowledge of the projects concerned, precisely because it is, of course, in this gestation period that diplomatic or other efforts are likely to be most effective. In some cases (most famously the early Soviet nuclear programme) proliferation is also enabled or accelerated by active intelligence-gathering about other nations' earlier breakthrough research. Whatever the precise circumstances, states are always going to be interested in conducting or frustrating intelligence-gathering on proliferation. But the ways in which intelligence can be used will depend on the legal, political and military contexts of the future.

I also take it to be self-evident that intelligence is useful for policy and military reasons: its purpose is to allow better decisions and not for itself. Areas offering fewer or less important decisions will tend to attract a lower concentration of intelligence resources. Therefore, today, detailed intelligence on weapons proliferation is primarily about so-called weapons of mass destruction (WMD) – i.e. nuclear, biological and chemical weapons (NBC) – and their delivery systems, and it is about WMD that I am going to speak. I shall use the generic term for brevity but I am well aware of their wide differences in specific effects and significance.

I do not, of course, suggest that it will not remain important to keep a general idea of others' *overall* military capabilities. Entirely conventional forces will remain of great interest for order of battle as well as technical intelligence reasons. But close-up study of the microprocesses of proliferation – of specific transactions, procurement routes and likely in-service dates – will be rare for anything except operationally or politically critical weapons, like NBC, and the means which can either deliver them, like ballistic missiles, modified space launchers, or terrorist groups, or which can interdict them, like missile or air defence systems.

More than ever in the unpredictable post-Cold War world, intelligence organisations will find it impossible to study all weapons types, areas and developments. Prioritisation inevitably happens, based on judgements about where national forces are likely to fight and what would pose the greatest threat to them, and to the home population. The sheer world-wide scale of small arms exports, for example, means that studying this kind of proliferation intensively would be enormously expensive in intelligence resources. It would also at present improve relatively few decisions open to Western governments. I think this suggests that, unless effective international enforcement measures to limit small arms proliferation are legislated in some way, small arms proliferation will not become a major Western intelligence preoccupation.

Special Features

How special is intelligence on WMD proliferation? It does not involve special collection methods: it combines human sources, signals intercept, overhead imagery and open-source information just as in other fields. But for WMD, assessment often requires very specific, and hard to come by, technical and scientific advice about the meaning of revealed information and what it implies about the sophistication, technical method, maturity, outside assistance and organisational competence of a proliferation project. Those states which have themselves in the past already developed missiles or NBC weapons will find it generally easier to interpret intelligence data on states of proliferation concern. In addition, there may be a greater pooling of information between various national organisations than in other intelligence areas, since non-proliferation is a fairly widely shared common interest and policy goal.

The Functions of Intelligence against Proliferation

Broadly, I think we need intelligence about WMD proliferation for three reasons:

1. To stop, or at least to slow, it, or to raise its cost and difficulty. This can be achieved *domestically* by well-informed government decisions over export controls, by legal prosecutions of delinquent supplier firms, or, if approaches can be detected in time, by alerting genuinely ignorant suppliers to the intentions of would-be customers. University departments can also be discreetly warned of the track record and connections of foreign applicants in sensitive technical disciplines.

Internationally, intelligence contributes to maintaining and updating export control regimes such as the Australia Group on Chemical and Biological Materials, the Missile Technology Control Regime, the Nuclear Suppliers Group and the Zangger Committee. Meetings of these groups involve information exchanges between members about recent evidence to refocus the attention of export licensing officials, or to reframe and develop the multinational export restrictions.

Diplomatic action can also be taken, based on secret information, to dissuade proliferants, or, often more realistically – since most are obviously not persuadable – to dissuade their suppliers: the willing or unwitting proliferators. Governments may be quite genuinely unaware of how questionable export contracts, even by state-owned firms, can be. Here intelligence channels can themselves form an effective alternative conduit, permitting subtle approaches to well-disposed supplier countries. These can be even more discreet than formal diplomatic dealings. They have achieved some – obviously unacknowledgeable – successes in frustrating WMD-related deliveries. Whatever channels are used, the case for exposing intelligence indications of proliferation to implicated governments will depend on the estimated chances of inducing them to halt or reverse it.

The spread of Nuclear Non-Proliferation Treaty (NPT) and Chemical Weapons Convention (CWC) membership, with their resultant obligations, increases the chances of being able to use intelligence to appeal to other supplier states to live up to their undertakings. There are now 187 parties to the NPT and over 130 to the CWC. Shame is a collective emotion and is strengthened by the number of those that feel it. The more who take vows of chastity, the harder it is to get away with whoring around. Complete universality, which is the aim of the NPT, the CWC and the BTWC (the Biological and Toxic Weapons Convention), would intensify these pressures.

Intelligence also aids in the *renunciation* of WMD. In those rare cases, where so-called 'repentant states', such as South Africa, have given up nuclear weapons programmes, diplomacy assisted the decision and was helped by outside knowledge of those emerging capabilities, as well as by regime change. And in the chemical and biological weapons field, the many states which have renounced active programmes are likely to have been encouraged to do so by the practical calculation that cheating against the indefinite probing of outside intelligence would be difficult and costly to sustain. Not only would deeply covert illicit weapons programmes be more expensive and less reliable, but indications of security concern about them can impact on general national economic well-being by reducing a country's attractiveness for inward investment.

2. The second function of intelligence is to mitigate the effects of successful proliferation: it does this by informing the military ability to attack, deter or defend against specific NBC threats. That could mean finding warning indicators for immediate WMD attack to allow timely responses. These could include not only appropriate alert procedures for defensive systems, but also pre-emptive counterforce attacks (though this, outside an actual conflict, is so politically controversial, as the US has found in Sudan, that openly avowable intelligence of very high reliability will be particularly sought after to justify the decision in the inevitable ensuing dispute). In the longer term, intelligence can suggest selective improvements in overall military potential, to reduce vulnerabilities and create offsetting capabilities. We see

this in the current debate over National Missile Defence in the US, where decisions will be very much affected by the intelligence assessments of long-range ballistic missile threats. The time-scales for these reactive programmes can be very long, putting premiums on early discovery of proliferation projects of concern, and on the avoidance of strategic surprise.

Mitigating proliferation's security consequences needs a range of intelligence requirements: at the highest level, understanding a proliferant's strategic culture, doctrine, and perception of its potential opponents' strategic personalities and their probable responses to its introducing new WMD into the situation. All this would help establish what would be necessary for deterrence. Planning counterforce responses requires knowledge of weapon types, production, storage, dispersal and launch sites. Planning active defence measures involves knowing about delivery methods and the worst ways they might be used against friendly forces. Finally, acquiring and preparing passive defence measures, like NBC suits or vaccines, necessitates the best available knowledge of the potential enemy's selection of specific C and B (chemical and biological) agents.

Institutional innovation can improve intelligence-sharing and resultant collective action of this sort between allies. The common understandings reached in NATO about the proliferation threat through the Defence Group on Proliferation have led to a successful and continuous programme of systematic reduction of Alliance vulnerabilities. The new WMD Centre now being set up in NATO will continue and improve this process of sharing assessments.

3. Intelligence can also illuminate the wider consequences of proliferation: it does so by making sober and correct military assessments of the balances and outcomes which WMD could effect. Here we should not forget the invaluable reassurance that can be conferred by intelligence's contribution to the proof of negatives. However strong the prevailing apprehensions, objective

information on a state or group may suggest that it does *not* in fact have specific WMD of concern, and that finance or technical resources, strategic doctrine, ideology or theology make it unlikely that it will obtain them – at least in a given time-scale.

Where proliferation has occurred, or is clearly under way, I shall return to the various widening complications for intelligence assessment later on.

Non-State Actors

I've been talking so far about national proliferation programmes. Intelligence on the WMD acquisition and attack plans of non-state actors is important for all the obvious reasons that make intelligence the most critical resource against any terrorist activity. But, additionally, to the extent that WMD terrorism might be state-financed or technically supplied, the plausible fear that the linkage would be discovered, or, with the addition of forensic evidence, retrospectively reconstructed, will be a heavy disincentive. While fanatical terrorist operatives may not themselves be deterrable, the regimes of potential state sponsors are usually much more cautious. Excellent intelligence – if we could get it – should therefore have multiple direct and indirect pay-offs in preventing catastrophic terrorism from those groups which are not entirely independent of states.

Looking into the medium or long term, however, as CB expertise sufficient to allow informal production and weaponisation of CB agents diffuses more widely within the advanced economies – above all through the biotechnology revolution – outside state support may become less critical for groups interested in such weapons. The same process suggests a relative future shift towards understanding terrorists' intentions, motivations and targeting criteria rather than tracking equipment, material and competences, which will all become increasingly widespread.

But I do concede in advance how difficult this will be to

achieve with these groups – apparently, at least, until we improve their co-operation in recruitment by evolving a form of cocktail party which we *can* get Hezbollah and Aum Shinrikyo to attend.

Special Problems over Intelligence on WMD Proliferation

Having tried to demonstrate how effective intelligence can be in addressing proliferation, now let us look at the practical difficulties in collecting, assessing and using it. I would sum these up as numerous, growing, but not insurmountable. They include:

(a) The classic dilemma between protecting sources and methods of intelligence and making the maximum use of it. For example,

(i) The inhibitions on sharing data with exporters other than close intelligence allies;

(ii) The difficulties in revealing sensitive intelligence material publicly to back legal action on export controls.

(b) The likelihood of remaining one step behind the proliferant as new technologies emerge.

(c) The very small number of very senior and trustworthy people in many states of concern who are involved in decisions on WMD operational concepts or intentions.

(d) The extreme measures taken by proliferants to safeguard communications channels relating to proliferation, or to hide domestic activity, even by heroically scaled underground excavations as in the Korean or Libyan tunnel projects. The revelations of what Western intelligence could discover in Iraq may have stimulated further world-wide efforts to improve deception techniques.

(e) The fact that there may not be anything to discover which would equate to a Western concept of use behind a decision to acquire WMD – which means that there may be no comprehensible and predictable rationale to pin down and plan for. With such uncertainties over intention, the risk of strategic mirror-imaging or of simple worst-case prediction may be dangerously hard to avoid.

(f) The elaborate, though expensive, deception and denial methods now used for proliferation-related international procurement: false end-user certificates and bogus end-users, offshore dealing, diversionary routes, front companies, use of diaspora businessmen.

(g) The spreading use of encryption for commercial transactions of all kinds worsened by the inexorable expansion of the Internet, and the practical and legal difficulties of controlling intangible technology transfer.

(h) The pressures of servicing increasing numbers of export control regimes: each is now 'a rolling event' imposing extra demands on intelligence resources. Control lists may need to be amended through a fast track for rapid consensus as new technical threats to the regimes are identified.

(i) The spread of dual-capable technologies, especially new key-enabling technologies which, like accelerometers, for example, are now commercially available in Integrated Circuits, for missiles.

(j) The related need to cover exports into civil and military technology bases, above all for biological weapons.

(k) Very worryingly, the spread of networks of secondary and tertiary proliferation. For example, the original Russian SCUD designs (based on the Nazi V2) were exported to North Korea, further modified and sold on to other states, where they are once again developed to form the basis of an indigenous missile manufacturing capability. The jokey journalistic term for such networking is 'Club Mad' – but these are serious, carefully planned developments intended to circumvent the West's ability to use its diplomatic, financial or technical resources to prevent the spread of weapons it finds threatening. It is clear that such networks will be hard for intelligence to penetrate and offer little leverage to apply against whatever developments may be discovered.

(l) Finally, there is the possibility that such regimes may not conduct the monitorable testing which would be considered necessary in Western procurement systems before new weapons are taken into service or put up for sale. Given these countries' strategic cultures, the enormous consequences of using, say, an untested ballistic missile to carry an untested nuclear or biological weapons warhead, may make its technically successful use in a crisis hard either to discount or confirm in advance.

Quite a long list of structural difficulties. But I would insist that the *major problem* overhanging the proliferation field is not an intelligence one: *it is the sheer difficulty of finding usable, diplomatic military or economic tools to halt or reverse proliferation* (especially when achieved by indigenous development or production) once it has occurred. This is even true in the special and high-profile form of non-proliferation known as Arms Control and its verification.

Intelligence, of course, plays a key role in designing and policing arms-control arrangements. It may even be indispensable for their negotiation – it is hard to see how the US-Russian Strategic Agreements could have been reached without overhead satellite imagery. But I think that we need to see arms-control verification, and intelligence's contribution to it, not so much as a technical problem (which we might call 'The Science of Distrust') but, critically, as a matter of persuasion – almost a branch of Rhetoric. The key difficulty may not be in technical detection or acquisition of proof. Providing investigations and relevant challenges can be pursued into areas of doubt with the real co-operation of the inspected state, as stipulated by the treaty or convention, technical problems should become secondary.

The key question is whether those guaranteeing each treaty or convention can in fact be expected to respond to non-compliant behaviour to remove suspicion and re-establish co-operation. In bilateral treaties like START, this is much easier. Single states can rapidly form their own views of their co-signatory's conduct, raise it in the Special Consultative Commission and then act as they judge necessary – though I don't underestimate how hard and slow this process can be in practice, as over the disputed status of the purportedly ABM radar at Krasnoyarsk during the 1980s. But, for multilateral agreements, the Iraqi case seems to demonstrate that the danger is less from sensationally detected cheating than endless, persistent, shameless lying, obstruction, provocations and counter-accusations.

After UNSCOM's considerable early successes – which certainly relied heavily on intelligence from friendly states – persistent Iraqi obstruction has worn down the will of the international community. Long-term obstruction works. It has demonstrably eroded the overall determination of the Security Council. Some permanent members have shown themselves much less concerned about acting on evidence of non-compliance than others. This is the point which Richard Butler, the former UNSCOM Executive Chairman, now grimly stresses – emphasising the indispensability of a united Security Council as the ultimate judge and guarantor of multilateral treaties. Yet intelligence – even supplemented by information from on-site inspections by UN bodies – does not seem strong enough by itself to persuade those states – even permanent Security Council members – who don't want to be convinced of Iraq's continuing culpability.

The prolonged division in the Security Council shown over Iraq suggests that intelligence may be more effective in privately alerting nations to others' non-compliance than enabling it to be demonstrated internationally in ways which can stop it. How prepared will the international community be in future to pursue intelligence leads into further potentially endless disputes over arcane technical evidence, specialist judgements and complex documentation? We now know this process would have to be conducted in a political atmosphere that must be expected to become poisoned and polarised. The precedent of Iraq won't be forgotten and it may be fateful.

It seems clear then that, however high its quality, intelligence on verification arrangements may not always be directly usable. Acting on it may not seem likely to succeed in generating consensus judgements that would in turn lead to effective politico-military or economic responses. If that is the prospect, intelligence will probably not be used to prompt a challenge inspection except, possibly, where it can be supported by some degree of open-source corroboration. The best way to allow for these realities may be to look on verification as a mechanism of persuasion and motivation that is little use unless it can work in particular, invariably highly political, contexts, in which the alleged cheat is always likely to have allies and sympathisers for other, wider reasons.

So not only is verification not science, but it is unlikely even to resemble an impartial intelligence assessment process.

One further implication of this is that verifiability and the role of intelligence may vary significantly with time and place. The international political climate for verification and compliance issues may initially encourage both responsible states or cheats, for opposite reasons, to sign up to a treaty. But the climate can then change, both globally and in regional scenarios that falsify initial expectations. The role of intelligence in the enforcement of the treaty would then depend upon the political context at the time and in relation to the country about which allegations might be made and followed up.

It is not impossible to imagine a future diplomatic atmosphere in which convincing intelligence – even against large, influential and well-supported states – could be relied upon eventually to correct all cases of non-compliance, but it won't be created without great effort and a widened world consensus.

In arms control, as in ordinary life, intelligence by itself may
not be able to overcome lack of will. It is salutary, in conferences of this kind, to remember how many around the world
resent the general inequalities of globalisation and especially
growing Western superiority in high technology conventional
military power, backed by legally privileged US, UK and French
nuclear arsenals. I am always surprised how often in such discussions I find it necessary to try to ventriloquise the voice of the
Angry Arab Masses. (I'm not particularly convincing in this but
I think somebody has to try.) From this kind of perspective –
whether or not one regards it as irrational or short-sighted – the
spread of missiles, chemical, biological and even nuclear capabilities, can appear as an understandable, necessary or inevitable
equaliser – a way of bringing down strategic apartheid. Non-
proliferation efforts can seem designed to inhibit technological
development and maintain general economic advantage, and
high-technology Western intelligence capabilities can be
portrayed as particularly sinister, mysterious and non-objective.

There may not, therefore, be any widespread international will
to believe and act upon sanitised summaries of exotic foreign
intelligence, or to endorse a judgement of non-compliance.
Especially where controversial and morally troubling sanctions
regimes are at stake, as in Iraq, governments may be particularly unwilling publicly to convict a transgressor without demanding impossibly convincing detailed evidence with unacceptably
revealing indications of its intelligence basis. There is already
some explicit opposition to export control regimes which restrict
sales of sensitive materials even to treaty signatory states, on the
basis of intelligence judgements reached by privileged supplier
nations. And non-aligned countries have quoted the Sudanese
case as proof that information derived from national technical
means is biased and should not be admissible in arms-control
regimes.

For both the arms controller and, I think, the intelligence

professions, this is all very depressing. But we should also remember that comprehensive measures to control or abolish weapons are relatively recent and not fully tried. And against these negative trends and tensions we can set the increasingly universal normative effects of the obligations under NPT, CWC and BTWC that I have already mentioned, and their practical application as paper procedures become operationalised and accepted. The expansion of open-source information and the imminent availability of commercial satellite imagery down to one-metre resolution may also help somewhat in allowing corroboration of suspicions through publicly producible evidence. The overall balance of likely outcomes fluctuates and is hard to judge.

Part of this uncertainty is how far, in the next decades, states with sophisticated intelligence resources committed against proliferation will be able to work out satisfactory intelligence liaison with relatively new international bodies such as the Organisation for the Prohibition of Chemical Weapons, and its Biological counterpart, if that is ever successfully created. There have been decades of successful international co-operation with the International Atomic Energy Agency, which is an encouraging precedent. But, Iraq apart, the IAEA has not had to mount a contested or controversial challenge inspection, and the difficulties and allegations of non-neutrality and information leakage (in various directions) which arose during the UNSCOM experience indicate the frictions and suspicions that can occur in such activities.

All this requires us to think about how proliferation and non-compliance may combine to complicate intelligence on the future strategic landscape.

Here, I think the difficulties in detecting and preventing proliferation and reliably enforcing arms-control agreements imply an increasing differentiation of national positions over WMD possession and threat of use. It is unlikely that there will be any mass international move away from non-proliferation efforts. But, even so, on behaviour already exhibited or alleged, we can expect a widening spectrum. It would be reasonable to predict at one end shameless so-called rogue states and proliferation suppliers under regimes regarded as capable of suicidal nuclear aggression. Then we might have nuclear weapons states suspected of deliberate proliferation assistance to build up influence, create nuclear allies, or simply earn money. Then factor in those countries that have demonstrated nuclear weapons capabilities but are not, and cannot become, accepted nuclear weapons states under NPT definitions. Then allow for tough-minded non-treaty joiners who seem to be developing chemical or biological weapons as cheap, ultimate national deterrents. Then consider nuclear weapons states which might be anxious to preserve the NPT and deter threatened CBW use, but whose willingness to resort to nuclear retaliation is deliberately ambiguous, and so might be misinterpreted. Finally, at the other extreme, assess the impact of righteous nations who constitute impeccable pillars of the various regimes, but whose willingness to stand up to WMD-backed aggression may not be taken as self-evident.

The most worrying category of all would be states that become widely suspected, but, even if challenged, could not be proven to be cheating over WMD. While remaining parties to arms-control regimes, they could campaign from inside for the dismantling of export controls applying to any treaty signatory. The debilitating suspicions spreading from that boil-like configuration would tend to undermine the credibility of all such treaties.

Decoding the dynamics and interactions of these varied and often mutating players on this more complex strategic terrain is going to pose extra problems for intelligence specialists. Not only will real military WMD capabilities become more varied, but intentions and strategic personalities will assume greater importance. Varied and intangible national willingness to acquire, and then variously to threaten or to use, or to abstain, or be deterred from employing WMD, will be increasingly significant. Different propensities to ignore treaty or moral inhibitions will also have to be estimated to judge how much difference world-wide normative expectations on WMD use, or the commitments of formal arms control, can actually be expected to make to strategic realities in specific confrontations. An assessed intention to brandish unconventional weapons may not carry the same strategic implication as a motivation to use them – but those implications may still not be trivial and they are unlikely to be benign. Meanwhile, the potential operational radii of states of WMD concern will extend, will pose uncertain potential threats to more and more countries, and will increasingly overlap.

Those widening intangibilities will in turn bring growing uncertainties about deterrence and security relationships, regional strategic balances, the practicability of coalition intervention against regional aggressors, and the likelihood of pre-emption, escalation, or retaliation if chemical, biological or nuclear weapons respectively are used or threatened.

Offsetting defensive developments are already occurring, in a search for greater assurance against proliferation threats. But these in turn imply additional, second-order, technical and political uncertainties about the anticipated effectiveness, over various time-scales, of counter-force, or of new active defensive systems such as: air defences, theatre missile defences and national missile defences.

Further uncertainties arise over the adequacy of passive defence measures among national forces, local allies and coalition partners.

Judgements of these factors will in turn inform assessments of varying national determinations to commit to and sustain policies or actions in the face of WMD – and proliferants' perceptions of the degree of such determination.

There is obvious scope for reaching very different assessments of all these intangible and hypothetical factors. The extra challenges for intelligence organisations from growing technical uncertainty, strategic instability and multiplication of international security dilemmas, vividly indicate the dangerous undesirability of proliferation as a global process. *Proliferation increases the potential for mistaken assessments, leading to unwise decisions, and magnifies the fatefulness of their outcomes.*

Conclusion

My overall assessment, if a policy-maker can use that privileged term, is that: intelligence from all sources has a vital role to play in WMD proliferation. It is often a precondition for all other efforts. Open-source, producible intelligence is likely to be especially useful.

Intelligence organisations can detect international transactions, frustrate them by contacts with counterparts in well-disposed states, support more formal diplomatic *démarches*, and supply background – though often not publicly discoverable evidence – for prosecutions of those suppliers who ignore legal restrictions. Intelligence can also persuade other export regime members to keep their regulations up to date. But there are very considerable limits on intelligence's effectiveness if supplying states do not, in reality, want to prevent the export of WMD materials, or if the proliferant becomes technically self-sufficient.

Where there are formal arms-control agreements, intelligence can alert nations and their allies to breaches. It may be assisted in this by the access and transparency that arms control can help create within previously closed states. But the ability to end non-compliance by invoking verification arrangements will depend heavily on the specific, unavoidably highly charged, political context and the effective working of internationally organised challenge inspection arrangements.

The global strategic landscape is likely to become increasingly determined and complicated by proliferation and the resultant uncertainties about who has precisely what WMD and delivery systems, how effectively they would perform against anticipated counter-measures, and how far proliferants would be deterred or inhibited in use. All this will add great uncertainty into the analysis of many regional balances and scenarios. But, even if this complexity renders high-confidence strategic prediction well nigh impossible, intelligence will retain a very important operational, tactical and technical role in managing and mitigating the military consequences of WMD acquisition and use. Demonstrated success in this may itself help deterrence, and hence reduce the subsequent apparent attractiveness of WMD acquisition.

To sum up, we should expect effective intelligence to help reduce and delay the scale of WMD round the world and lessen its consequences in peace and war. In this, intelligence will work reciprocally with political commitment. Intelligence input must remain objective, cautious and well grounded to avoid acrimonious suspicions of threat inflation and deliberate justification of policy intentions, which would rapidly undermine its subsequent credibility and international usefulness. Complacency or over-confidence poses its own dangers. But crying wolf, or hyping up Rent-a-Threats, is the worst way for intelligence organisations to oppose proliferation.

Nevertheless, however responsible and accurate intelligence authorities are, their contribution and the way it is made will depend on the political background. Above all, that means the long-term demonstrated overall will of the international community to halt or reverse proliferation – and therefore also to solve the multitudinous regional security dilemmas and apprehensions which drive it. The requirements for intelligence – in every sense of the word – of that wider project would be a subject for another conference, or perhaps another discourse.

DISCUSSION

John Lauder

John Lauder is the DCI's Special Assistant for Non-Proliferation. He also serves as both the intelligence community's and the CIA's Issue Manager for Non-Proliferation and, since 1987, as Director of the DCI Non-Proliferation Center. He served in the United States army from 1969 to 1972, when he joined the staff of the Committee on Standards of Official Conduct of the US House of Representatives. He attended courses at Edinburgh University and the JFK School of Government at Harvard, and in 1974, after taking an MA in International Relations at Yale, he joined the CIA. His first assignment was in the former Office of Strategic Research conducting analysis on military and conventional arms-control issues. In 1985 he became Chief of the European Assessments Division in the Office of Soviet Affairs, and served in Vienna for four years as a senior adviser to several US delegations for conventional arms-control negotiations. In 1989 he was appointed Deputy Chief for Intelligence in the DCI Counter-Terrorist Center in Washington.

First of all, let this time slot on Sunday morning be an answer to all of you who say that in countering proliferation we haven't a prayer of success. This is a Sunday morning time of prayer and reflection for many of us, and indeed Paul Schulte's excellent presentation and paper move me to a two-part prayer of both thanks and petition. The thanks is: thank God for consumers of intelligence like Paul and for his rich insights into the relationship between intelligence and non-proliferation policy; and the petition: please God, give us far more consumers like Paul. Paul is indeed an ideal consumer of intelligence and he is quite right when he notes the profound links between intelligence and non-proliferation policy.

In fact, I envy my UK colleagues in some respects in this

regard. Their community is smaller and more tightly linked than ours, on our side of the Atlantic. The UK's CIG and JIC processes are excellent vehicles for addressing disagreements and enhancing consumer/producer dialogue on such questions. We have made improvements in the United States in this regard, in large part through DCI George Tenet's reorganisation almost two years ago of the non-proliferation intelligence community that strengthened that community and the role of the Special Assistant for Non-Proliferation, the position that I occupy. We also have a rich and productive dialogue on proliferation issues with key members of what Jim Woolsey called our Congressional Board of Directors.

Paul makes it clear in his paper that proliferation involves highly charged political issues; and our duty in intelligence is often to speak truth to power and to describe factually and soundly our understanding of developments that may suggest a current policy is not working, that our diplomats have been lied to and that new measures may be required. In addition, Foreign Ministries and intelligence agencies are likely to differ about the application of the tools of policy. For example, they often differ on such questions as how much intelligence to share at the risk of sources and methods to make diplomatic *démarches* persuasive. And policy agencies differ among themselves about how much of a share of scarce intelligence resources each policy agency should receive. I've actually had policy colleagues who have called me and have actually said, 'You are giving too much attention to the intelligence needs of my good friend over in Department X and we need more over here in Department Y.'

And this problem I think is actually more difficult and contentious than even Paul suggests in his paper, largely because of the great range of consumers of proliferation intelligence: bilateral diplomats, arms-control negotiators, defence planners, war fighters, export controllers, law enforcement, health services, consequence managers, first responders, international bodies, Parliaments, publics, and the list could go on.

The additional challenge, as Paul observes, is that each of these consumers requires a somewhat different focus and time-line, and different levels of confidence and detail, for the intelligence collection, exploitation, analysis and dissemination that they need. I almost wish that I had had the presence of mind a month or so ago to suggest that we invite my Russian colleague, Gennadiy Yevstafiyev, to be part of the panel, because it would have been interesting to have heard the extent to which the Russians and others share the same problems that Paul and I have seen from the UK and the US angle. Maybe others here can speak to that as we go on to discussion. I think the key to all of this is to recognise that policy and intelligence agencies are in this together. Our failures and successes are indeed collective, as we fight the good fight, as Elie Weisel challenged us, to keep fanatics from being armed with the power of weapons of mass destruction.

Now Paul has appropriately reminded us why success in this endeavour is so hard, and about why the proliferation problem is so intractable. His paper listed thirteen or fourteen potential difficulties in collecting, assessing and using intelligence related to proliferation. I was stunned by the length of that list. When I have given similar papers I normally have stopped my list at six or seven. But the good news is that Paul has introduced his list by noting that, although the challenges are numerous and growing, they are not insurmountable, and indeed we in the intelligence services represented here are making progress in surmounting those challenges. We certainly have not surmounted all of them, and let me spend just a minute or two more on why that is the case.

My boss, George Tenet, has often said before Congress that no issue better illustrates the challenges, complexities and uncertainties that we in the US intelligence community face than halting the proliferation of weapons of mass destruction and their delivery means. I've got to say that over the past year and a half, we have not had a particularly good year in the proliferation community. We have witnessed nuclear tests in South Asia, continued concern about Iraq's weapons of mass destruction programmes, broader availability of technologies relevant to biological and chemical warfare, and accelerated missile development in Iran, North Korea and most recently in Pakistan and in India. Particularly worrisome in this regard is the security of weapons of mass destruction materials and expertise in the former Soviet Union that has been appropriately a focus of a number of US and Russian and other bilateral and multilateral programmes. Worrisome too has been the increased co-operation among states that Paul mentioned, more effective efforts by proliferants to conceal illicit activities, and growing interest by transnational, sub-national and terrorist groups in acquiring weapons of mass destruction capabilities.

Our efforts to deal with all this are complicated by the fact that most weapons of mass destruction programmes are based on technologies and materials that have civil as well as military applications, and that is a particular special problem for intelligence. The difference between a pharmaceutical plant and a biological weapons facility, or between a fertiliser plant and a chemical weapons facility, is often just the arrangement or the turning of a few valves within that facility. National Technical Means cannot reliably tell the difference, and in such cases analytical judgements about capabilities are essentially the same as analytical judgements about intentions. Successfully divining intent is the hardest thing for any of us in intelligence to do. As Paul reminded us, this problem spills over into arms control and non-proliferation agreement monitoring as well. I heard a speaker at another conference earlier this year, in talking about the Biological Weapons Convention, note that the Biological Weapons Convention in essence limits 'evil intent'. Try monitoring 'evil intent' from space.

Clearly to attack that problem, to make those judgements, relies on spies, relies on the synergism between spies and technical attack or technical means of one sort or another, and relies on all of those '-INTs', and every one of those '-INTs' that some of you have mentioned. Because of these problems, and despite the fact that we have increased our resources in many of these areas, there is a continued and growing risk of surprise. We focus on a handful of states, and even there, there is much that we don't know. The proliferation problem – including suppliers, conduits and potential proliferants – is a global issue of which there are some sixty-seventy states in which there are activities that are occurring that are of concern.

In the interests of time, I am not going to give additional examples, particularly from the biological weapons area, but we could come back to that in discussion. I think it's enough to say that as groups that have international networks, like Osama bin Laden's, seek to develop or acquire chemical or biological weapons capability – not only for attacks against humans, but even for economic attacks against crops and livestock for example – there will be still more enormous challenges for intelligence.

These are challenges that I would say that we are beginning to meet. We are forging new partnerships beyond traditional national security communities, we are applying old tools in creative ways, we are developing new tools, and, I would argue most impressively, we are recruiting, developing and training a new generation of collectors and analysts to deal with these types of questions. Those of us in this room who have been in the business for so long will be able to pass the torch to a new generation that I think can deal effectively with these problems. Still, there will be great uncertainties and there is enormous risk of surprise.

GENERAL DISCUSSION

The general discussion was opened on a light note by a former MOD official, who pointed out that the 'customer', i.e. Paul Schulte of the MOD, deals with 'proliferation' which at least in English is a fairly neutral term, while the intelligence analyst, John Lauder of the CIA, deals with 'non-proliferation', which is a more directed term. More seriously, he asked whether intelligence can study proliferation as a discrete subject. John Lauder had talked about limited resources, he said, and also the fact that intentions – evil intentions – also had to be analysed. In his own experience as an intelligence analyst, his remit had covered a great band of proliferating countries, beginning with Iran and narrowing down to Pakistan, India, China, and ending with North Korea, the only country on which his department was required to study proliferation only. He questioned whether it was really possible to study proliferation in a single country, and asked whether in the future it was a single subject that should be studied, or a single country.

On the question of nomenclature, Paul Schulte replied that the reason he is called Director of Proliferation and Arms Control is that his predecessor had been an Oxford Latin scholar who thought it would be 'immense fun' to announce the formation of PACS on Epiphany Sunday. This meant, among other things, that he occasionally gets letters sent to the Chief Proliferator of the Ministry of Defence.

On the wider question, he suggested that modern intelligence services have always studied proliferation, although they may not have called it that. (About this time last century, he noted, it would have been the spread of pre-Dreadnoughts and iron foundries, for example. Naval intelligence would have looked closely at predicting these processes.) As in most disciplines, there seem always at least two ways of getting into the same phenomenon: structural or functional analysis in social science, proliferation or regional studies, and country-specific work in intelligence. Both add to the other. It was his view that a proliferation policy went hand-in-hand with a regional policy. Similarly, there could be no proliferation understanding without a regional understanding.

John Lauder agreed with these remarks. Both he and Paul Schulte have, he said, discussed partnerships between policy and intelligence among intelligence organisations, and he added that some key partnerships exist among those that have insights into the motivations of states that are seeking programmes, and those technical experts that understand nuclear weapons and biological weapons. He urged the need for such synergy and co-operation, and was against excessive narrowing of the use of resources. It was important, he concluded, to ensure that both the regional experts and the functional technical experts are driving each other towards meeting the challenge.

Sir David Hannay noted the pessimism that he detected in Paul Schulte's presentation, and asked both speakers to comment on the relative value of slowing down or preventing proliferation. He felt that by assuming that this is a black-and-white issue, that you either win or lose, makes for excessive pessimism, when in actual fact serious slowing down of weapons proliferation, combined with political changes, can in itself achieve the desired objectives, as the experience of South Africa, Argentina and Brazil has shown.

He then asked the speakers to comment on the relative value of multilateral and bilateral approaches to a situation like North Korea. Referring to the fact that the IAEA had never conducted a challenge inspection, he pointed out that it was precisely their intention to conduct a challenge inspection that triggered off the whole North Korean saga, and that, in his view valuably, brought out into the open just what the North Koreans were up to, and thereby at least probably slowed down what they were doing very significantly. After that, the United States administration, too, quickly abandoned the multilateral route and chose the bilateral route. He asked for comments on the value of those two routes, recognising that the United Nations would never impose mandatory economic sanctions because of the Chinese position, even though this did not mean that the Chinese want the North Koreans to have nuclear weapons, far from it.

Thirdly, having noted Paul Schulte's pessimism about Iraq and UNSCOM, Sir David asked the speakers to comment on the extent to which the West may have prejudiced its ability to use anti-proliferation policies against Iraq by muddling up two issues: one, the use of sanctions to get rid of Saddam and, the other, the use of sanctions to get rid of his weapons of mass destruction. He regarded this as having been very damaging, and the longer it has gone on the more damaging it has become, and he concluded that if that analysis is correct, then we ought to learn from our mistakes and not repeat them in the future.

John Lauder agreed that seeing the problem in black-and-white terms – winning or losing – makes for pessimism, but he also believed that in this 'great chess game' the best approach was to play for a stalemate, because over time states get tired, their basic security needs are met in some ways, and they abandon their effort towards programmes. What leads to the pessimism, he said, is that the problem is extremely broad, there are some enormous stresses at the moment on the systems, and the next few moves on the chessboard are very difficult, and it is not entirely clear whether the next decade will be as good as the last in rolling back and preventing additional programmes.

Paul Schulte added that the distinction between slowing down and stopping is not completely watertight. Slowing down is worth doing. It was good that there wasn't a nuclear-armed Iran in 1990, and it was good that its biological programmes had been delayed as well, due to the imprecise scrutiny that was available at the time. This should not be ignored. There are, he said, innumerable tiny invisible gains and losses in this game. But if the eventual prospect is that things will only be slowed down, that makes it harder to expect people to renounce real economic advantage, or to sign up to inconvenient and intrusive arms-control arrangements, when the eventual general gain in long-term security is not very great. If one has to concede that the only prospect is a slightly slower drift towards a very proliferated world, how much can individual state actors be expected to give up to help non-proliferation efforts? He conceded that this represented quite a complex interaction in terms of motives and incentives.

On multilateral versus bilateral ability to affect North Korea, he felt that it came back to shame and pressure. Countries that are well integrated into the world, in economic or other ways, are probably relatively more susceptible to multilateral pressures. But hermit kingdoms, like North Korea, may be largely immune to multi-directional pressure, and issues involving shame and world-standing. They may only be interested in concrete pay-offs, or promises from what they see as their major concern, their major Satan. In such situations, he expected bilateral efforts from the US to be more effective.

On the question about Iraq, he asserted that he has never muddled up UN sanctions and their purpose with the wider question of policy towards Saddam. Nor did he think that the UK or many of the countries involved in advocating the case for sanctions have muddled them up. The question, he argued, is theoretical in any case. 'We have not reached the point – and we must not allow it to be argued without refutation, especially in the media, that we are close to the point – where there is any question about withdrawing sanctions for arms control and compliance reasons,' he said. He went on, 'Whether you would then keep sanctions on in order to bring down Saddam is a different and hypothetical question. That is the way I've set things out when this argument came up in the Commission (though it's not essentially a question for the Commissioners). I think it's possible and necessary to address the here and now problem of lack of compliance with arms control without taking on the wider problem of the future of Iraq.'

A former SIS officer asked John Lauder, who had referred to dealing with his Russian opposite number in a committee, what his reaction was and what possible influence he had been able to bring to bear when a defector first reported in 1992 that Russia was still making biological weapons, and it was impossible to dissuade Russia from selling cryogenic rocket motors to the Indians, without which they would not have been able to make their bombs. To their credit, the speaker added, the Russian press had reported this, while nothing seems to have appeared in the Western press. The question was, what real effect was John Lauder able to achieve through the Russians on his committee in perhaps slowing down or preventing such a thing happening again?

John Lauder replied that there is much to be done, bilaterally and multilaterally. As for the Russians, there was a need to discuss proliferation issues about the relationship of Russian entities and entities in other countries, and about how to protect the vast infrastructure for weapons of mass destruction, including the development of delivery vehicles, developed in the former Soviet Union and that are now located in Russia and other states. 'Had we invited our Russian colleague to join us here,' he went on, 'I could imagine a dialogue in response to such a question, where I would say, "We flagged some issues of concern, I thought in substantial detail, for appropriate follow-up," and my Russian colleague might say, "Well, you didn't quite say enough for us to tell exactly where the culprits were."'

A British academic noted the parallels between proliferation and drug trafficking, stressing the central role of intelligence, and yet the difficulties involved in using interdiction of supply and shame in order to reduce the overall problem of drug trafficking. He asked whether special measures have a role in proliferation, e.g. disruption, the West buying things that it doesn't want other people to buy, or supplying materials that look as if they are the right thing but are not. He wondered if intelligence could be used a little more aggressively.

John Lauder noted that there have been cases reported in the press of various services in the West buying up certain materials.

Paul Schulte added that it is not just intelligence that can make a difference. He agreed that there is a substantial but necessarily discreet role for active measures. But some important things can be openly acknowledged, like the US Co-operative Threat Reduction Programme in Russia that is trying to get rid of the large-scale nuclear and chemical legacies of the Cold War. He concluded that this is something that can make a difference and is both speakable and creditable.

Admiral Martini asked how it was possible to carry out covert operations in non-proliferation policy and at the same time to pursue non-proliferation in an international body, such as the United Nations.

John Lauder responded that the unilateral activities of intelligence and support of international bodies that are carrying out verification and other measures are reconcilable, and are indeed reconciled on a regular basis, if discreetly.

Admiral Martini replied that the non-proliferation operations he had carried out in Libya had shown that this type of work required a high degree of covert activity, and added that a multilateral approach was likely to put the services into difficulty.

John Lauder responded that there are precious few non-proliferation, counter-proliferation tools available, in any event, and those that are used are chosen almost on a case-by-case basis. There are times when a multilateral approach is the best way to get at a particular problem, and indeed that is why multilateral arms-control agreements have been crafted, why resolutions, such as the one that set up UNSCOM, require states – the US, the UK, Israel, Russia and others – to support the work of UNSCOM and other bodies. Equally, there are times when the non-proliferation agencies act in a variety of ways on their own initiative, bilateral and multilateral diplomatic endeavours, and sometimes through other bilateral ways.

A British academic, while accepting the need for a high priority being given to weapons of mass destruction, pointed to the relative neglect of other areas, such as the light weapons trade, which he saw as a very serious problem. He cited as an analogy peace-keeping operations, where the UN is failing to disarm the societies that it is beginning to administer, and he argued that these more short-term problems are important, but they are not getting the attention they require.

Paul Schulte agreed completely that concentrating more on one thing means relatively less on the other. He had intended making a reference to small-arms proliferation, but had been prevented by the time constraint. He said that governments are beginning to look at the issue of small-arms proliferation. He came back to the point he had made about intelligence having to be prioritised against its ability to contribute to decisions: there are relatively few decisions that at the moment Western governments can make in relation to the small-arms proliferation. Unless and until there is some kind of international legislation to stop it, it is often hard to see how it is possible to intervene. In discussion with NGO advocates, he has repeatedly asked the question, often without getting a satisfactory answer, whether if we pass these resolutions, attempt to set up these regimes and increase resources going into studying the situation, just what practical difference it can make? If the problem is governance – having adequate customs control to stop and adequate policing to take away these weapons – then none of this expensive attention and high-sounding political commitment will by itself actually make much difference to the slow tides of weapons movements throughout Africa and central Asia.

A British academic commented that Paul Schulte had hit on the ultimate area of turf wars between different intelligence organisations. In Britain MI5 are supposed to deal with operations within Britain and MI6 abroad. To trace the movement of illegal arms from suppliers within Britain down to the ports is the business of one organisation, to trace their destination is the task of another organisation. Making this an international task will create far worse problems of co-ordination. He noted that maritime and air transport is a centralised area of commercial and governmental consideration. The insurance of dangerous cargoes and the legislation of agreements, concluded in international maritime organisations, govern this area, and he thought that intelligence organisations ought to concentrate on it. His research had shown that, in the past, naval intelligence was regarded as having to do with warships, and all other forms of intelligence were entirely land-bound. Yet most of these goods, if they are at all heavy, have to travel by sea, and if they are light, they have to travel by air; and since these forms of transport are controllable, it ought to be possible to use this machinery much more than it is being used at the moment.

John Lauder agreed, adding that it is something that needed attacking on both sides of the Atlantic. First, on the question of enforcement, he was already collaborating with the FBI committee that deals with these cases. Secondly, on the maritime issue, there was acute awareness of how materials are being moved, and the agencies are doing what they can to track those movements. On his visits to London, for example, he usually calls on the CINC US NAVEUR (C-in-C US Navy, Europe).

Paul Schulte noted that there is a distinction between tracking and interdicting, adding that a lot of this trade moves by

sea, rather than by air. Taking as a theoretical example a North
Korean ship going to an Iranian port, he asked precisely what
could be done about it. 'You can be aware of a ship movement,
you may or may not have a hunch about what is in it, but you
have no legal right to interdict it.'

SEVEN

INTELLIGENCE IN THE
SERVICE OF ECONOMIC
SECURITY

Loch K. Johnson

War and commerce are but two different means of arriving
at the same aim, which is to possess what is desired.
Benjamin Constant[1]

*L*och K. Johnson is Regents Professor of Political Science at the
*University of Georgia and author of several books, including most
recently* Secret Agencies: US Intelligence in a Hostile World *(Yale
University Press, New Haven, 1996). He has been awarded the
Certificate of Distinction from the National Intelligence Study Center
(1986) and the VO Key Prize from the Southern Political Science
Association (1993). He has been Secretary of the American Political
Science Association and President of the International Studies
Association, South; and has served in the US federal government as
special assistant to the Chair of the Senate Committee on Intelligence
(1975–6), staff director of the House Sub-Committee on Intelligence
Oversight (1977–9), and special assistant to former Secretary of
Defense, Les Aspin, Chair of the Aspin-Brown Commission on
Intelligence (1995–6).*

Introduction

This is a report on the status of economic intelligence in the Government of the United States. For purposes of context, it begins by providing a brief examination of American intelligence priorities on the threshold of the third millennium.

When the Soviet Union disappeared in 1991, so did the central concern of US intelligence. Throughout the Cold War, between 60 and 75 per cent of America's intelligence resources were focused in one way or another on the USSR.[2] The primary goal of foreign policy officials in Washington had been to curb the spread of Communism; but now, in the new order of things, the CIA (or 'the Agency') and its dozen companion organisations in the intelligence community faced a reshuffling of their missions and targets – perhaps even the need to invent new ones in order to justify the continued existence of a large bureaucracy with a $27 billion annual budget.[3]

According to a former DCI, Robert M. Gates, the demise of world Communism ushered in 'a set of tasks assigned to the Agency [that] are both more complex and more numerous than during the Cold War'.[4] Debate over the proper objectives of a refashioned intelligence agenda heated up during the Clinton administration as it began to navigate the uncertainties of a new age without the reliable compass of the containment doctrine.

Observers of American foreign policy wondered if life after Communism would produce a dramatically different approach to international affairs in Washington, as befitting the radical change in global politics that had occurred. Within the hidden confines of the National Security Council, the Pentagon and the intelligence community, planners devised fresh lists of enemies – real and potential – now arrayed against the United States in lieu of the Soviet Union.[5] The White House and Congress created a special joint commission on the roles and capabilities of the United States intelligence community (the Aspin-Brown Commission), viewed widely as an opportunity to revamp the nation's secret agencies for a different kind of threat environment. Public officials and media pundits spoke of how economics would now supplant the nation's more traditional concern about military security.

Even the intelligence community displayed a certain resilience in adapting to the new global environment, contrary to the expectation that these agencies (in the standard caricature of bureaucracies) would prove sluggish and resistant to change. By 1994, the CIA had extensively reoriented its world-wide operations, maintaining only about 15 per cent of its assets for purposes of intelligence collection and analysis against Russia and other former Soviet states. Gates, the first post-Cold War DCI (1991–3), viewed this fresh orientation as a 'massive reallocation of resources'.[6] Much of the former Soviet empire, once hidden behind an 'iron curtain', was now on public view to outsiders. Russia alone had hundreds of neophyte newspapers, magazines and other media outlets, as well as a handful of competitive political parties. Secrets were fewer, the need for espionage by the CIA less.

Yet, despite this impressive reshuffling of intelligence assets, America's foreign policy goals remained relatively static in the post-Communist world. The list of adversaries changed, to be sure, with 'rogue nations' like North Korea and Iraq moving to the forefront where the USSR had once stood like a colossus. International economic matters also gained added interest at high levels. Yet, this interest remained far less extensive than foreshadowed by the early hoopla over the Clinton administration's creation of a new National Economic Council. Moreover, the Aspin-Brown Commission on Intelligence proved largely an exercise in modest adjustments to, rather than sweeping reform of, the fifty-year-old CIA and the rest of the intelligence community. In the loftier councils of government, questions of military security continued to hold sway over other agenda items, and the military intelligence agencies continued to receive the lion's share (85 per cent) of the annual budget for espionage.[7] *Plus ça change.*

Old Wine in New Bottles

Military Security: Abraham Maslow is famous for observing that human beings exhibit a hierarchy of needs, from basic survival to enlightened self-actualisation.[8] Nations, too, set priorities according to their needs. 'Our first and most important foreign policy priority is peace – for ourselves and for others,' declared the director of the Policy Planning Staff in the Carter administration.[9] In a bipartisan echo, the Reagan administration emphasised the importance of 'seeking to protect the security of our nation and its institutions, as well as those of our allies and friends'.[10] Above all, America would keep up her military guard during the Cold War, carrying a big stick and – if necessary – using it.

With the fall of the Soviet Union, it seemed for a moment that military matters might be less pressing. A series of arms accords – on intermediate-range nuclear forces (INF), strategic arms reduction talks (START I and START II) and chemical weapons – augured well for a decline in military confrontations throughout the world. Democracy took root in once inhospitable soil. Juntas fell in Latin America; liberated citizens cast aside Communist regimes in Central Europe. For the first time in history, a majority of nations began to experiment with some form of representative government.

Not all of the news was good, though. The US-Soviet stand-off had come to an end, but for many nations (as well as ethnic and tribal factions) the use of force to achieve objectives remained an attractive option. Much of the world looked just as hostile as it had during the Cold War. Nations boasted new weapons capabilities, as when India and Pakistan exploded powerful nuclear devices underground in 1998, and North Korea fired a test missile over Japan in 1999 and reportedly planned on testing a longer-ranged missile capable of striking the United States. The American people learned in 1999 that China had evidently engaged in widespread espionage activities inside the United States, stealing computer data on state-of-the-art (miniaturised) nuclear warheads.

Some nations went beyond the provocative display of new weaponry or old-fashioned spying. Iraq invaded Kuwait in 1990; and savage internecine warfare erupted in Somalia, Burundi, Rwanda and the Balkans. Media reports of mass rape and genocide in Central Africa, Bosnia and Kosovo became regular occurrences throughout 1998 and 1999. The world remained a hostile place despite the end of the Cold War.

Nations become not what they may wish to be but what they must be. In light of enduring military threats in the world after the Cold War, the United States set aside hopeful thoughts of a 'peace dividend'. Reinforced by the dynamics of the military-industrial complex (alive and well even without the Soviet *bête noire*), Washington officials maintained US defence and intelligence budgets at near Cold War levels – indeed, in the crucible of the Kosovo crisis in 1999, GOP legislators (who held a majority in both chambers of Congress) sought and gained large spending increases for national security purposes.[11] If America wished to be the world's leader, it would have to have a credible military capability to intervene near and far – or so the nation's leaders seemed to think (and, in Iraq and the Balkans, to act). The intelligence community would be given the task of tracking global military threats – from the proliferation of weapons of mass destruction and the perils of chemical and biological terrorist attacks against the United States to support for military operations on every conceivable foreign battlefield.

Political Security: As Clausewitz tutored, war is the conduct of politics by other means. Consequently, the United States must

understand the political machinations of other powers, not only
the workings of their war machines. Just as during the Cold War,
the dawning of the twenty-first century brings with it an over-
mastering concentration by America's intelligence agencies on a
combination of military and political targets – what Joseph S.
Nye, Jr, refers to as 'strategic' considerations (in contrast to
economic and humanitarian interests).[12] Does North Korea
intend war against South Korea or Japan? Do the leaders of
China have imperial aspirations in Asia, perhaps starting with
an invasion of Taiwan? Will Iraq resume its quest for nuclear
weapons? Who will replace the ageing President Boris N. Yeltsin
in Russia, and what are the likely views of the new leader with
respect to US–Soviet relations?

Economic Security: This abiding interest in the military and political dimensions of international affairs has typically relegated
the desire for economic prosperity to a secondary position
among America's leading foreign policy (and, therefore, intelligence) objectives.[13] Priorities in this new era have proved no
exception.

At the beginning of the Clinton years, however, it seemed as
if issues of international economics were about to displace
America's long-standing primary interest in military and political security. With the Cold War swept into history's dustbin, the
new administration could afford to concentrate more on domestic policy considerations – especially economics. 'The Clinton
administration has given priority to "commercial diplomacy",
making the promotion of American exports a primary foreign
policy objective,' observed Samuel P. Huntington in 1997.[14] Or
as President Clinton's US Trade Representative, Mickey Kantor,
put it: 'The days when we could afford to subordinate our
economic interests to foreign policy or defense concerns are long
past.'[15] The President's first DCI, R. James Woolsey, reinforced
these sentiments: 'The days are gone when international econom-

ics could be labeled low politics to separate it from the higher, loftier plane of political-military issues.'[16]

President Bill Clinton's Under-Secretary of State for Political Affairs further emphasised that 'our economic interests are paramount'.[17] Director of the FBI Louis Freeh concurred: 'We've entered a phase and a century where our economic independence and security and strength is really identical to our national security. . . .'[18] Throughout the Presidential honeymoon period, Clinton seemed determined to focus on rebuilding the American economy. Our 'national security rests more than ever on our economic strength', he declared.[19] His administration believed, according to a close observer, that 'international issues (other than commercial ones) could be for the most part marginalised'.[20]

Then the pressure of security problems began to crowd in on the President's economic aspirations: Iraq, Somalia, Burundi, Rwanda, North Korea, Bosnia, the terrorist Osama bin Laden, Chinese threats against Taiwan, Israeli-Palestinian flare-ups, rising tensions between India and Pakistan, and the war in Kosovo that threatened to embarrass – some said unravel – NATO, America's oldest defence alliance. The front seats in the bus were no longer reserved for international economics.

'Most of the threats to global stability – and ultimately to the security and integrity of American civilisation – have had less to do with the intricacies of "geo-economics",' Pietro S. Nivola has recently written, 'than with a primal fact of international politics, namely, states and peoples intimidating one another by force of arms.'[21] While some authorities maintained that recent American foreign policy had become largely a battle over international economic supremacy,[22] by 1996 the Clinton administration knew better. It was up to its scuppers in problems that chiefly involved the Pentagon and the Department of State, not the Departments of Commerce and Treasury or the US Trade Representative.[23]

This is not to say, of course, that commercial interests no longer mattered. They have always mattered, from the days of Thomas Jefferson's naval duels with the Barbary pirates in the Mediterranean (the use of military force to protect economic interests) to contemporary diplomatic tussles with Japan and China over worrisome trade imbalances. Today, as Thomas L. Friedman underscores, 'economic crises can spread rapidly from one continent to another'.[24] America cannot afford to ignore the ramifications of an increasingly global economy. Relatively speaking, though, the initial euphoria for things commercial during the early Clinton days gave way to a greater concern for military and political affairs – even if 'the dismal science' was never far out of mind.[25] Intelligence has mirrored these policy interests, with a rising concentration on economic intelligence from 1993 to 1997, followed by a decline as intelligence support for military operations regained ascendancy in the light of open conflict in Iraq, Bosnia and Kosovo.

The Security of a Quality Life with Human Dignity: The United States has foreign policy goals beyond the military, political and economic domains. Though generally less well supported by the American people,[26] a cluster of lifestyle issues that threaten humanity attract the sympathies of many citizens: adequate health care; quality housing and education; clean air and drinking water; the protection of woods, lakes and streams; defence against drug dealers and other international criminals; and freedom from the biggest killer of all, infectious diseases.[27]

Many Americans care, too, about global injustice, particularly the violation of human rights in other lands. A major impetus for US military involvement on the Horn of Africa and in the Balkans since the end of the Cold War was a heartfelt concern for the suffering of people in those regions, whether victims of hunger or warfare. Americans hope as well to see the benefits of democracy spread world-wide – a dominant theme in the

Clinton administration, with its goal of democratic 'enlargement' meant to take the place of Communist containment as a guiding doctrine for US foreign policy.

Here, then, are the objectives that animate America's external relations: above all, the physical protection of the United States and its allies (a shield that relies on military strength and political awareness), followed by a concern for economic prosperity. Also on the agenda – though often an interest more rhetorical than real – is a concern for the social well-being of people in other nations and their freedom from coercion: the moral and humanitarian impulse in foreign policy that underlies American foreign aid programmes, cultural exchanges, support for struggling democracies, the Peace Corps and some military interventions abroad (notably Kosovo). From this rich intelligence agenda in the post-Communist era, this essay focuses on the role played by America's secret agencies in support of economic security for the United States.

Intelligence and Economic Security

An understanding of foreign military threats and the politics that fuel them has been, and will continue to be, the first responsibility of the US intelligence community; here, after all, are matters of life and death – including the still-present spectre of nuclear annihilation. Nevertheless, matters of economic security have always been high on the nation's agenda, too.[28] Samuel D. Porteous succinctly explains its importance to a nation: 'In its most basic form, intelligence of this nature is designed simply to assist government leaders to better manage the economy.'[29]

As the interest in economic intelligence surged to the forefront for a brief time during the first term of the Clinton administration, roughly 40 per cent of the intelligence community's resources shifted to matters of international economics.[30] Even during the Cold War when Moscow's political and military machinations

attracted most of the community's attention, the secret agencies
still dedicated an enormous amount of funding and human talents
to the monitoring of the Soviet economic system – the 'largest
single project in social science research ever undertaken'.[31] The
CIA managed to track the demise of the Soviet economy closely
in its declining stages from 1984, despite failing (like everyone
else) to anticipate its complete collapse in 1991.[32]

Economic security is, thus, by no means a fresh entry on the
New Intelligence Agenda; the topic has long been an area of
concentration for the CIA and America's other intelligence agencies. The world changes, though, and new economic challenges
arise. Specific economic issues of interest to policy-makers (and
therefore to the managers of the intelligence community) have
fluctuated over time: wheat production in the USSR and oil
pricing by the Organisation of Petroleum Exporting Countries
(OPEC) in the 1970s, for example; and the effectiveness of trade
sanctions against Iraq and the flow of petroleum into a bellicose
Serbia in the 1990s. Still, the generic categories of economic
topics considered important by intelligence planners have
remained fairly constant. They include information on global
economic trends; international financial and trade issues; the
availability of critical resources; negotiating strategies at international economic conferences and world-wide technological
developments.[33] They do not include industrial espionage.

Industrial Espionage: The purpose of economic intelligence is to
support policy-makers in the US Government with information
about the economic decisions and activities of foreign *governments,* not foreign businesses. This support is based on insights
derived from sources both open (legal) and closed (illegal espionage), in a ratio of about 95 per cent to 5 per cent, respectively.[34] For a variety of reasons, the intelligence community has
rejected industrial espionage, that is, providing clandestinely
derived intelligence to private American companies.

In the first place, these companies have rarely asked for assistance. The largest ones already have their own capacity for spying on foreign competitors. Besides, the network of agents recruited by the CIA and military intelligence, and in place around the world, are burrowed into foreign governments, not foreign companies (although in some nations selected industries, such as aerospace and telecommunications, are run by the government and this becomes a distinction without a difference).[35] Moreover, were a CIA agent caught with his hands in the safe of Toyota headquarters at midnight, the repercussions for US-Japanese relations might be so severe as to make the attempt an act of folly – especially since, these days, Japanese autos are often assembled in America through joint ventures, creating jobs at home for US workers.

Given the intermingling of American and foreign components in automobiles and other manufactured goods, along with the multinational boards and stockholders of major companies, the CIA would run into baffling dissemination problems even if it gathered intelligence against a 'foreign' company. Would the company the CIA decided to help be sufficiently American to receive top-secret intelligence?[36] The Boeing aircraft corporation in Washington provides a classic illustration of the complications inherent in today's global economy. If the CIA provided intelligence to Boeing about Airbus (its European competitor), might this not harm another American company, General Electric, which produces jet engines for Airbus? Some US firms make a greater profit in overseas markets than in the United States (General Motors in Europe, for one). Further, what about when three or four American industries are in competition: which would receive the information? Should labour be informed as well as management? And, if these groups were all on the dissemination list, could the sensitive sources and methods on which the intelligence is based be kept secret?

The world of international commerce has become so

interwoven and complex that industrial espionage by the CIA
has consequently raised many red flags. In a different metaphor,
former Defense Secretary Harold Brown warns that the hazards
of industrial espionage by America's secret agencies represent
not just a 'slippery slope' but a 'ravine'.[37] As a result of these
considerations, the CIA has decided flatly that it will 'not
conduct economic espionage against foreign firms for the
benefit of US companies', a position firmly endorsed by DCIs
Gates and Woolsey while they were in office (and since).[38] This
policy stance is popular among intelligence officers, one of
whom proclaimed (with a modern geo-economic twist to
Nathan Hale's famous declaration upon facing the British
gallows in 1776): 'I'm prepared to risk my life for my country,
but I'm not ready to put my life on the line for General
Motors.'[39]

   This is not to say that everyone endorses a hands-off attitude towards industrial espionage. Former DCI Stansfield
Turner (1977–80) is convinced that the rejection of this option
by the CIA is equivalent to a form of disarmament – and unilateral at that, given the support for this approach by virtually all
other major nations.[40] In light of the growing world trade
competition, economic secrets might help the United States as
much as military secrets, in the Admiral's view, and they ought
to be pursued in the same fashion with the same determination.[41] So far, Turner has lost this argument. Sometimes,
though, in the course of their normal espionage activities the
intelligence agencies do come across seemingly important
economic intelligence about specific foreign companies. The
CIA and the other secret agencies are allowed some discretion
over whether to pass this information along to the Commerce
or State Departments. Inside these Departments, the intelligence is stripped of tell-tale signs that might reveal sources and
methods, then (from time to time) forwarded to US companies in what can only be described as an ad hoc relationship

between the Government and various US firms.[42] These murky arrangements, poorly conceived, follow no uniform guidelines and appear vulnerable to public disclosure of classified information, however inadvertent.

On the Defensive: The intelligence community helps the American business community more systematically and legitimately in another manner: through counter-intelligence. According to DCI Gates in 1992, some twenty nations have engaged in economic espionage against the United States since the end of the Cold War; four years later, a Senate document indicated the number had climbed to over fifty nations which had tried to obtain through clandestine means advanced technologies from American industries.[43] Another survey in 1996 claimed that China, Canada, France, India and Japan have been (in descending order) the most aggressive nations in the conduct of non-defence related economic espionage against the United States, with Germany, South Korea, Russia, Taiwan, England, Israel and Mexico close behind; and, in 1999, the Cox Committee discovered a remarkable Chinese espionage prowess directed against US defence targets as well.[44] An additional study has pointed to aggressive economic espionage operations against the United States carried out by France, Israel and South Korea.[45] 'There are no friends or allies in this international [economic] spy game,' cautions an FBI agent.[46] It is a point of view reinforced by none other than a former director of the French intelligence service, Pierre Marion. 'It would not be normal that we do spy on the [United] States in political matters,' he opined on the NBC show *Expose* in 1991. 'We are really allied, but in the economic competition, in the technological competition, we are competitors; we are not allied.'[47]

Through such training programmes as the Developing Espionage and Counter-Espionage Awareness (DECA) and an economic counter-intelligence programme (ECP), the FBI has provided advice to US companies on how to protect themselves against espionage, whether by a foreign company or an intelligence service.[48] A more recent Bureau programme, the Awareness of National Security Issues and Response (ANSIR), serves as a further channel of education and warning to American firms about foreign intelligence activities that might be directed against them. During fiscal years 1993 and 1994 alone, the FBI reports briefing almost 20,000 companies about how to safeguard proprietary information, and has conducted comparable seminars for universities, laboratories and local governments – although, as the Chinese spy scandal of 1999 indicates, the lessons apparently failed to protect the nation's nuclear secrets at the Los Alamos labs.[49] As an additional initiative against industrial spying, the Economic Espionage Act of 1996 has made it a federal crime to steal trade secrets.[50] The Departments of State and Defense have also blocked some commercial sales programmes supported by the Department of Commerce, in an effort to prevent sensitive scientific information from falling into the hands of potentially hostile nations – an illustration of how long-standing export-control laws may be used to curb or slow the spread of military technologies around the world. A recent instance is the block placed on the sale of a Hughes Space and Communications satellite to China for the establishment of a mobile telephone network that would cover much of Asia. State and Defense Department officials feared that the technology to place the satellite in orbit might also contribute to improvements in the accuracy of China's fleet of long-range missiles.[51] This is but one of many battles that have taken place between the Department of Commerce, with its domestic orientation and interest in advancing US business deals, and the more traditional departments like State, Defense and Treasury, with their greater concern for security issues.

The Purposes of Global Economic Espionage

Industrial espionage aside, the intelligence community is busy enough simply responding to the requests of policy-makers for information about more globally oriented issues – 'a dazzling range of questions about economics', according to a former Vice Chairman of the National Intelligence Council, the panel of community-wide senior analysts located at the CIA.[52] 'We are being asked today to do much more on a whole set of world economic issues,' testified DCI Woolsey in 1995.[53]

State Economies: Foremost among the intelligence community's global economic responsibilities is simply helping America's leaders better understand the 'objectives, motivations, and constraints' that shape the economic decisions of other nations.[54] The community attempts to track the progress of economic reforms in Eastern Europe, for instance, as well as in the former Soviet republics.

The economic future of Russia is in itself a subject of enormous significance. America's secret agencies can ill afford to ignore the question of economic stability in a nation armed with thousands of nuclear-tipped intercontinental ballistic missiles and harbouring a lingering hostility toward the United States.[55] According to Russia's top prosecutor, Yuri Skuratov, half of the commercial banks in his nation are mob-run and criminals control about half of the GNP.[56] A polling in 1998 indicated that Russians believe that the distribution of power in their nation is far more in the hands of 'criminal structures and mafia' than in the Presidency or the national assembly (Duma) combined.[57] This is a situation that warrants scrutiny, and the CIA and the FBI may be in the best position to provide reliable information on these unfortunate circumstances.[58]

Valuable, too, is intelligence on economic conditions within closed and unfriendly societies like North Korea and Iraq –

again, information often difficult to acquire through means other than espionage. Knowledge of a nation's economic health can reveal much about both its prospects for stability and its military capabilities, making it doubly important for foreign policy officials to acquire.

In this, as in all other international economic activities, a large number of agencies in the US Government are participants, and they often have information that is as good, if not better, than the intelligence community's. The Departments of Treasury, Commerce and State have first-rate economists who may know more about international finance than any CIA analyst. Yet often the intelligence community can provide a perspective that other entities may have overlooked – especially secret 'nuggets' of information derived from, say, a telephone tap or an asset deep within the trade ministry of a foreign economic rival. Moreover, sometimes the more open departments in America's government are simply too busy and understaffed (especially at the State Department) to prepare detailed economic reports for US officials. Even the basic task of collecting open information on economic topics overseas has been eroded by substantial cutbacks in State Department personnel in US embassies around the world. As these staff cuts have occurred, officials have turned to the intelligence community to take up the slack.

Nor do the various policy departments have a good track record for co-operating and sharing information among themselves or with the intelligence agencies. 'Many policy-making entities jealously guard their analytical functions,' accurately notes a Canadian observer of international economic policy as practised in Washington, 'and [they] see intelligence service analysis as an unwanted and not very useful intrusion into their territory.'[59]

Such obstacles to the contrary notwithstanding, the CIA has taken a leadership role – just as it did with arms-control issues during the Cold War – in providing useful economic information to policy-makers, because it has the staff at its headquarters in Langley, Virginia, and the world-wide network to do so. Furthermore, the Agency boasts elaborate around-the-clock publishing facilities that support analysts in the preparation of eye-catching, four-colour graphics of economic statistics presented on glossy paper. The CIA has also become skilful in the writing of reports that eschew the numbing diction of professional economists in favour of a lively prose that is more palatable to busy policy-makers with limited training in econometrics.

Beyond these advantages of institutional resources – far more than the Department of State – is the secret information the CIA has on tap to fold into its open-source reporting. An added flourish is the 'secret' or 'top-secret' stamp the Agency places on the report covers, a beguiling inducement that fairly shouts 'READ ME FIRST!' to harried officials. Finally, the CIA has developed over the years a quick distribution system for inserting its reports into the interstices of Washington's highest government echelons.

So the CIA is not necessarily smarter on international economic questions, but it is extraordinarily well organised for information-processing and dissemination. 'The capacity to handle both open and clandestine sources of information for now remains uniquely within the intelligence community,' Porteous astutely observes, 'rendering it the sole choice for all-source intelligence.'[60] The policy departments also understand another advantage of letting the CIA and its sister agencies fill their information gaps: analytic support from the intelligence community 'is available at zero marginal cost to the requesting agency'.[61]

As a result of these capabilities, the intelligence community frequently takes the initiative in preparing the economic portfolios sought by policy officials. As the intelligence community's chief economics analyst stated candidly in 1995:

The intelligence community is not a source of mainline

economic analysis. Our strength – and our principal mission – lies in winkling out the key bits of non-public information and then blending this non-public information with, typically, a much larger volume of openly available material to build a picture of foreign government plans and intentions that is comprehensive (the phrase we often use is 'all-source') and, equally important, tailored to the specific immediate needs of US policy-makers.[62]

The resourceful policy official, though, will pay attention as well to economists in the Departments of State, Commerce and Treasury, the Federal Reserve Board, the Office of the US Trade Representative and various international organisations. The prudent policy official widens his or her knowledge base further by gleaning information from leading newspapers and periodicals, trusted business lobbyists and opinion on Capitol Hill.

Level Playing Fields: Also high on the list of intelligence priorities, and a newer role, is the monitoring of unfair trade practices engaged in by foreign governments. This is a responsibility that at least one DCI (Woolsey) reportedly approached 'with particular gusto'.[63] The goal here is to assure fair access for American businesses in the international marketplace, or, in the popular Washington cliché, to seek 'a level playing field' – as when American companies are bidding for contracts against foreign competitors (in so far as 'American' and 'foreign' can be ascertained in this age of multinational corporations). The CIA's global network of agents watches for signs that a foreign government might be rigging bids on a contract, gaining preferential access to information, taking bribes from foreign firms, receiving kickbacks, or otherwise engaging in unfair business practices.

'We collect intelligence on those efforts to bribe foreign companies and foreign governments into, for example, awarding an airport contract to a European firm rather than an American firm,' Woolsey explains. The State Department will then warn the offending government that it is about to jeopardise its relations with the United States. Continues Woolsey: 'frequently, but not always, the contract is re-bid and the American firm gets a share of it. . . .'[64] The Aspin-Brown Commission reported that diplomatic interventions of this kind netted billions of dollars in foreign contracts for American firms from 1993 to 1996 alone that otherwise would have been lost.[65]

Dossiers for Diplomats: Further, the intelligence community gathers information that might be helpful to US negotiators at international trade conferences – what Gregory F. Treverton calls 'tactical tidbits'.[66] While en route to a conference on (say) the North American Free Trade Agreement (NAFTA), or the General Agreement on Trade and Tariffs (GATT), American diplomats may benefit from studying intelligence insights on which coalitions are likely to form around what issues and how various nations are apt to vote.

Popular among negotiators are personality profiles of the foreigners who will be facing them across the bargaining table. This information is organised into a 'baseball card' format for easy reading and carrying, and is laced from time to time with racy insights into the private lives of foreign diplomats.[67] Valued, too, are telephone intercepts of conversations held by foreign negotiators on the eve of an economic conference (courtesy of the NSA).[68] Wise recipients of these 'insights' understand, however, that this signals intelligence (SIGINT) can be a risky source of information; it is subject to deliberate deception, or the individuals being recorded may simply be poorly informed.

In 1993 American intelligence assets in the European Union reportedly provided information that helped US diplomats prepare for the Uruguay round on international trade negotiations; and, in 1995, the intelligence community is said to have gained access to revealing data on Japanese negotiating positions with respect to automobile trade with the United States.[69]

The economic agenda for diplomats and spies expands from time to time. In 1999, for instance, President Clinton encouraged the International Labor Organisation to adopt a treaty that would prohibit the most abusive forms of child labour practices, including the exploitation of children in prostitution and pornography. In support of the proposed treaty, the President issued an executive order that mandates preparation of a list of countries and products that might be engaged in forced child labour.[70] This data will no doubt require clandestine, as well as open, investigation, and the CIA will be given yet another assignment related to international economic policy.

Monitoring Sanctions: As the United States has turned increasingly to the use of economic sanctions in recent years as punishment against nations opposing its global interests, the intelligence community has been called upon to monitor their effectiveness. This involves tracking the activities of individual foreign trading companies, including their ties to money and their use of various communications channels (telephone, fax, e-mail). As well, the CIA is expected to monitor the flow of oil, international transportation and arms into and out of offending nations – a vast, complicated bundle of transactions. For these purposes, the CIA houses inter-agency sanctions-monitoring teams, which have followed shipping and other modes of trade affecting Iraq, Pakistan, Iran, China and Serbia. The information analysed by these teams is then forwarded to the Treasury Department, whose Office of Foreign Assets Control is in charge of enforcing trade sanctions. Should the President order the US navy to check on suspicious ships at sea bound for (say) Iraq, the CIA is able to conduct a quick computer run on each ship to see if its owners have been guilty of previous attempts to violate an international blockade.

America for Sale: As well, the secret agencies have been assigned the task of keeping track of foreign attempts to invest in the

United States, or to purchase American real estate and other assets. This responsibility, known in the Government as 'foreign acquisitions review', requires the intelligence community to provide information about such activities to the Committee on Foreign Investment in the United States, an inter-agency panel in which the Commerce Department is a major player.

Protection against Predators: Within the intelligence community's rich database on international economic subjects are detailed profiles of companies that have been engaged in unsavoury business activities, whether violating sanctions, laundering money, spreading weapons and fissionable materials, or selling to known terrorist organisations. Here are the 'bad actors' of the world's marketplace. The Federal Reserve Board, the Treasury Department and the Commerce Department have extensive corporate memories in this regard as well; but the intelligence agencies are often able to contribute valuable information to the Government's storehouse of knowledge on disreputable foreign companies. The intelligence community funnels these data to the Department of Commerce and to the Department of Treasury's Office of Foreign Assets Control; in turn, they alert American banks and firms to stay away from these perpetrators of sharp practices.

Drug Busting: In the shadowy domain of 'underground economics', the intelligence community has been drawn into the war against international organised crime, especially drug trafficking (highlighted by a recent DCI as the 'main money-making venture' of international criminals).[71] America's secret agencies have taken on this counter-narcotics mission reluctantly for the most part, sensing that law enforcement officials in the FBI and the Drug Enforcement Administration (DEA) are more experienced and better armed to deal with the low-life – and dangerous – thugs who pedal cocaine and heroin in the back streets of New York, Chicago and Los Angeles.

The DCI Crime and Narcotics Center is located at the CIA and is the repository for data collected by the intelligence community on the profits ('narco-dollars') and money-laundering operations of drug dealers.[72] Suspected ties between drug cartels and international banks are monitored for tip-offs on illegal drug deals, and the CNC rapidly alerts FBI and DEA officers if opportunities for an arrest seem propitious.

While this concept of intelligence support to law enforcement agencies may sound good in theory, in reality the narcotics cartels are winning the drug war hands down (even if from time to time a few of the major cartels are 'brought down' by the US Government, including the notorious Cali druglords). Of the total amount of illegal substances bound for the United States, only about 30 per cent are ever intercepted. Although an improvement over the 10 per cent of a decade ago, this statistic is still discouraging since the remaining 70 per cent more than meets the US demand. This losing effort has led critics to conclude that success lies not in the interception of drugs – akin to finding a needle in a haystack, given the thousands of ships, aeroplanes and motorised vehicles that enter the United States each year – but in discouraging the desire of consumers to purchase harmful drugs in the first place.[73]

Clearly, the United States must adopt an even more aggressive education programme to better inform Americans about the physiological dangers of drugs, one that specially targets America's major drug-users: white, affluent males in their late twenties and early thirties. The current funding of about $18 billion has proven inadequate to defeat what President George Bush referred to during his first year in office as America's 'public enemy number 1'. Important in a more extensive education campaign would be publicity debunking various drug misconceptions, including the widespread belief that inhaling heroin (as opposed to injecting it with a needle) will avoid addiction.[74] Necessary, too, are more effective treatment programmes to wean current addicts.[75] The constructive role that intelligence agencies (or, for that matter, the FBI and the DEA) can play in counter-narcotics is relatively limited compared to the results that could be derived from additional resources dedicated to improved anti-drug education and health care – a shift of attention away from the supply side to the demand side of this seamy business.

Weapons Transactions: Drugs are not the only illicit and dangerous commodities in the underground commerce that takes place among nations and groups. As part of America's non-proliferation efforts, the intelligence community seeks out information on trafficking in arms and related materials – especially nuclear, biological and chemical weapons of mass destruction. An important component of chemical weapons, for instance, is the substance Empta, a precursor for the production of the deadly nerve agent VX. The CIA would like to know whenever a foreign country is manufacturing Empta and related compounds. The intelligence community claimed that this was the case in a factory near Khartoum in 1998, leading to bombing of the plant by American aircraft. The attack became controversial when the Sudanese Government claimed that the only chemicals produced by the plant were aspirin and other common medicines.[76]

A Period of Transition: As these examples illustrate, America's secret agencies expend considerable resources on questions related to international economics. Yet, just how important this assignment really is remains 'unresolved' as the twentieth century comes to an end, according to a senior intelligence official: 'We are still in a transition period.'[77] The global financial crises that arose in the waning years of the century stimulated a greater concentration on the collection of international economic intelligence than ever before; questions linger, however, about whether the secret agencies really have much value to add to analyses already provided by the Departments of Treasury and Commerce as well as other government agencies – not to mention the highly regarded reporting on economic issues by the *New York Times,* the *Wall Street Journal* and the *Economist.*

In support of the CIA's economic role, its officers are quick to emphasise that the needs of Washington officials are often quite different from those of Wall Street investment analysts. Besides, they maintain, the CIA has become adept at 'making things easier to understand' for distracted Washington officials.[78] The Agency focuses on economic problems at the top of the policy-maker's in-box that very morning, delivering information and insight that is timely, lucid and attractively presented – a composite of open and secret sources of information directly relevant to the official's immediate concerns. That at any rate is the aspiration, not necessarily what really happens in the hurly-burly of daily life that transpires inside the pressure-cookers around Washington that pose as government buildings.[79]

Recently, the CIA has tried to concentrate on carrying out three activities especially well with respect to economic intelligence.[80] First, the Agency attempts to serve the needs of the new National Economic Council (NEC), created during the first year of the Clinton administration (1993) as a specialised economic companion to the National Security Council. Bo Cutter, the NEC deputy director, developed the Council into an important focal point for economic intelligence, treating the CIA as an extension of his own staff and giving strong credibility to the Agency's 'value added' in this domain.[81] The NEC has been particularly interested in trying to understand the politics of shifting coalitions at international trade conferences and, according to Cutter, the CIA has proved helpful. Most important, though, has been the daily 'tactical' information the CIA has been able to provide about economic events around the world – everything from figures on world crop production to maps on international oil shipments.[82]

Second, the CIA has tried to rise above its past focus on the

economies of individual countries. Shaken by the Asian financial crisis of 1997–8, Cutter and other consumers of economic
intelligence in the executive branch sought a broader assessment
of the world economy – an 'integrated transnational analysis', in
the current Washington jargon. What's going on inside a particular country is no longer enough; more important is an understanding of the economic global interactions among nations and
the unexpected dynamics they may create. Recently, the NIC
conducted a one-day game involving intelligence officers and
policy-makers (chiefly deputy assistant secretaries), an experience
considered useful by participants for the vivid sense it gave them
of the dynamics that characterise contemporary geo-economics.[83]

Third, intelligence analysts in the community – from the most
senior NIOs down to the newest, the rookie analyst – are attempt-
ing to provide greater nuance in their written economic assessments. These days, economic intelligence reports are filled with
possible scenarios, laying out a panoply of likely directions the
international economy might take and assigning probabilities to
each pathway. The intention is to remind policy-makers that
intelligence analysts – mere mortals like the rest of us – never
know for sure what is going to happen; rather, they are only able
to draw upon their expertise and experience to suggest the odds
of certain events unfolding. Unlike during the Cold War era,
policy-makers today are presented with fewer black-and-white
intelligence assessments; shades of grey are now the order of the
day. This approach is often frustrating for the nation's leaders,
who seek sure guidance and certain answers; but it is also less
misleading, conveying to those who must make decisions only
the best-guess hunches for various options.

Conclusion

'Our national security is inseparable from our economic security,' declared President Clinton's first Secretary of State, Warren

Christopher.[84] Similarly, President Clinton vowed that – despite the Chinese spying on the United States – he would pursue better security at the nation's weapons labs *and* improved economic engagement with the Chinese, 'because both of [these objectives] are in the national interest'.[85]

Most of the economic information sought by US policy-makers can be acquired through open sources. Officials will continue to read newspapers and journals, as well as interpretations of economic trends proffered by economists in Treasury, Commerce, State, the Federal Reserve, the Office of the US Trade Representative, the International Trade Commission and the NEC. Still, the CIA has demonstrated a skill for sifting through open foreign materials (especially hard-to-find 'grey' sources, like speeches by Saddam Hussein and esoteric papers delivered by Japanese economists at scholarly meetings), then combining them with valuable bits of information derived from clandestine operations. This service has been a generally appreciated time-saver for busy policy-makers.[86]

The trick is to ensure that the assessments of analysts labouring in both the open and the secret agencies are brought to the attention of key decision-makers in a timely, synergistic manner. Here, unfortunately, one runs into the problem of institutional fragmentation that has long plagued the US intelligence community. During America's clumsy response to the Mexico financial crisis of 1995–6, Ernest R. May, the noted historian and intelligence scholar, observed that 'neither the Treasury nor the Federal Reserve had a comfortable relationship with the intelligence community'.[87] Unfortunately, this phenomenon of institutional estrangement remains all too prevalent.

Even though most of the time military and political security concerns will crowd out other interests at the top of America's foreign policy agenda, and even though a vast amount of valuable data on international commerce can be found in the public domain, the intelligence community will remain a player of consequence in the US Government's deliberations over global economic policy. The secret agencies are well staffed and experienced for providing timely information to policy-makers on events and conditions related to military, political and economic affairs (which is not to say the agencies are always correct).

The community will also continue to shoulder the added counter-intelligence assignment of helping US firms protect themselves against economic espionage by other nations and foreign companies. Finally, the White House on occasion may order the CIA to employ disruptive economic covert actions ('special activities') to counter America's adversaries, as with the mining of harbours and blowing up of fuel depots in Nicaragua during the 1980s.[88] In sum, for as long as nations seek commercial advantage in the global market, economic intelligence will remain an important assignment for the secret agencies.

DISCUSSION

Mark Heathcote

Mark Heathcote is currently Vice-President of Group Security for BP Amoco. As such, he is responsible for the oversight and motivation of the company's security network, but he specialises in the security and political risks facing the company, travelling widely in the process. Until 1994 he served in the Foreign and Commonwealth Office, serving in Pakistan, where he dealt with the Afghan issues; he was involved in the run up to the Falklands War and also served in Greece. In the 1970s he spent a period on loan to the Northern Ireland Office where he worked for the Secretary of State, writing political assessments. He was mainly a specialist on Latin America. Previously he had worked for P&O in London, India and Pakistan.

First, I'd like to thank St Antony's for very kindly inviting me to this meeting. I then ask myself why have I been invited, because I am no academic, I'm afraid. I take it it's because of my commercial background now as Head of Security for a large, multinational company, BP Amoco. Although I did have a fleeting knowledge of some intelligence affairs in the past, so maybe there is something there. But I have been away from the Government for about six years now and this has been something of an exercise in nostalgia coming back here. It is interesting to find people still talking about the Cold War, and indeed the 1940s, and 1950s, but I suppose this reflects the age of us as Cold Warriors now attending the meeting. One might wonder now how a young intelligence officer would react to our discussions. I believe the 'changing world' has changed more in the last ten years than ever before, and a young intelligence officer nowadays would be thinking much more in terms of crime, weapons of mass destruction, economics, industrial intelligence and the sorts of things that are now the stuff of a modern intelligence service.

And the other interesting thing is that there really isn't anybody here from what I would call para-intelligence – the police, the Customs; these are the sort of people nowadays who are playing a big part in the partnership we have to have in the modern areas of intelligence.

I have been asked to comment on the excellent paper by Professor Loch Johnson on economic espionage in the US. I feel his paper is very comprehensive and there is not a lot to add regarding the scene in the US. Indeed, he is a lot better qualified than I am on this subject. I therefore thought that I would comment briefly on the role of intelligence services and their suitability for carrying out economic espionage. In doing this I will be able also to comment on some of the points made in Professor Johnson's paper. I also feel we cannot talk about economic espionage without talking about industrial espionage.

I thought also I would discuss the role of other countries in economic espionage and, since I work for a commercial organisation, would say a little more about espionage from the point of view of a commercial organisation. I will not speak of industrial espionage as carried out corporation on corporation, even though this is a huge and fascinating subject generating in the US alone allegedly £300 billion a year.

There is a lot of confusion about the difference between economic espionage and industrial espionage. Economic espionage is defined by the US Government as the use or the facilitation of illegal, clandestine, coercive or deceptive means by a foreign government to acquire economic intelligence. Whereas industrial espionage is described as illegal or covert intelligence collection sponsored by individuals or private business to gain a competitive advantage. In fact, foreign intelligence services stealing industrial and technological secrets should be described as indulging in industrial espionage, and for the purposes of this talk I intend to do just that.

To my mind, the difference between political and economic intelligence, as opposed to industrial espionage, is very small. Indeed, there is no clear dividing line. Very often governments are collecting information to support their political agenda. For example, information on attitudes of governments to the World Trade Organisation, the machinations of OPEC and the economic intentions of Asian states in respect of their debt and negotiations with the IMF, are really semi-political in nature; whereas the CIA's targeting of a Japanese trade delegation during Japanese/American automobile trade negotiations is nearer the bone – if they indeed did do so. They deny it.

On the other hand, the stealing of commercial secrets for the benefit of national industry should be described as industrial espionage, as many governments see this as a legitimate target for their services.

Loch Johnson has already raised an interesting issue about the problems that intelligence services have in collecting industrial and commercial secrets as technology or contract-type information. They create all sorts of problems in terms of dissemination, and an embarrassing political minefield for a country that does it. The French have partly solved the problem of which national contractors to favour by supporting 'approved' consortia. Politically, countries have frequently been embarrassed by revelations that their national intelligence services have been stealing economic, commercial or technological secrets, and when CIA officers are expelled for this sort of thing, as occurred in France, there is widespread publicity.

There is also the question of whether the intelligence services are indeed well equipped to carry out economic or industrial espionage. Most operational intelligence officers are generalists. They are supported by teams of analysts who may be expert or semi-expert in their field. To embrace the finer points of a country's debt negotiations is fine for a central banker, but generalist intelligence officers are not always the best for this purpose, and when it comes to industrial secrets they are unlikely to have the insight that is needed to support the position of a commercial organisation.

Therefore, there is a real danger that intelligence officers are collecting information that is already known by commercial organisations and, indeed, by financial experts in specialist ministries in their own governments. Having said this, there will always be some hard targets which, with a bit of luck and good intelligence work, will produce nuggets of information that will prove key to understanding an economic or commercial problem. In other words, I believe large numbers of national intelligence services are deluding themselves that they are collecting really valuable information in these fields.

The CIA is almost unique in having in the DI an analysis division which can prepare rounded economic assessments, including open- and secret-source information, for their customers. The BND has some of the same capability. Elsewhere intelligence services, especially in the UK, have to rely on the departments of state to provide necessary analysis and briefing on intelligence requirements, and these departments of state have other priorities than the collection and analysis of intelligence. They are bogged down in day-to-day issues. This is one of the reasons why the Foreign Office Research Department was created and the I&R in the US State Department. Intelligence services in some countries enjoy a unique position in being alone able to provide the rounded assessment that other departments of state do not have the time or capacity to provide for ministers.

Little has been said about communications intelligence that undoubtedly could and probably does play a big role in the collection of economic and industrial intelligence. You will no doubt have seen the debate in the European Parliament about the capabilities of the Echelon network in being able to hoover up vast quantities of commercial communications. The question must be, how much is GCHQ and NSA making use of this potentially invaluable information for the benefit of their commercial firms? If I was an unscrupulous government with this tool in my hands, I believe I could hugely aid any national export industry.

Loch Johnson also mentioned drugs. Many intelligence services have much to offer in this area in supporting the main drugs investigators, such as the UK Customs and Excise, overseas where the Customs may not have the appropriate resources.

On counter-intelligence, the Security Service in the UK has reason to be jealous of the FBI's resources in assisting companies with economic counter-intelligence. To an outsider, some of this sensitivity seems overblown, but no doubt by exaggerating the threat a greater awareness is created. I believe the emphasis needs to be in vulnerable areas, such as the threat to technology. In the same way, we have cause in the UK to be jealous of the Overseas Security Advisory Council, which is a partnership between business and the State Department to help US companies on security issues.

Speaking about the vulnerability of commercial organisations, such as mine, to the work of foreign intelligence services overseas, I have to say that we are all extremely vulnerable. Unlike embassies, we cannot control the environment in which we work. It is very easy for foreign intelligence services to support or recruit any member of our local staff by appeals to patriotism or by intimidation. The threat is therefore much more from theft of information than from the more usually quoted electronic eavesdropping. I do not need to tell people here that it is probably far easier for an employee to steal information than to carry out a technical operation. If you add to this the fact that many of these countries can use their intelligence services to support their national state organisations, such as a national oil company, then a commercial organisation is in deep trouble. We have to work hard to protect that 2 per cent or so of commercial information which we believe we need to keep away from a foreign government. I could talk for a long time about threats from espionage overseas.

According to the US Government services (and unlike other nations the US documents these things), there is little doubt that the sophisticated services, such as the UK, France, Germany, China, Russia, Japan, South Korea, Cuba and Italy, collect economic intelligence. In a way, why shouldn't they? Even the UK Intelligence Service Act speaks of the 'economic wellbeing' of the nation. This is all information needed for the conduct of international affairs. It is in the one area of industrial espionage by national intelligence services and their commercial allies that things become interesting. The DCI, William Casey, said in 1984 that the activities of certain Japanese computer companies posed a direct threat to the security of the USA in terms of the US lead in semi-conductors and proprietary information. I am straying into the area of pure commercial espionage, but in 1997 the

annual report for Congress on foreign economic collection and
industrial espionage claimed that US companies lost $2 billion
worth of information every month to economic espionage and
the theft of trade secrets.

The list of those countries which steal industrial secrets
according to US sources is a little different from those that are
listed as carrying out economic espionage. There is a general
view in the US that foreign companies are receiving direct help
from their intelligence services in carrying out attacks on US
companies, e.g. the attacks by the French firm St Gobain on
3M. But I am not clear what real evidence there is for this. The
countries in the US lists include (and I am going to skate over
these for lack of time):

Japan: They claim that most intelligence is collected by
Japanese firms in association with the Ministry of International
Trade and Industry, but I am not sure that this is not really a
case of straight commercial espionage.

France: There are a number of documented cases of the DGSE
targeting technology in the US including against Loral Systems,
Lockheed Missile and Space Company and others. And the FBI
– this is something that affected us as a company – briefed us
in Houston the other day that there had been a recent case of
foreign diplomats 'dumpster-diving', as they call it, going through
the rubbish from companies and collecting information.
'Dumpster-diving', I like the expression.

South Korea: According to the DIA, information has been
stolen on computer, aerospace and nuclear technologies.

Germany: The BND is said to have set up a classified computer
intelligence facility called RAHAB to access foreign commercial
data.

Israel: Israel is said to have an active programme to gather
proprietary information.

Russia: Russia is increasingly focusing on industrial espionage
and numerous ex-KGB officers are working for Russian

companies in their 'security departments', and espionage must be expected from many East European firms.

China: Industrial espionage has always played a huge part in China's economic development.

Although this is straying a little, I would like to finish up by talking a little bit about what a commercial organisation might like to receive in the way of commercial intelligence from its national intelligence service (we, BP Amoco, are a multinational!), and how in reality it acquires it. The information comes under the following headings:

Competitor Information: What are the plans and commercial tactics of competitor companies?

Proprietary information: This refers to leads by other companies in technology and in our area of information, such as seismic data.

Contract information: This would be information during a negotiation in a contract and the position of rival companies.

Price data: This may be related to our own costs and market advantage related to price.

Market information: This is related to our market position and data which is market-sensitive related to share prices, etc. All this information needs to be protected by the company and is vulnerable to threat by other companies and is therefore of interest to any commercial company in the field.

Political/Security Risk information: e.g. the effect East Timor might have had on foreign investment/economic sanctions on Indonesia.

As far as acquiring this information is concerned, I think sometimes intelligence services delude themselves into thinking that they are the only people available that can collect such information. As I have already said, in fact they are not very well equipped for this. There is a vast amount of information available from open sources including the Internet itself. There are also now many consultants in the market who are intelligence services themselves in all but name. They employ 'correspondents' from different countries and can compete very effectively with the agent-running of intelligence services. It would therefore be rare for an intelligence service to be able to provide the key nugget to open up a particular intelligence problem for a company, and it is highly unlikely it could meet the sort of time constraints imposed by a company. Civil Services are much slower than commercial organisations!

Finally, there is competitor intelligence. Again there are a number of consultants active in this field – in the US there is a Society of Competitive Intelligence Professionals – but the company, too, can co-ordinate its own intelligence collection, especially if it's a large organisation. The difficulty is to focus the disparate parts of a company to target on the information that is needed. This is rarely done 100 per cent successfully.

GENERAL DISCUSSION

The discussion was opened by the chairman of the session, Robin O'Neill, a former Chief of the Assessments Staff of the JIC, who made two comments from his own experience. First, the JIC came back into the study of economic issues in 1983, when an economic section was re-established, an earlier one having got bogged down writing papers so long, and so slowly, that the government departments concerned were not interested in them. In 1983 a very good economist was recruited and told to work on the Soviet economy. After two weeks he reported that the Soviet economy 'just didn't add up' and was bound to grind to a halt. Hardly any of the information used in the report he wrote was secret, coming almost entirely from open sources. It was one of the first warnings that the Soviet Union was entering its terminal phase. Equally interesting was the fact that nobody elsewhere in the Government was interested in conducting that sort of broad study. They were interested in limited banker-type questions about repayment of debts, etc. Robin O'Neill's second comment was on the danger for those who use secret intelligence thinking that just because it's secret, they can believe it. As an example of this, the people who collected statistics on East European countries and the people who used them were fooling themselves and their governments, as it was rubbish. The statistics themselves were indeed the official statistics of the countries concerned, but they were false and hence misleading, and essentially useless, both to the governments who relied on them and to foreign intelligence analysts. 'Merely because a document has "top secret" stamped on it doesn't mean it's true.'

An American academic then pointed out that a large proportion of the personnel in the private sector, who are engaged in commercial and industrial intelligence, in collection, analysis and counter-intelligence, were trained in the various intelligence agencies of the public sector. They work in a variety of consultancies, some mentioned by the speakers, others not, including private-eye operations, in-house detective operations, political-risk analysis, sub-sections of business firms, and obviously the security departments of companies. Governments therefore do not need to do these things. By analogy, many former KGB officers in Russia were now working in various forms of security jobs and using at least some of the skills they learned in an earlier life. He remarked that there was much to commend this arrangement.

Mark Heathcote agreed, adding that in many ways a commercial organisation that can afford to pay for this service has more control than if it depended on government whim to hand a few crumbs from its table.

A French participant stated his belief that government had no business in economic intelligence. Good intelligence, in his view, means good relations between the supplier and the client, and therefore industrial intelligence should be sought by industrialists in their particular branch, probably 99 per cent of it open intelligence. He then observed that economic espionage had come to play a major role in the information war, which is now a topic of great concern to military thinkers in the West who are concerned with the evolution of military strategy and new kinds of mission, and are rediscovering, for instance, psychological warfare.

Loch Johnson remarked that a Director of French Intelligence of recent vintage had said precisely the opposite, namely, that it was wrong to steal military and political secrets from one's allies; but economics were a different matter. He agreed that information warfare is a 'hot-button issue'.

A German academic raised the question of government involvement where two monopolists or near-monopolists from different countries are in competition. He asked what the legal position in the United States was on giving government support in such a situation, and what is current ethical thinking? When the issue of multi-billion dollar losses through foreign economic espionage is raised, for instance, in the US Congress, and a solution is demanded from government, it seems ethics is abandoned in favour of pragmatism.

Loch Johnson replied that there is no significant legal history on this matter. There is no law on what the American intelligence agencies can do when it comes to foreign economic espionage. The ethics is a different matter. Ethically speaking, the intelligence community has decided not to spy either in terms of economic espionage or industrial espionage against America's closest friends, including the United Kingdom. A general decision has been made, as Loch Johnson pointed out in his paper, that the US will not get into the domain of industrial espionage, except where a foreign national government actually owns the industry concerned. A publicly owned company, in his view, was 'fair game' for economic espionage.

A British academic noted that both speakers had mentioned

the cut-off between political intelligence and economic intelligence and industrial and economic intelligence, and he asked whether it was not the case that S&T (Scientific and Technological) intelligence naturally tailed off into industrial intelligence?

Loch Johnson replied that this was so only if the S&T companies concerned are overseas state-run companies. He acknowledged that complex relationships made it difficult to draw the line, and that the decision to launch an intelligence exercise was made on a case-by-case basis, and he concluded that in general, if it is a private S&T firm the US intelligence community would not be targeting it.

An American economist with experience of both intelligence assessment and analysis in the CIA, and now working with the JIC, stressed the importance of economic analytic tools for the future and argued that there is almost no current intelligence problem, including weapons proliferation and terrorism, that is not illuminated by useful economic analysis. The espionage issue was admittedly a different story. There are, nevertheless, mysteries that can be better probed by good economic analysis than by covert espionage. For instance, answering the question of when the North Korean economy will collapse, and so on. It is the case, this participant continued, that clients have not always welcomed the messages of economic analysts in the intelligence business, Mexico being one example, the East Asian financial crisis another. In conclusion, all the new techniques and tools and analysis that economics can bring should be exploited, and in a multi-disciplinary way, as clients rarely ask single-point questions.

A retired FBI official pointed out that there is a society of 6,000 competitive intelligence professionals around the world, and that they have a very strong ethics code within their organisation. He pointed out that Jan Herring, a former NIO who left the CIA to become the Director of Competitive Intelligence for Motorola and Nutrasweet, has stated that 20 per cent of a firm's information budget can answer 80 per cent of the questions asked by its decision-makers, and he wondered what Mark Heathcote thought of that.

Speaking as Deputy Chief of Security for BP Amoco, Mark Heathcote replied that his company does not put a lot of weight on competitive intelligence or political-risk analysis, partly because they take the view that the best thing one can do is to try to highlight some of the things that might go wrong, though on balance trying to predict the future is a waste of time. On the competitive intelligence issue, until BP took over Amoco the company never had a department for this purpose and did quite well without it. They are now experimenting to see what they think of this new animal, and it is too early to make a judgement as to its value.

A former CIA officer and current intelligence academic made the point that it is difficult to motivate intelligence officers to collect against private industry compared to the motivations that professionals felt during the Cold War, for example, or may feel in the area of non-proliferation intelligence collection. He suggested that, for example, it might it be very difficult for the CIA Director and for senior officers to demand of their professional clandestine officers that they go out and endanger themselves and others for the purpose of collecting against private enterprise, and he asked if there is a dramatically, profoundly different motivational issue.

Loch Johnson agreed that it is much more difficult to motivate someone to conduct this kind of espionage than when the target presents a real military and political threat to the survival of one's country.

Mark Heathcote suggested that the people who are motivated to work for King and country, or President and country, are usually not people who get involved in commercial espionage, where there is a lot of money to be made, but a lot of people will do a lot of things for money, and this might even include ex-CIA officers.

A British Government-trained imagery analysis consultant referred to the frequent mention at the conference of the impact of commercial and satellite imagery on various areas. He wondered whether the availability to a lot of people, at a fairly low cost, of air imagery was thought to be a threat to a company like BP Amoco, from the security point of view, or even from the industrial espionage point of view.

Mark Heathcote replied that he had never encountered it as a security threat. On the commercial side, what is happening is that his company is using imagery more and more for developing commercial aspects, for instance, looking for oil. He pointed out that the oil business is quite an open one, and that there is not much secrecy about it. He did not see it as a threat, while remarking in conclusion, 'but maybe you know something I don't'.

Notes to Loch Johnson's paper

The author would like to express his appreciation to Amy Elizabeth Early for research assistance and Leena S. Johnson for editorial guidance in the writing of this essay.
1. Quoted in Albert O. Hirschman, *National Power and the Structure of Foreign Trade* (University of California, Berkeley, 1945; expanded ed., 1980), pp. 14–15. In his classic study of international affairs, E.H. Carr stressed that 'power is indivisible' and 'the military and economic weapons are merely different instruments of power' (*The Twenty Years' Crisis: An Introduction to the Study of International Relations* [Harper and Row, NY, 1939], pp. 117, 120).
2. Remarks by Robert M. Gates, Conference on US Intelligence, Langley, Virginia (11 June 1984); and, while serving as DCI, remarks, Economic Club of Detroit, Michigan (13 April 1992).

3. For this budget figure, see *New York Times* (16 October 1997), p. A17.

4. Robert M. Gates, 'In War, Mistakes Happen', *New York Times* (12 May 1999), p. A27.

5. The US intelligence community consists of thirteen major agencies, including the CIA, the Federal Bureau of Investigation (FBI), the National Security Agency (NSA), the National Reconnaissance Office (NRO), the National Imagery and Mapping Agency (NIMA), the Defense Intelligence Agency (DIA), and additional entities within the Departments of State, Defense, Treasury and Energy. See 'Factbook on Intelligence', CIA (Office of Public Affairs, Washington, DC, undated, but evidently printed in 1999), p. 15; Mark M. Lowenthal, *US Intelligence: Evolution and Anatomy* (Praeger, Westport, 2nd ed., 1992); and Jeffrey T. Richelson, *The US Intelligence Community* (Westview, Boulder, 4th ed., 1999).

6. Author's interview, quoted in Loch K. Johnson, 'Reinventing the CIA: Strategic Intelligence and the End of the Cold War', in Randall B. Ripley and James M. Lindsay (eds), *US Foreign Policy after the Cold War* (University of Pittsburgh, Pittsburgh, 1997), p. 152.

7. Loch K. Johnson and Kevin J. Scheid, 'Spending for Spies: Intelligence Budgeting in the Aftermath of the Cold War', *Public Budgeting & Finance* 17 (Winter 1997), pp. 7–27.

8. Abraham H. Maslow, *The Farther Reaches of Human Nature* (Viking, NY, 1971) and *Motivation and Personality* (Harper and Row, NY, 1987).

9. Anthony Lake, *Managing Complexity in US Foreign Policy*, Bureau of Public Affairs, US Department of State (14 March 1978), p. 1.

10. *Fundamentals of US Foreign Policy*, Bureau of Public Affairs, US Department of State (March 1988), p. 1.

11. See 'Congress and Kosovo', unsigned editorial, *New York Times* (29 April 1999), p. A28.

12. Joseph S. Nye, Jr, 'Redefining the National Interest', *Foreign Affairs* 78 (July/August 1999), p. 35.
13. See Michael Mastanduno, 'Economics and Security in Statecraft and Scholarship', *International Organization* 4 (Autumn 1998), pp. 825–54.
14. Samuel P. Huntington, 'The Erosion of American National Interests', *Foreign Affairs* 76 (September/October 1997), pp. 28–49.
15. Quoted in 'Cool Winds from the White House', *Economist* 326 (27 March 1993), p. 58.
16. R. James Woolsey, 'World Threat Assessment Brief', Statement for the Record, *Hearings*, Select Committee on Intelligence, US Senate, 104th Cong., 1st Sess. (10 January 1995), p. 8.
17. Quoted by Daniel Williams and John M. Goshko, 'Reduced US World Role Outlined but Soon Altered', *Washington Post* (26 May 1993), p. A1.
18. Testimony, 'Economic Espionage', *Hearings*, Select Committee on Intelligence, US Senate, 104th Cong., 2d Sess. (28 February 1996).
19. President William J. Clinton, *National Export Strategy: A US Strategic Response to Foreign Competitive Practices* (Trade Promotion Co-ordinating Committee Washington, DC), p. 4.
20. Pietro S. Nivola, 'American Trade Policy after the Cold War', in Ripley and Lindsay, *op. cit.*, p. 249.
21. *Ibid.*, p. 254.
22. See, for example, Jeffrey E. Garten, *A Cold Peace: America, Japan, Germany, and the Struggle for Supremacy* (Times Books, NY, 1992); and Edward N. Luttwak, *The Endangered American Dream* (Simon and Schuster, NY, 1993).
23. Mastanduno notes that mid-way through the Clinton administration, 'foreign policy initiative within the US government . . . shifted from the economic revisionists to the security traditionalists' (*ibid.*, p. 846).

24. Thomas L. Friedman, 'A Manifesto for the Fast World', *New York Times Sunday Magazine* (28 March 1999), p. 43.

25. The usual pre-eminence of military over economic matters can be seen as well in America's reaction to the theft by foreigners of US military and economic secrets. Discovery of the former stirs an outrage, as when Jonathan Pollard of the Office of Naval Intelligence passed highly classified military documents to Israeli intelligence in the 1980s, and when a Chinese-American scientist at the Los Alamos labs was thought to have provided the Chinese Government with US nuclear-weapons designs in the 1990s. Yet when French intelligence infiltrated American aerospace firms, when Israeli intelligence penetrated Recon/Optical (an Illinois company that manufactures satellite cameras), and when South Korean intelligence targeted the acquisition of microwave technology used in the F-16 fighter, the American response was in each case little more than a slap on the wrist. See Duncan L. Clarke and Robert Johnston, 'Economic Espionage and Interallied Strategic Co-operation', *Thunderbird International Business Review* 40 (July/August 1998), pp. 413–31, who point out that nations involved in economic espionage against one another also seek mutual assistance with respect to such transnational threats as terrorism, nuclear proliferation and organised crime; therefore, nations are prepared to accept some level of economic espionage aimed at them, even by allies, in return for co-operation on these greater dangers.

26. See the polling data in John E. Rielly (ed.), *American Public Opinion and US Foreign Policy 1991* (Chicago Council on Foreign Relations, Chicago, 1991), p. 15.

27. Mary E. Wilson, 'Infectious Diseases: An Ecological Perspective', *British Medical Journal* 31 (23 December 1995), pp. 1681–4.

28. See Maurice C. Ernst, 'Economic Intelligence in CIA', *Studies in Intelligence* 28 (Winter 1984), pp. 1–22, reprinted in

H. Bradford Westerfield (ed.), *Inside CIA's Private World* (Yale University Press, New Haven, 1995), pp. 305–29; Arthur S. Hulnick, 'The Uneasy Relationship between Intelligence and Private Industry', *International Journal of Intelligence and Counterintelligence* 9 (Spring 1996), pp. 17–32; Philip Zelikow, 'American Intelligence and the World Economy', in *In from the Cold,* Report of the Twentieth Century Fund Task Force on the Future of US Intelligence (Twentieth Century Fund Press, NY, 1996), pp. 137–262; and Philip Zelikow, 'American Economic Intelligence: Past Practice and Future Principles', in Rhodri Jeffreys-Jones and Christopher Andrew (eds), *Eternal Vigilance? 50 Years of the CIA* (Cass, London, 1997), pp. 164–77. Zelikow notes that 'historically, the need to infer military capabilities has been the great motive behind collection of economic intelligence' ('American Intelligence and the World Economy', p. 165).

29. Samuel D. Porteous, 'Looking Out for Economic Interests: An Increased Role for Intelligence', *Washington Quarterly* 19 (1996), p. 192.

30. This increased percentage dedicated to global economic matters evolved as a response to a survey of key policy agencies conducted by the Bush administration in an attempt to clarify the Government's projected intelligence needs between 1991 and 2005 (National Security Review Directive 29, November 1991, Washington, DC).

31. David M. Kennedy, 'Sunshine and Shadow: The CIA and the Soviet Economy', *Case Program,* No. C16-91–1096.0, Kennedy School of Government (Harvard University, Cambridge, 1991), p. 2.

32. Kristen Lundberg, 'CIA and the Fall of the Soviet Empire: The Politics of "Getting It Right"', *Case Program,* No. C16-94-1251.0, Kennedy School of Government (Harvard University, Cambridge, 1991).

33. See Loch K. Johnson, *Secret Agencies: US Intelligence in a*

Hostile World (Yale University Press, New Haven, 1996), ch. 6.

34. See the Report of the Commission on the Roles and Capabilities of the United States Intelligence Community, *Preparing for the 21st Century: An Appraisal of US Intelligence* (US Government Printing Office, Washington, DC, 1 March 1996), p. 22 (hereafter the Aspin-Brown Commission). Intelligence community information derived from legal (open) methods and provided to private firms (usually through intermediaries, like the Department of Commerce) is commonly referred to as 'business intelligence'.

35. In 1995, French counter-intelligence authorities caught the CIA in an espionage operation against the government-affiliated telecommunications company France-Telecom, temporarily setting back US-French relations (David E. Sanger and Tim Weiner, 'Emerging Role for the C.I.A.: Economic Spy', *New York Times* [15 October 1995], p. A1).

36. According to a report from the General Accounting Office (GAO), fifty-four American defence contractors were part of parent companies owned by foreign interests ('Defense Industrial Security: Weaknesses in US Security Arrangements with Foreign-Owned Defense Contractors' [GAO, Washington, DC, February 1996]).

37. Comment, public meeting of the Aspin-Brown Commission, Washington, DC (19 January 1996).

38. Statement provided to the author by the DCI's Office of Congressional Affairs, Langley, Virginia (7 February 1995). The Gates and Woolsey reaffirmations may be found, respectively, at: Gates, remarks, Economic Club of Detroit, *op. cit.*, p. 9; and Woolsey, 'The Future of Intelligence on the Global Frontier', address, Executive Club of Chicago (19 November 1993), as well as Woolsey, testimony, *Hearings*, Select Committee on Intelligence, US Senate, 103rd Cong., 1st Sess. (2 February 1993).

39. Quoted in Zelikow, in *In from the Cold, op. cit.*, p. 236.

Hale's more eloquent expression was, 'I regret that I have but one life to lose for my country.'

40. For the involvement of other nations in industrial espionage, see Mike Frost and Michel Gratton, *Spyworld: Inside the Canadian and American Establishments* (Doubleday, Toronto, 1994), pp. 224–7; American Institute for Business Research, *Protecting Corporate America's Secrets in the Global Economy* (1992), pp. 41, 45; Craig Whitney, 'Germany Finds that Spies Are Still Doing Business', *New York Times* (9 September 1993), p. 1; and Randall M. Fort, 'Economic Espionage: Problems and Prospects', *Consortium for the Study of Intelligence* (Washington, DC, 1993), p. 3.

41. See Stansfield Turner, 'Intelligence for a New World Order', *Foreign Affairs* 70 (Fall 1991), pp. 151–2. Then-Chairman of the Senate Select Committee on Intelligence, David L. Boren (D, Oklahoma) endorses this view; see his 'The Intelligence Community: How Crucial?', *Foreign Affairs* 71 (Summer 1992), p. 58. In the early 1970s, the President's Foreign Intelligence Advisory Board (PFIAB) also advocated industrial espionage by the United States (Ernst, *op. cit.*, p. 328).

42. See John Maggs, 'From Swords to Plowshares', *Journal of Commerce* (18 August 1995), p. 1; author's interviews with senior officials in the Departments of Commerce and State, Washington, DC (24 June 1999).

43. Robert M. Gates, testimony, *Hearings*, Sub-Committee on Economic and Commercial Law, Judiciary Committee, US House of Representatives, 102d Cong., 2d Sess. (29 April 1992); the Senate figures are from S. 1556 (104th Cong., 2d Sess., 2 January 1996), reported by Edwin Fraumann (an FBI official), 'Economic Espionage: Security Missions Redefined', *Public Administration Review* 57 (July/August 1997), p. 303.

44. The survey was published by the American Society for Industrial Security in 1996 and reported in John J. Fialka,

'Stealing the Spark: Why Economic Espionage Works in America', *Washington Quarterly* 19 (1996), p. 180; for the Cox Committee findings, see *Report*, Select Committee on US National Security and Military/Commercial Concerns with the People's Republic of China, US House of Representatives, 106th Cong., 1st Sess. (Government Printing Office, Washington, DC, May 1999).

45. See Clarke and Johnston, *op. cit.*, p. 415.

46. Fraumann, *op. cit.*, p. 308.

47. Quoted in 'Votre Secrets, Monsieur?' *Security Management* (October 1992), cited by Merrill E. Whitney and James D. Gaisford, 'Economic Espionage As Strategic Trade Policy', *Canadian Journal of Economics* 29 (April 1996), p. 627.

48. Fort, *op. cit.*; Fraumann, *op. cit.*, p. 308.

49. Fraumann, *op. cit.*, p. 306.

50. 18 USC, secs. 1831–9.

51. Jeff Gerth and David E. Sanger, 'Citing Security, US Spurns China on a Satellite Deal', *New York Times* (23 February 1999), p. A1. The Clinton administration subsequently allowed the sale.

52. Gregory F. Treverton, 'Intelligence since Cold War's End', in *In from the Cold, op. cit.*, p. 115.

53. Woolsey, 'World Threat Assessment Brief', *op. cit.*, p. 9.

54. C.R. Neu, NIO for Economics, 'Comments on Economic Intelligence', Institute for International Economics (25 April 1995), p. 2.

55. On this hostility, see Michael Wines, 'Straining to See the Real Russia', *New York Times* (2 May 1999), p. 1 (Sec. 4).

56. Nicholas D. Kristof and Sheryl WuDunn, 'Of World Markets, None an Island', *New York Times* (17 February 1999), p. A9.

57. The poll was conducted by the Russian newspaper *Izvestiya* (23 January 1998) and provided to the author during an interview with the director, DCI Crime and Narcotics

Center, Central Intelligence Agency, Langley, Virginia (21 June 1999).

58. 'The struggle of the last half century was to defeat Communism,' writes Representative James A. Leach (R, Iowa), with respect to Russia's economic troubles, 'the challenge in the years ahead will be to constrain corruption' ('The New Russian Menace', *New York Times* [10 September 1999], p. A27).

59. Porteous, *op. cit.*, p. 199. For ample documentation of this institutional jealousy during recent international financial crises, see Zelikow, 'American Intelligence and the World Economy', *op. cit.*; and Ernest R. May, 'Intelligence: Backing into the Future', *Foreign Affairs* 48 (Summer 1992), pp. 63–72.

60. Porteous, *op. cit.*

61. Neu, *op. cit.*, p. 6.

62. Neu, *op. cit.*, pp. 2–3.

63. According to Neu, *op. cit.*, p. 3.

64. R. James Woolsey, during a question-and-answer period following his address, 'The Future Direction of Intelligence', Center for Strategic and International Studies, Washington, DC (18 July 1994).

65. Aspin-Brown Commission, *op. cit.*, p. 23. Intelligence officials claim to have uncovered bribes affecting $30 billion in foreign contracts between 1992 and 1995 (James Risen, 'Clinton Reportedly Orders CIA to Focus on Trade Espionage', *Los Angeles Times* [23 July 1995], p. A14).

66. Treverton, *op. cit.*, p. 115.

67. Author's interviews with senior government officials, Washington, DC (21–24 June 1999).

68. *Ibid.*

69. Maggs, *op. cit.*; Weiner (1995), *op. cit.*

70. Jane Perlez, 'Clinton Pushes for Treaty to Ban the Worst Child Labor Practices', *New York Times* (17 June 1999), p. A17.

71. Woolsey (1995), *op. cit.*, p. 10.

72. The Center has other concerns related to economic matters as well, including corrupt business practices, contraband, financial fraud, environmental crime, alien smuggling, arms trafficking, and the kidnapping of women and children for illegal labour practices.

73. Loch K. Johnson, 'Smart Intelligence', *Foreign Policy* 89 (Winter 1992–3), pp. 53–70.

74. Christopher S. Wren, 'A Purer, More Potent Heroin Lures New Users to a Long, Hard Fall', *New York Times* (9 May 1999), p. 27.

75. David Broder, 'To Win the War on Drugs', *Washington Post* (2 May 1999), p. B7.

76. The CIA continues to claim it has solid evidence that Empta was in fact being made, and that the plant in question had ties to Osama bin Laden. The Agency refuses to provide proof to the public, however, on grounds that its *modus operandi* would be compromised for future operations (author's interviews with senior intelligence officers, Langley, Virginia [18 February and 15 June 1999]). Other government 'officials' have suggested to a reporter that the plant 'was probably making nothing more dangerous than pharmaceuticals', Daniel Schorr, 'Washington Notebook', *New Leader* 82 (17–31 May 1999), p. 5.

77. Author's interviews, *ibid.*

78. *Ibid.*

79. Loch K. Johnson, 'Analysis for a New Age', *Intelligence and National Security* 11 (October 1996), pp. 657–71.

80. *Ibid.*

81. Author's interview with Bo Cutter, Washington, DC (26 June 1995).

82. *Ibid.*

83. Author's interviews with senior intelligence officers, Langley, Virginia (18 February 1999).

84. Testimony, *Hearings*, Foreign Relations Committee, US Senate, 103d Cong., 1st Sess. (4 November 1993).

85. Quoted by John M. Broder, 'President's Sober Response Assures Public of Counterespionage Measures', *New York Times* (26 May 1999), p. A15.

86. Highly placed policy-makers are frequently unaware of the intelligence origins of information they receive in staff briefings and government reports. As a result, they may blithely dismiss the secret agencies as largely unhelpful, while the deputy assistant secretaries who actually read the intelligence reports often have a more charitable view.

87. May, *op. cit.*, p. 65.

88. On this most secretive of the CIA's international economic activities, see Johnson, *Secret Agencies, op. cit.*, pp. 168–9.

EIGHT

MODERN INTELLIGENCE SERVICES: HAVE THEY A PLACE IN ETHICAL FOREIGN POLICIES?

Michael Herman

Michael Herman did his National Service in the Intelligence Corps and after reading modern history at Oxford joined GCHQ in 1952. He served there until 1987 with secondments to the Cabinet Office and the Ministry of Defence. After retirement he was a Gwilym Gibbon Research Fellow at Nuffield College, Oxford, and an Honorary Research Fellow of King's College, London, and Keele University. He has taught academic intelligence courses and published numerous intelligence articles. His book Intelligence Power in Peace and War *was published in 1996 by Cambridge University Press in conjunction with the Royal Institute of International Affairs, and has been reprinted twice.*

[An earlier version of this paper was published in Irish Studies in International Affairs 1999.*]*

Intelligence services are integral parts of the modern state; as Sir Reginald Hibbert put it in the late 1980s, 'over the past half-century secret intelligence, from being a somewhat bohemian servant or associate of the great departments of state, gradually acquired a sort of parity with them'.[1] They have not withered away with the end of the Cold War. There has been some reduction in this decade, but not to the same extent as in the armed forces, and intelligence budgets have recently levelled off.[2] American expenditure has been declared as $26 billion annually, around 10 per cent of the cost of defence, perhaps with some recent increases in human source collection.[3] The equivalent British budget is probably more than £1 billion, rather more than the cost of diplomacy.[4]

Does this investment pose questions of international morality? Most Western governments recognise issues of democratic accountability and restrictions on domestic targeting, but like the rest of the world accept the need for 'foreign intelligence'.[5] On coming to power the present Labour Secretary of State, Robin Cook, emphasised the ethical dimension of his foreign policy, but at the end of his first year spoke with unexpected warmth of the intelligence support he had received.[6] The Clinton administration sponsored a study of the CIA's ethics, but what emerged focused on intellectual integrity, not morality.[7] The media makes great play with intelligence leaks, whistle-blowing and failures, but remains thrilled by secrecy. Its ethical concerns over intelligence tend to be inward-looking, on its part in what is criticised as the domestically repressive 'national security state', rather than on its foreign coverage. *The Times* pronounced in 1999 that 'Cold War or no Cold War, nations routinely spy on each other.'[8]

Nevertheless an underlying liberal distaste is evident for 'stealing others' secrets'.[9] Peter Wright's autobiographical account of his 'bugging and burglary' of foreign embassies in London is frequently quoted.[10] John le Carré's novels denigratingly portrayed Soviet and Western intelligence as two halves of the same apple.[11] CIA-bashing remains a world industry, an element in the *bien pensant* view that the US is 'becoming the rogue superpower'.[12] At a more thoughtful level, two British academics have dismissed all espionage as 'positively immoral' apart 'from certain extreme cases' (undefined).[13]

This points to a genuine if muted question about intelligence and ethical foreign policy. An Oxford student recently asked his college chaplain whether a Christian could apply in good conscience to work in intelligence; what was the right reply? Intelligence as an institution is an accepted part of the fabric of international society, but does it make for a better world or a worse one? Does it make any ethical difference at all? These are questions for intelligence practitioners as well as governments and publics. This paper seeks to explore them.

Starting Points

Intelligence has to be judged in the first instance by its obviously observable consequences. One test is whether it increases or decreases international tension and the risks of inter-state war.[14] Another, more topical test is whether it promotes or retards international co-operation in a world that now has elements of 'a true world community, with global responsibility for the preservation of a just order'.[15]

Yet judging it solely in this pragmatic way seems incomplete. The code of conduct that deters individuals from reading each others' mail does not rest only on the risks and consequences of being found out, and states are arguably also bound by more than reciprocal self-interest. The American authority on the history of codebreaking concluded (even during the Cold War) that it was 'surreptitious, snooping, sneaking . . . the very opposite of all that is best in mankind'.[16] Kant condemned wartime espionage not only for its consequences (that it 'would be carried over into peacetime'), but also since it was 'intrinsically despicable' and 'exploits only the dishonesty of others'.[17] Ethics is right conduct. The moral absolutist or intelligence pacifist cannot be kept entirely out of the discussion.

The 'foreign intelligence' to be judged in these ways is basically the Western model: an institution with some commitment to telling truth unto power, and some separation from the power itself. Contrary to Bacon's over-quoted dictum that knowledge is itself power, Western intelligence has on the whole not sought power or exercised it. Intelligence under Communism and in other authoritarian states has a quite different tradition and would require a separate critique. But the Western ideal of objectivity is not a purely regional one, and has some wider currency. Military intelligence everywhere seeks to know its enemy, and Western intelligence applies the same aspiration more widely, as part of government by reason rather than ideology or caprice. It now has a place, albeit inconspicuously, in liberal democracy's world-wide baggage. However much it is criticised for its failures, democratic rulers are in trouble with their electorates if they are known to have disregarded it.

Intelligence on this Western model needs to be considered in its two different aspects: the knowledge it produces, and the activities through which it produces it. Their effects differ. Thus the knowledge gained from Western overflights of the Soviet Union in the 1950s benefited international security through scaling down some exaggerated Western estimates of the Soviet threat; yet the flights themselves were threatening and provocative, culminating in the Soviet shoot-down of the U-2 on 1 May 1960 which wrecked the East-West Paris Summit a few days later.[18] Knowledge and activities can be examined separately but then have to be integrated into an ethical balance sheet.

Intelligence Knowledge

General Effects:
Intelligence knowledge is itself of two overlapping kinds: first, the product of special, largely secret collection and, second, assessments on those foreign subjects – mainly bearing on

national security – on which intelligence is the national expert.[19]
The common factor to both is some separation between intelligence and policy-making.

Some of this knowledge has no obvious ethical connotations.
Intelligence on the other side's negotiating positions may have figured in the 1999 US-European Union dispute over banana imports, but if so it is difficult to see a moral dimension for the intelligence or the diplomatic bargaining it served. Yet where intelligence knowledge bears on more obviously ethical issues of international security, justice and humanity, it can have some moral influence on its own account. If truth-seeking by the intelligence producers is linked with governments disposed to listen, the result is an improvement in international perception which – arguably – reduces what have been termed national leaders' 'war-conducive' acts of insensitivity, thoughtlessness and recklessness.[20]

Of course these conditions do not necessarily apply. Evil regimes are served by self-seeking intelligence, and even in better states leaders use intelligence as selectively as domestic statistics. Intelligence cannot stop governments being wicked or misguided, and it provides no magic key to the future. But (like statistics) it can do something in favourable conditions about governmental ignorance and misperception. John Gaddis argues that the Soviet documents from the Cold War show 'the dangers of making emotionally based decisions in isolation' when authoritarians do not consult experts.[21] Recent writing about the Indo-Pakistan crisis in 1999 has brought out leaders' mutual sense of siege, and the importance of 'methods of deployment, intelligence capabilities and command-and-control systems in reducing the risks of the antagonists' nuclear momentum; one hopes that intelligence in both countries is up to the job'.[22]

Even if this has some credence as a general proposition, good intelligence can still be accused of applying its own institutional 'spin', a *déformation professionelle* towards hawkish, 'worst case' assessments. Intelligence is partly a warning system; and as a former British JIC Chairman has put it, it specialises in 'the hard world of shocks and accidents, threats and crises . . . the dark side of the moon, history pre-eminently as the record of the crimes and follies of mankind'.[23] So it is not surprising if intelligence exaggerates threats and demonises enemies. It is bound to be sometimes misleading (again like statistics),[24] but the charge is that it tends to be misleading always in the same direction, giving policy and decisions a systemic bias.

Yet historically this is a caricature, not a measured judgement. There is indeed a danger of military intelligence reflecting the interest of the military-industrial lobby in increased defence expenditure, as was an element in the Cold War. Soldiers in any circumstances have to dwell on 'worst cases' since they pay the price of complacency. Intelligence's secrecy – 'if you knew what we know' – does not make criticism of hawkish assessments easy. But the overall intelligence record is far more varied than this image suggests. There are more instances of failing to detect surprise attacks than of ringing alarm bells for imaginary ones, and as many examples of underestimating opponents as exaggerating them. Moreover, institutional checks and balances can be devised to provide some safeguards against bias, as in the way the British JIC system allegedly produces an interdepartmental synthesis of military pessimism with diplomatic optimism – itself another caricature, but with a grain of truth in it. International discussion of intelligence estimates is even more effective in improving standards. Intelligence can err by striving too hard to be 'useful' to its customers, but this is balanced by the ethic of professional objectivity, the practitioner's self-image of exposing 'all those who won't listen to all the things they don't want to know',[25] and the importance of international reputation. The effect over time is that governments that take note of Western-style intelligence behave as better international citizens than those that operate without it.[26]

Specific Applications:

This conclusion is supported by more specific connections with international morality, many of them springing from America's world role and its unmatched superpower intelligence. Intelligence is part of the American security umbrella over China's and North Korea's intentions towards their Pacific neighbours. It figures in America's role as international mediator, providing stabilisation and reassurance. As part of the settlement after the 1973 Yom Kippur War, Henry Kissinger undertook to provide Egypt and Israel with intelligence from regular airborne sorties.[27] The power of satellite surveillance has subsequently given a new dimension to this part of the American security toolkit. The effect of intelligence briefings given to India and Pakistan in 1990 to prevent their drifting towards war illustrates intelligence satellites' place in the armoury of American power.[28] Similar intelligence support will presumably be offered to Israel in compensation for eventual withdrawal from the Golan Heights.

Nevertheless intelligence contributions of this kind to international security are by no means limited to the American ones, and they extend beyond specific situations to a group of worldwide and long-term security issues. Terrorism is one such; the limitation of weapons of mass destruction and other arms proliferation is another, through the Missile Technology Control Regime, the Nuclear Suppliers Group and others of this kind; and international sanctions are a third category of wide-ranging, intelligence-driven co-operation. International arrangements between intelligence professionals underpin these political agreements. National intelligence tips off collaborating nations, or is used to keep them from backsliding.

It also supports the many agreements that now exist for arms control and other confidence-building measures. Historically it bore the main weight of arms-control verification in the Cold War; the US-Soviet strategic arms-control agreements of the

1970s depended entirely on intelligence for verification, since on-site inspection was still unacceptable to the Soviet Union. These agreements even had provisions for co-operative displays to each party's imagery satellites, and limitations on the encipherment of radio-telemetry from missiles. Astonishingly, the superpower antagonists undertook in this way to facilitate each other's secret intelligence collection.[29]

Arms-control and confidence-building agreements now have large symbolic elements, but where there are real tensions, as between India and Pakistan, intelligence still operates in synergy with any agreements reached for transparency. Intelligence triggers treaty-based inspections; inspections plus declared confidence-building data provide leads for intelligence; each checks and steers the other. National Technical Means of collection (the Cold War euphemism for intelligence) were recognised in 1996 in the Comprehensive Test Ban Treaty as legitimate triggers for international on-site inspection.[30] The power of modern intelligence is a prop, perhaps not sufficiently recognised, for the advocates of nuclear reduction or elimination.

Intelligence's most dramatic impact in recent years has however been in support for international intervention. Iraq since the Gulf War has been a classic intelligence target of almost Cold War difficulty, and UNSCOM-IAEA inspections of Iraqi compliance with the Gulf War peace terms leaned heavily on national intelligence inputs, with as many as twenty nations contributing data.[31] Action over the no-fly zones and the Kurdish sanctuary has been similarly intelligence-steered.

Iraq may be *sui generis*, but Bosnia and Kosovo have represented what seems the new pattern of intelligence support for international intervention of all kinds. All those responsible for such operations, from the UN Secretary-General downwards, have emphasised the need for good intelligence.[32] A deluge of information is available from the many non-intelligence sources – the media, diplomatic reporting, deployed military units,

NGOs, international officials – but all concerned echo T.S. Eliot's cry in *The Rock*: 'Where is the wisdom we have lost in knowledge?/Where is the knowledge we have lost in information?'

National intelligence is relied upon to fill gaps, validate other sources and, above all, *assess*. The concept of graduated force, surgical strikes, low casualties and minimum collateral damage is intelligence-dependent. Military forces deployed in peace-enforcement and peace-building need virtually the full range of wartime intelligence support, and providing evidence on crimes against humanity now adds a whole new set of intelligence requirements.[33] International intervention is snowballing and – as put in one of the British agencies' recruitment literature – 'government cannot make the right decisions unless it has the full picture'.[34] Kosovo has dramatically demonstrated the paradox of highly public international operations depending crucially on secret intelligence.

Meeting the need poses many problems. America's leading role cannot be guaranteed,[35] and in any case other participating nations have to be accommodated in the intelligence structure. Its intelligence dependence on America is a current issue for the European Union; coalitions of the willing need shared information, with some confidence that it is not being rigged by the US with British connivance. Small powers have the dilemmas posed by supporting international action while taking others' intelligence assessments on trust.

Yet the problems should not obscure modern intelligence's ability to deliver the goods. Satellites' scope is ever-increasing, as is the capability of high-flying aircraft and drones. So too are the opportunities provided by the electronic world in which every detachment commander, insurgent leader, terrorist director, hostage-taker or international drug-dealer has his mobile phone or communicates via the Internet. The cases of collateral damage in the bombing of Serbia should not divert attention from what the campaign showed of the power of sophisticated technical collection combined with precise weaponry. 'There are now no places on Earth that cannot be subjected to the same relentless harrowing . . . . The World Order looks better protected than it did the day before the bombing began.'[36]

This support for international order may at last be making intelligence respectable; or at least *some* intelligence. In her aid programme for developing countries, Clare Short as Britain's Secretary of State for International Development has endorsed strengthening 'the capacity of [local] intelligence services to assess genuine outside threats'.[37] Considering her radical background, this could be taken as game, set and match for intelligence's ethical justification.

Intelligence Activities

The Ethical Spectrum:

But if this applies to intelligence's knowledge, there is still the problem of its activities. About 90 per cent of intelligence expenditure is on secret collection; is this a form of anti-social international behaviour? Absolutists hanker after a Woodrow Wilson-like world of open information openly acquired. Pragmatists may have no objection to covert methods *per se* but may worry about the effects. International law suggests some constraints, though actually not many. From any of these viewpoints it might be held that intelligence's activities undo the good done by the knowledge they produce.

Here a first approach is to consider the collection methods intelligence uses, to recognise their variety and broad ethical spectrum. At one extreme no questions of propriety are posed by intelligence's use of public information and the results of military and diplomatic observations and contacts. Something of the same applies to some of its own peacetime collection, despite the secret intelligence label. Ships and aircraft collect intelligence in international waters and airspace without accusations of illegality, as do armies when deployed overseas (though the media always tags similar civilian observations as 'spying').[38] Satellite photography violates no international law and is now more or less accepted as a commercial as well as an intelligence activity.[39] *Pace* Kant, wartime intelligence-gathering is free from any legal or moral restraint, except on the torture of prisoners under interrogation. (There is also a legal concept of 'treachery',[40] but it has not yet been applied to intelligence.) Yet a wartime effort has to be operational in peacetime and cannot sit twiddling its thumbs.

Other types of intelligence collection and exploitation have less legitimacy, but are tolerated provided that they remain undeclared. Most electronic interception is at relatively long ranges and provides no indication of its precise targets; despite national privacy legislation, transmission via the ether is intrinsically a public means of communication. Routine anti-Americanism does not usually extend to condemning US technical collection.[41] Russia now has a separate and probably effective codebreaking organisation, but no one loses much sleep over it. Armed forces assume intelligence coverage of them, and diplomats are not fussed by having their telegrams intercepted. Intelligence collection in these categories does not seem particularly intrusive. Governments' attitudes to it have echoes of current American policy over homosexuality in the armed forces: 'Don't ask, don't tell.'

Some other collection has bigger ethical question-marks against it. The Western overflights of the USSR in the 1940s and 1950s, by balloons as well as aircraft, were clear breaches of territorial integrity, as was the West's intelligence collection in Soviet territorial waters incompatible with maritime law on innocent passage.[42] There is also the doubtful status of embassies, as both intelligence targets and intelligence bases. Suborning foreign embassy staff to provide documents or ciphers has a long history, but the Cold War added the new dimension of bugging and electronic attacks against their premises. The new US embassy in Moscow has had to be abandoned, unused, hopelessly penetrated with microphones and bugs.[43] Gordievsky's autobiography recounts the claustrophobic precautions taken in the Soviet embassy in London.[44] An American diplomat has written with honesty of the effects on his diplomatic judgement of being under intelligence siege in Moscow: 'it was hard not to let that situation impact on your own view of the former USSR'.[45]

The converse of this targeting of embassies has been the development in this century of 'diplomatic cover' for agent-runners and recruiters, after diplomats became too respectable to do this work themselves. Some embassies subsequently became bases for electronic interception; sixty-two Soviet listening-posts of this kind were reported to be in action late in the Cold War.[46] On most counts these various features of twentieth-century diplomatic life sit awkwardly with the 1961 Vienna Convention which governs it. On the one hand, this provides for the inviolability of diplomatic missions and their premises. On the other, it describes diplomacy's function as ascertaining conditions in the host country *by all lawful means*, with the stipulation that diplomatic premises are not to be used 'in any manner incompatible with the function of the mission as laid down in the present Convention or by other rules of general international law or by any special agreements in force between the receiving and sending state'.[47]

Most questioned of all is peacetime espionage, irrespective of any diplomatic involvement. In reality some human agents are just extensions of diplomatic sources; governments need some inconspicuous and unavowed contacts, as with the IRA before the 'peace process'. Others are like confidential press sources. But the dominant image is of the spy engaged in deeply concealed espionage. Some even of this espionage is defensive, part of the conflict between intelligence attack and defence; despite the American shock-horror over Ames as a Moscow agent in the

CIA, his effect was to reveal US espionage in Russia.[48] Some spies have patriotic or ideological motives, though avarice and other human weaknesses loom equally large; in 1995 the CIA was restricted over recruiting 'unsavoury' agents.[49] Whatever the motives, espionage is feared for the damage it can do, and evokes the reaction associated with the betrayer, the Judas, the traitor, akin perhaps to the 'moral panic' over some domestic crime.[50] In England the betrayal of secrets to the Crown's enemies was identified with treason even before the 1351 Treason Act. The same feeling attaches itself to foreign covert action, for which intelligence is usually the executive agent. The intensity of Soviet espionage and covert action left a deep imprint on Western attitudes, reinforcing atavistic fears of the enemy within, and ambivalence about using such methods oneself.[51] Authoritarian regimes share the fears, though not the scruples.[52]

This survey suggests some inverse correlation between ethical acceptability and the degree of intrusion in intelligence's methods, but the picture is not clear, and international law does little to clarify it. The laws of war permit the execution of spies, but wartime espionage is not itself illegal; 'the spy remains in his curious legal limbo; whether his work is honourable or dishonourable, none can tell'.[53] No one knows what the Vienna Convention's 'lawful means' and 'rules of general international law' actually signify for diplomatic collection methods. Violations of national territory are illegal, but there is no code of conduct for information-gathering *per se*. The liberal repugnance for covert means cannot be discounted, but there is no international law of states' privacy. Moreover, the state cannot defend its own secrets properly without being up-to-date on offensive techniques; the effective gamekeeper has to be a competent poacher.

Thus considering methods *in vacuo* does not get us very far. In reality the scale of intelligence operations may be as important as the precise methods used, particularly since all intelligence tends to be tarred with the brush of espionage (as in the way the media always refers to the British SIGINT agency, quite inaccurately, as 'the Cheltenham spy centre'). Most Western airborne and shipborne collection around the Soviet periphery did not infringe national airspace; yet the sheer weight of it probably reinforced Cold War tensions and threat perceptions. Some forty American aircraft were shot down in the first decade and a half of the Cold War, as well as the two innocent South Korean passenger aircraft much later, with grievous losses.[54] The political circumstances are equally important; the Indian shooting down of a Pakistani electronic aircraft in August 1999 reflected the state of tension as well as exacerbating it. Ethical judgements probably need to link methods with scale and cumulative effects, but the nature of the targets and reasons for targeting are also a factor.

Targeting of Non-States and International 'Baddies':
Here a shift over the last decade is important. Foreign intelligence is now directed more than previously towards two relatively new targets. One is the 'non-state' category, ranging from fragmented and dissolving states, through independence movements, terrorists, international criminals and illegal dealers in nuclear material, to others at the security-threatening end of the trading spectrum. The other, linked with the first group, is the small group of rogue states, exemplified by the Milošević regime or states supporting terrorism. Many of these new targets, whether state or non-state, are either international 'baddies', or actors in scenes of actual or incipient mayhem. In targeting them, most governments have altruistic motives overlaying narrow national interests, with intelligence's tasking manifesting ethical foreign policy in a direct way.

Arguably this combination of targets and policy objectives moves intelligence's ethical goalposts virtually to a wartime position; in a sufficiently good cause, against such targets, almost anything goes. Intelligence may be needed on potential victims of violence to effect their protection. Foreign non-state entities and failed states have no international rights of privacy, and rogue states have forfeited them by bad conduct, especially if they are gross violators of human rights. The baddies are at war with international society, deliberately or implicitly by rejecting civilised standards. Unlike armed force, intelligence does not kill or cause suffering. Though he was speaking of military intelligence rather than covert collection, a thoughtful Victorian officer pointed out that 'the pursuit of intelligence has not, like swollen armaments, any tendency to bring about war'.[55]

Yet it can still be argued that some intelligence methods are ethically unacceptable in any circumstances. Using robust methods in special cases may be seductive; 'the exception would become part of the norm'.[56] Intelligence may be harmless in itself, but there is a danger of slipping into the defence that 'guns do not kill people; people kill people'. Whatever the morality of the bombardment of Serbia, intelligence power was a prime element, not just an incidental supporter.

Ideally such problems of conscience might be solved by UN mandates. Thus at the end of the Gulf War the Security Council's request to all states to give UNSCOM 'maximum assistance, in cash and in kind' was interpreted to include intelligence.[57] Yet it is difficult to see the UN leading with ethical criteria over intelligence methods. Its image is one of rectitude and transparency, and indeed has suffered from the allegations that UNSCOM cover was used for covert CIA operations.[58] It can be expected to favour the 'don't ask, don't tell' approach to the sources of the national intelligence it receives. In the long run the UN will need to sponsor some intelligence collection and assessment on its own account, in the way UNSCOM had its own analysis unit plus American U-2 collection at its disposal; but that is a separate issue. For the time being the absolutist probably has to deal with intelligence's ethical problems without much UN guidance.

For the pragmatist, of course, the problems *on these targets* – the limitation must be repeated – these absolutist concerns do not carry great weight. The greater the ethical emphasis in foreign policy, the less concern is needed over intelligence's methods and scale, always assuming that this collection is necessary. The scale of international suffering and crimes against humanity is a powerful warrant for intrusive collection, as is rogue states' sponsorship of terrorism and assassination of their political opponents overseas.

Targeting of Legitimate States:
But most intelligence is still directed against normal states whose behaviour does not put them beyond the pale, and here other considerations apply. International society is a society of states bound by co-operation, or at least toleration; they do not behave as if in a complete state of nature. The avoidance of inter-state aggression and war remains one of the world's highest priorities. Governments' reticence about intelligence collection is not related only to source protection, and implies a conflict with a tacit code of international behaviour over information-gathering, albeit a shadowy one. Some states with particularly close relationships refrain from regular covert collection against each other; much as they would like it, the US and Canada probably do not tap each other's telephones to get access to the other's bottom line in their many economic and other negotiations. Even where special relationships do not exist, responsible states think twice about using the more intrusive and risky intelligence methods against others; not all states are fair game for anything. Even against antagonists, issues of prudence arise over covert operations which (if discovered) will be taken as insults or confirmations of hostility. Cold War documents show British Ministers balancing the intelligence benefits from airborne collection, including U-2 flights based on Britain, against the effects on Anglo-Soviet relations.[59]

Of course states' behaviour depends on the facts of particular cases: the targets, the methods and the risks of being found out. But generally speaking it has not been assumed in the West that peacetime intelligence had complete *carte blanche*, whether the targets were friendly states or unfriendly ones. Vestiges persist of British Victorian rectitude over covert methods and the pre-Second World War American maxim that 'Gentlemen don't read each others' mail', even though neither has been observed with any consistency (and the American quotation was a post-1945 rationalisation).[60]

These inhibitions exist; yet over the last decade they do not seem to have significantly limited intelligence's scale and methods. Press reports suggest the opposite; more espionage cases hit the media now than in the Cold War. Most of the permanent members of the Security Council have been accused of spying on each other, and membership of the European Union does not seem to convey immunity from being targeted by fellow-members. Russia seems to have sought an intelligence *détente* in the early 1990s – the last head of the KGB handed over the bugging plans for the new US Moscow embassy; there was some release of Soviet intelligence records; public statements claimed that its successor Foreign Intelligence Service was contracting its overseas collection and sought international co-operation[61] – but this period has now passed. The KGB's foreign intelligence successors are now flourishing, active and influential; and China's coup in acquiring American nuclear secrets is said to rival the Soviet successes of the 1940s. The Russian Federal Security Service claimed to have caught eleven foreign agents and thwarted thirty-nine attempts to send secret information abroad in the first half of 1997.[62] Other countries are following these leads. Early in the 1990s a respected historian foresaw that claimants to regional dominance would seek superiority in intelligence collection, producing 'upward spirals and a new intelligence war'.[63] Reports that intelligence expenditure in the Far East had doubled from the end of the Cold War to 1997 may support his prognosis, as has the Chinese and North Korean concern reported over Japanese proposals to launch intelligence satellites within four or five years.[64] The media may exaggerate, but it seems that the global Information Age has in no way reduced states' interest in acquiring others' secrets.

Does It Matter?:

Does this affect inter-state relationships? Much of it is accepted as part of the international system. Except in special relationships, intelligence collaboration between states has never been seen to rule out some discreet targeting of each other. It cannot be *demonstrated* that collection on either friends or enemies has affected the climate of the 1990s. Its economic espionage has not caused France to be blackballed in the European Union. Intelligence threats have not consistently increased military confrontation in Korea, South Asia or South Lebanon, and did not provoke the war between Eritrea and Ethiopia. Conventional wisdom tolerates espionage on *The Times*'s grounds that everybody does it.

Yet it seems unrealistic to exclude intelligence from the unquantifiable grit of international friction. Collection is necessarily *against* someone; attack necessitates defence. Even if collection has been somewhat reduced from the Cold War scale, it is difficult to believe that its more intrusive aspects do not have cumulative effects in reinforcing conflicts and impairing international co-operation. The targeting of diplomacy, and the facilities which diplomacy itself provides for intelligence, hardly promote the diplomatic function described by Alan James as 'the communications system of the international society'.[65] Ernest Bevin as Foreign Secretary said that a better world would involve being able to cross the Channel without a passport; his modern successors might say that it would involve discussing secrets abroad without worrying about foreign bugging. Being able to operate without reckoning with covert intelligence attacks may be a factor – if only a minor one – in the special quality of the English-speaking transatlantic and Old Commonwealth relationships, and perhaps of those of the Scandinavian countries. Intelligence-gathering within the EU hardly makes it easier for it to stagger towards its Common Foreign and Security Policy. Espionage is said to be a factor in the low state of US-Chinese relations.[66] Most important of all, the continuation of the Cold War pattern of intelligence attack and defence surely has some influence on relationships between Russia on the one hand and the US plus NATO on the other.[67]

Perhaps the more open modern world helps to make covert intelligence more disturbing. In the age of world-wide investigative journalism, intelligence is now far more exposed than formerly; few secrets remain secrets. Foreign policies are now more influenced by domestic politics, and it is difficult for politicians and opinion-formers to accept foreign intelligence attacks as natural parts of the international game. The modern humanitarian morality that 'something must be done' takes effective intelligence for granted, yet at the same time prizes international legality and clean hands. Even before the present British Government's ethical foreign policy, its predecessor endorsed a 'moral base' for its defence doctrine; the 'concept of propriety, which seeks to ensure that the activities of the armed forces are viewed universally as being justifiable, fair, and apolitical'.[68] It can be argued that intelligence everywhere – an aspect of national power, like armed forces – needs a similar ethical foundation.

Balance Sheet and Desiderata

Despite intelligence's modern status, what states do is worth more ethical scrutiny than the intelligence they use and the activities that produce it. Some intelligence knowledge does not affect the ethical standards of the foreign policies it influences, and many intelligence activities have no ethical significance in themselves. Nevertheless, part of intelligence's knowledge and a smaller proportion of its activities probably have some general (and contradictory) effects on the morality of international society.

The ethical case for this knowledge is fairly clear. Despite intelligence's failures and distortions, its rationales of information-seeking and objectivity tend to make those leaders who draw on it behave 'better' internationally than those less concerned with an intelligence view of reality, or less exposed to it. (Governments that encourage objective intelligence may well be inclined anyway to 'better' international behaviour than those that do not, but intelligence probably has some institutional influence.) The international community working *qua* community depends upon national intelligence inputs, particularly from American technical collection. It needs intelligence as much as the population, health and environmental data that are other foundations for international action.

Yet a minority of intelligence collection poses ethical problems. On some targets the ends justify the intelligence means, though perhaps not completely. (Should one torture terrorists to forestall imminent operations?[69] Perhaps one should.) On the other hand, the more intrusive methods of peacetime collection – espionage, some bugging, and perhaps diplomatic targeting and the exploitation of diplomatic immunities – probably are disturbing factors when used against legitimate states. The situation is not static. 'Since the end of the Cold War a universal international system has come into existence marked by the unprecedented situation in which almost all states are in diplomatic relations with other states.'[70] This aspect of globalisation sits uncomfortably with the prospect that 185 states and statelets may all invest in covert intelligence collection to keep up with the international Joneses. If international arms limitation is a desirable objective, why not limit intrusive intelligence?

This balance sheet suggests three *desiderata* for strengthening the international attitudes and norms that already exist. The *first* is to recognise that the Western idea of objective, all-source intelligence assessment on foreign affairs, with some separation from policy-making, is a necessary part of the modern, global standard of government. All states should be encouraged to develop the machinery, in the spirit of Ms Short's commendation of intelligence to the developing world.[71] The CIA's Directorate of Intelligence with its remit for analysis and assessment should be an international role-model, and it is tragic that historical accident has caused it to be identified with the covert collection and covert action of the Agency's Directorate of Operations.

Second is to emphasise the place of international exchanges between states at this 'finished intelligence' level. International action is no more cohesive than the intelligence exchanges that underlay it. The UN, EU, NATO and other regional institutions will eventually develop machinery for supranational intelligence assessment, but it will be a long haul and will have to build on inter-state exchanges. Two former American DCIs argued some years ago that American intelligence should become an international good,[72] and the US subsequently committed itself to intelligence support for international organisations.[73] To some extent this is already a *de facto* underpinning of international society, yet for its credibility the American input needs to be complemented by national intelligence institutions capable of critically assessing it for their own governments. States co-operating internationally need some kind of peer review of their own intelligence estimates. One wonders how far the *impasses* between NATO and Russia over Kosovo reflected different national intelligence inputs.

The *third* is to borrow the criteria of restraint, necessity and proportionality from Just War doctrine to discourage gung-ho

approaches to intrusive covert collection. Morality reinforces
the considerations of cost-effectiveness that covert methods
should only be used where overt material is inadequate. The
more intrusive the methods, the greater the justification needed;
recruiting additional human sources to fill the gaps in technical collection runs its own ethical risks. Ethics should be recognised as a factor in intelligence decisions, just as in anything
else, and the Western notion of elected leaders' accountability
for sensitive intelligence operations provides one way of reinforcing the ethical dimension. Similar considerations should be
applied to covert action, though the essential difference should
be recognised between the morality of information-gathering
and action. Perhaps more should be done to separate the two.

This restraint implies some re-ordering of collection priorities. National security matters should remain central and legitimate requirements. But to these can now be added those bearing
on international security, justice and humanitarian concerns.
John Keegan has argued that democracy's professional soldiers
are now international society's check upon violence; 'those
honourable warriors who administer force in the cause of
peace'.[74] *Mutatis mutandis*, national intelligence should now be
seen in this light.

The counterpoint to this approach is some limitation over
collection for purely national purposes, especially those unre-
lated to security. Throughout the 1990s it has been fashionable
outside the English-speaking countries to target covert collection on other countries' non-military secrets of economic, financial and technological kinds. Russia has seen this as a means of
solving its economic problems vis-à-vis the West. French publi-
cists have been rather proud of collection of this kind, though
it is by no means a purely Gallic activity.[75] The issues over government activity of this kind are complex, but as a generalisation it
is both provocative and overblown. The Soviet aircraft industry
is said to have copied stolen plans of Concorde; much good it

did them. Immediately after the Cold War some argued that US intelligence should be redeployed to the 'trade war' with Japan and Western Europe, and Washington deserves credit for substantially rejecting the case.[76] Even for governments that want to get into this field, using open and 'grey' sources and commercial information brokers is a better bet than tasking their intelligence agencies.

This restraint also implies extending the existing limitations on targeting other states for 'bargaining intelligence' on matters of purely national interest. Covert intelligence increases diplomatic effectiveness, but sometimes with the long-term costs already suggested. Firms in the private sector depend on reading their competitors' hands, but those that care about their reputations are careful about how they do so. Perhaps governments should exercise similar care over the intelligence methods used against friendly powers, and rely instead on journalists as the experts on intrusion.

These are desiderata for multilateral action, not for unilateral intelligence disarmament. They reflect Western views and Western cultural power – though a doctrinal restraint on intrusive methods would not come easily to the major Cold War powers, East or West. The US, Russia and Britain all have strong (and differing) reasons for keeping intelligence power unfettered. Yet the case remains for developing the present loose code of conduct through reciprocal or multinational understandings, probably inconspicuously. The problem is to demystify intelligence's role and make it a fit subject for international discourse.

Two features of international norms may be helpful. First, some evolve gradually through informal international contacts and the influence of 'world opinion'. The international patchwork of multilateral and bilateral intelligence relationships already provides scope for confidential discussion of intelligence purposes and priorities. In particular Western intelligence already has well-publicised links with Russia on international terrorism, drugs and other criminality, and evidence of war crimes, plus the military opportunities presented by the Partnership for Peace programme and other contacts. The publicity now given to intelligence objectives by Britain and America provides a basis for further discussion, with Russia and more widely.[77]

International understandings of any kind may seem an unlikely outcome, but are not impossible. Before the SALT I and II and ABM agreements of the 1970s, it would have seemed quite inconceivable that the superpowers would in effect legitimise aspects of each other's secret collection, yet they did.[78] Recently the OECD nations plus some others signed a 'bribery convention' in which 'the United States has got all the rich countries to play by roughly the same rules'.[79] This is still far removed from intelligence, but it is a reminder that unexpected things can happen when states are persuaded of common interests. Russia is reported to have pressed the UN Secretary-General in 1998 for an international treaty banning information warfare.[80] The possibility of mutual US and Russian reductions in espionage was raised, apparently from the American side, in July 1999 in Washington discussions between the US Vice-President and Russian Prime Minister, and remitted for further examination. The Prime Minister was removed from office shortly afterwards, but the idea has at least got to the conference table.[81]

Second, international law has a momentum of its own. An American naval officer writing on intelligence argued that there are limits of behaviour which 'create definable customary international norms . . . . To those who must work with these subjects, the norms are real, the boundaries tangible, and the consequences of exceeding them unacceptable – personally and professionally, nationally and internationally.'[82] Geoffrey Best takes us further by reminding us that 'much international law of the contemporary age . . . is "normative". Normative means standard-setting; adding to established State practice, the aspirational concept of State practice as it is expected, intended, or hoped to become at some future date.'[83] International law need not remain as silent on intelligence as it is now.

To sum up, intelligence is now a permanent part of the nation state. Even lesser states need it and will soon have it. There is plenty for it to do. But the new millennium should seek to emphasise internationally:

(a) the value of accurate knowledge and policy-free intelligence assessment of foreign affairs, based on all sources of information and not necessarily the product of covert collection. This should be recognised as a condition of good government in the globalised world;

(b) the increased relevance of national intelligence, both covert collection and all-source analysis, to the working of international institutions, and to other international action in the interests of security, justice and humanitarianism. International exchanges are a necessity for international society. International action is no more cohesive than the intelligence assessments that underlie it; and

(c) restraint in the use of the more intrusive methods of collection for purposes not geared to national security or support for the international community. Ethics should be a factor in intelligence decisions, as in all others.

In short, *The Times*'s dictum that 'Cold War or no Cold War, nations routinely spy on each other' provides a realistic starting-point for considering intelligence ethics, but is not the last word.

DISCUSSION

Admiral Pierre Lacoste

Admiral Pierre Lacoste fled to Morocco from occupied France in 1943 and became a French naval officer, serving for forty-two years, three times as a ship's captain, and also in signals and staff posts. He completed the Advanced Military Studies Centre and the Institute of Advanced National Defence Studies. He was promoted to Rear-Admiral in 1976 and became Commandant of the Advanced School of Naval Warfare. In 1978 he was military adviser to Prime Minister Raymond Barre, Commander of the Mediterranean Fleet in 1980, and in 1982 was appointed Head of Foreign Intelligence (DGSE). Since retirement in 1985, he has been President of the National Defence Studies Association (1986), Chairman of the National Defence Liaison Committee (DAN) (1989) and director of the Centre for the Scientific Study of Defence (CESD) at the University of Marne de la Vallée. His publications include Present-day Naval Strategies *(1986),* Mafias against Democracy *(1992),* An Admiral in the Secret Service *(1997), and* Intelligence the French Way *(1998) (all in French).*

I am honoured to have been asked to comment on Michael Herman's paper on ends and means of intelligence in an international perspective. As head of the French foreign intelligence service – DGSE – for less than three years, I do not consider myself to be a genuine professional in intelligence. Actually, from 1943 to 1982, during my career in the French navy, I was never directly involved in secret service activities. And later on, after I had retired in 1985, I made it a matter of principle not to interfere in the activities of my successors in the French Services, and therefore I no longer had access to confidential official papers.

However, for many reasons I am still interested in observing the intelligence world. As a former signals officer in the navy, I am particularly interested in developments in communications, electronics and computer sciences, and their applications in intelligence. Having headed a foundation for strategic studies, I still keep a close watch on relations between intelligence, national security, strategy and foreign affairs in the post-Cold War world. As a citizen and a democrat, I am troubled by the contradictions between secrecy and political transparency. I know how difficult it is to find a middle way between, on the one hand, clandestine collection that is an absolute necessity for collective security and national interest and, on the other hand, freedom of information that is a basic principle in all democratic regimes.

For this reason Michael Herman's paper is of genuine interest to me. Fifteen minutes being too short a time to make all the comments it deserves, I will restrict my intervention to three points.

1. The debate on ends and means is a fundamental one, but it is beyond intelligence, since many other aspects of the state's obligations are concerned; it is a matter of political philosophy.
2. Among the new factors of the present geopolitical situation, the rising power of 'non-state' actors has deeply modified the former conditions for intelligence practices.
3. The British model is unique, and other democratic regimes, even the US one, do not use intelligence in the same way.

In most public activities the question of ends and means is an ethical issue: how, for example, can we justify military violence? In what circumstances is it permissible? In the armed forces we know that it is seldom as clear as it is in wartime, as it was during the Second World War, when the aims of the Allies fighting against the Nazi and Japanese forces were perfectly sound. But nowadays national armies are involved in much more delicate situations: civil wars in foreign countries, peace-keeping, peace-enforcement, deterrence, coercion, and so on. Happily they have long known how to keep strict control of the organised means of military violence, how to apply extremely strict 'rules of behaviour' and 'rules of engagement'. Of course, this knowledge is at the root of the oldest military traditions. At the political level we observe similar obligations; in a regulated world, the United Nations Security Council has to legitimate military intervention.

I could find many other examples in different fields. Concerning the economy, the present globalisation of trade, industry, information networks, in a word, the 'world company syndrome', have profoundly modified the balance of economic powers; there is fierce competition, in which unilateral taxes, embargoes and other enforcement measures prove to be very effective weapons. However, who can say that they are really legitimate, especially when applied by a powerful country in order to protect its national interests without regard to the national interests of others?

As for intelligence matters, in wartime, espionage and 'dirty tricks' are traditional methods: 'the truth is so precious that it must be protected by a bodyguard of lies'. So the problem is to decide which wars are 'just wars'. When the Atlantic Alliance was fighting to protect and promote the values of democracy, the Soviet Union's objective was the success of the Marxist conception of human society. Many Islamic people are sincere when they become involved in a 'holy war' against the 'devilish' West.

In his presentation, Michael Herman mentioned the 'knowledge' aspects and the illegal sides of covert collection by human and technical means. But he has not mentioned other tasks of the secret services, such as invisible influence, covert action, or 'active measures'. Secrecy, discretion and professionalism are specific assets that are necessary in order to achieve such sensitive missions. Nowadays, in many sectors, I observe their development; for example, since the fall of the Soviet Empire, the behaviour of rich and powerful sects poses a real threat to certain eastern countries; but in the West who really cares? In terms of 'ends and means', is it acceptable to take advantage of a religion for espionage purposes? Adversaries of the secret services often point to some unacceptable methods of the dictatorial regimes in order to cast suspicion on all intelligence activities. We cannot disregard public opinion, which is always influenced by sensationalism, by the myths and fantasies of spy novels. But human rights include the protection of privacy; it is a right for individuals, for families, for corporations. Why then oppose the same rights for legitimate states? We must clearly affirm that a government is absolutely permitted to protect its own secrets and to launch investigations in order to obtain the confidential information that is necessary for its security and for the promotion of its vital interests. Prevention is now the primary justification for the existence of intelligence services. I am sure that most people are able to understand that argument.

I had the opportunity, in 1994, to present my personal views on the subject in a lecture at the Académie des sciences morales et politiques, a branch of the prestigious Académie Française. The title was 'Missions et éthique des Services spéciaux'. My conclusion was that, to perform their difficult tasks, the Services must rely upon men and women who are exclusively devoted to the public service, acting only for the collective interests of the nation. Just like judges, the police and the military, and many other civil servants in charge of sensitive situations, they must personally comply with the very strict moral obligations and ethical rules of their profession.

An important characteristic of present-day international society is the growing number of powerful new 'non-state' entities competing with the traditional legitimate states. In fact there are two worlds: the first one, symbolised by the United Nations, is in itself highly questionable, since single members can be so dissimilar, such as, for example, the US and the Bahamas, or Germany and Slovenia. Clearly, these states are not equals. Sovereignty is a myth, not to say mere hypocrisy, concerning many recently created 'mini or micro states'. The second world is also a mix of various structures. Some, like most multinational corporations or charitable NGOs – precisely called 'non-governmental' organisations – are truly honourable. Others, like some financial institutions or monopolistic media organisations, are more questionable. But another set of powers, the international mafias and large criminal organisations, do represent a very serious and dangerous threat to all societies. They are taking advantage of the opening of frontiers and they are skilfully using the discrepancies between various national laws and judicial procedures. That is why terrorists, war criminals, weapons and drug dealers, specialists in laundering and recycling dirty money, remain unpunished and are so prosperous. We know that law enforcement structures are drastically ineffective and that the balance sheet is clearly on the side of crime, not of the law.

Here is a new challenge for intelligence. The traditional limits between 'foreign intelligence' and domestic, police intelligence are blurred. The missions and the objectives of various official agencies overlap, increasing the opportunities for misunderstandings or fierce rivalries. International police co-operation is an obvious obligation, with the consequence that police officers are now posted to their national embassies abroad. At the same time, the foreign secret services, as well as military intelligence, have to collect police-related information and to track international criminal activities. Then another type of co-operation is necessary at the European and the international level, in which ex-enemies have to act together in their shared perception of common dangers.

Last but not least, it is fashionable today, for the sake of efficiency and cost cuts, to reject the bureaucratic state and to transfer its tasks to the private sector. Personally, I am not in favour of huge administrations, nor of state-owned industrial activities, but unfortunately my country is still the victim of old-fashioned Marxist ideas. On the other hand, I don't accept that privatisation can be extended to the specific obligations of a legal government, such as the armed forces or the secret services. Precisely in Bosnia, Africa, Afghanistan, it is well known that private companies are being used as a cover to equip and train local militias. I am shocked to see those who profess ethics, moral principles and democratic ideals actually involved with weapons dealers or fanatical Islamist mercenaries. But perhaps I am not 'politically correct'.

In his 1996 book *Intelligence Power in Peace and War*, Michael Herman revealed his own professional views perfectly plainly. His presentation offers a remarkable image of the British conception of intelligence. It is true to say that the British model inspired the origins of modern American intelligence in 1942. The experience of the Second World War proved the importance of technology: was GCHQ not the real 'father' of the NSA? One knows that nearly all the English-speaking countries have adopted similar principles to conduct their intelligence activities.

However, I believe that the Whitehall system of government remains a unique model. In fact, it is the result of long national traditions and political culture, where historical and sociological factors prevail. In the making of the British nation, sailors, merchants, businessmen and conquerors succeeded in the nineteenth century in building the largest empire in history. Fifty years ago its unique and extraordinary resistance to Hitler, its leadership for victory in the Second World War, offered exceptional opportunities for the leaders of this country to develop objective and reliable intelligence practices in the conduct of state affairs.

There is no similar background in other countries, even when they are genuinely democratic. In France, for example, the tradition is a very different one. In the UK, MI6 is placed under the authority of the Foreign Office, whereas the Quai d'Orsay has no institutional link with the foreign secret service; the majority of our diplomats ignore 'militarised' French intelligence; many of them are systematically hostile to '*les espions*'. Moreover, due to the collapse of the French army in June 1940, several generations of statesmen and military leaders have been totally unaware of the most secret aspects of the conduct of the war: for more than twenty years after 1945, nobody in French political circles, nor in the civil and military administrations, was conscious of the victorious role played by Enigma, Magic and other confidential aspects of Allied intelligence activities.

There is also an institutional aspect: successive French regimes have been profoundly different from Anglo-Saxon ones. To understand how intelligence matters are involved in the decision-making process, one must refer to specific French administrative regulations and political customs. The 'presidential' system of the Fifth Republic is by now quite different from the original 'Gaullist' model; it is possibly a paradox but, in my opinion, the present 'cohabitation' at the top of the double-headed French state has produced a better performance from the national intelligence organisation. And the post-Cold War crisis has opened the eyes of the politicians who are, by now, much more aware of its advantages, and support an increase in budgetary resources in favour of the secret services.

One cannot say that Michael Herman's model really fits American practice. Recent historical works have exposed some of the truth about the influence of political bias on the final product of the American intelligence community. This was especially clear under Henry Kissinger. Most recently, one can observe how the Presidential Foreign Intelligence Advisory Board (PFIAB), working on behalf of the White House, is trying to underestimate the success of the Chinese secret service in obtaining US nuclear secrets. That is clearly a partisan deviation, very different from the traditional neutrality of the British JIC. One knows also how very strange was the conduct of J. Edgar Hoover. He dominated the FBI for decades and never attempted to deal with drug issues or the Mafia; behaviour not so different from that of the boss of a political police force.

This is why I argue that intelligence is closely linked with the national culture. For instance, in France, as in several other Latin countries, the academic community ignores intelligence. For more than five years now, I have been trying to raise the interest of French scholars in the subject. Not a single French university department, nor any other branch of the academic world, has yet shown any concern. For the French universities, as well as for a great number of people who help to shape public opinion, intelligence is not a respectable activity; it is associated with dictatorial behaviour and military regimes.

To conclude, I will repeat that, in my view, the democratic nations must diligently nurture and develop their intelligence assets. They must keep them for the sake of a better-regulated international society in which, unfortunately, criminals and various kinds of 'trouble-makers' will always be active. Preventive actions are among the main specific responsibilities of the secret services in parallel with the law-enforcement activities of the police forces and the military actions of national armies.

To avoid the dangers and possible deviations in the delicate problems linked to intelligence practices, ethics remains the key word, both at the personal and institutional levels. That is why I am so affirmative when I say that governments must strongly resist transferring such responsibilities to the private sector.

[For lack of time, these two papers were regrettably not followed by a general discussion.]

Notes to Michael Herman's paper

1. R. Hibbert, 'Intelligence and Policy', *Intelligence and National Security*, vol. 5, no. 1 (January 1990), p. 115.
2. Contrary to the 'peace dividend' elsewhere, France planned a considerable expansion after the humiliation of depending on American intelligence in the Gulf War. (P. Kemp, 'The Rise and Fall of France's Spymasters', *Intelligence and National Security*, vol. 9, no. 1 [January 1994]).
3. 'Reborn CIA dusts off Cloak and Dagger', *Observer*, 14 March 1999. Expenditure for FY97 was $26.6 billion, and for FY98 $26.7 billion. Figures for FY99 have not been released; Congress is said to have approved an 'emergency' increase of $1.5–2.0 billion in the fall of 1998. (Press references summarised in Canadian Association for Security and Intelligence Studies *Newsletter* 34 (Winter 1999), p. 20.)
4. The three intelligence agencies have a published budget of about three-quarters of a million pounds, but the cost of MOD and other strategic intelligence needs to be added. For costs of 'the national intelligence capability', see the author's *British Intelligence towards the Millennium: Issues and Opportunities (London Defence Studies*, no. 38 [Centre for Defence Studies, London, 1997], pp. 7–9).
5. Within the European Union the Republic of Ireland may be an interesting exception.
6. Speech, 23 March 1998.
7. Kent Pekel, 'Integrity, Ethics and the CIA', in the CIA's *Studies in Intelligence* (Spring 1998), pp. 85–94.
8. Leader (26 May 1999).
9. The phrase 'stealing others' secrets' comes from a radio interview with one of the British secret agencies' recent whistle-blowers.
10. P. Wright, *Spycatcher: The Candid Autobiography of a Senior*

Intelligence Officer (Viking, NY, 1987), p. 54.

11. For a criticism of le Carré's moral stance, see J. Burridge, 'Sigint in the Novels of John le Carré', in the CIA's *Studies in Intelligence*, vol. 37, no. 5 (1994).

12. Attributed to Professor Huntingdon (as a comment on international opinion) by N. Chomsky, *The Guardian* (17 May 1999).

13. L. Lustgarten and I. Leigh, *In from the Cold: National Security and Parliamentary Democracy* (Clarendon Press, Oxford, 1994), p. 225. This work concentrates on intelligence's domestic aspects, but incidentally provides some ethical criticism of foreign intelligence.

14. Discussed in chapter 20 of the author's *Intelligence Power in Peace and War* (Cambridge University Press, Cambridge, 1996), written from the perspective of the early 1990s.

15. M. Howard, 'Introduction', in R. Williamson (ed.), *Some Corner in a Foreign Field: Intervention and World Order* (Macmillan, London, 1998), p. 9.

16. D. Kahn, *The Codebreakers* (Sphere edition, London, 1973), p. 456.

17. H. Reiss (tr. H.B. Nisbet), *Kant: Political Writings* (Cambridge University Press, Cambridge, 1991), pp. 96–7.

18. A US policy-maker of the time has claimed that the timing of the flight, on May Day before the conference, was taken by Khrushchev as a deliberately offensive US signal (Robert Bowie, BBC's *Baiting the Bear*, 8 October 1996).

19. In Russian usage the first is '*razvedka*' or '*shpionazh*', the second '*svedenie*'.

20. See H. Suganami, 'Stories of War Origins: A Narrativist Theory of the Causes of War', *Review of International Studies*, vol. 1, no. 4 (October 1997), for a typology of 'war-conducive' acts comprising contributory negligence and insensitive, thoughtless and reckless acts.

21. J.L. Gaddis, 'History, Grand Strategy and NATO

Enlargement', *Survival*, vol. 40, no. 1 (Spring 1998).

22. *The Economist* (22 May 1999), p. 5.

23. Percy Cradock, *In Pursuit of British Interests: Reflections on Foreign Policy under Margaret Thatcher and John Major* (Murray, London, 1997), p. 37.

24. Compare intelligence with the many statistical failures, such as over British earnings in 1997–8, set out for example in *The Economist* (5 March 1999), p. 38.

25. Vice Admiral Sir Louis Le Bailly, letter to *The Times* (3 August 1984).

26. For a discussion of American intelligence and policy in the Cold War, see C. Andrew, *For the President's Eyes Only* (HarperCollins, London, 1995). For the CIA's record in estimating the Soviet Union, see D.J. MacEachin, 'CIA Assessments of the Soviet Union', CIA's *Studies in Intelligence*, (semi-annual unclassified edition, no. 1, 1997), and K. Lundberg, *CIA and the Fall of the Soviet Empire: The Politics of 'Getting It Right'* (Harvard Intelligence and Policy Project, 1994).

27. H. Kissinger, *Years of Upheaval* (Weidenfeld and Nicolson/Michael Joseph, London, 1982), p. 828. Similar proposals were also made as part of the Israeli-Syrian settlement, p. 1254.

28. Statement by Robert Gates, BBC Radio programme *Open Secrets*, 21 March 1995.

29. For discussion see my *Intelligence Power in Peace and War*, ch. 9.

30. Article 23 (Verification) permits NTMs to be used to back up a call for on-site inspection if the data has been collected 'in a manner consistent with generally recognised principles of international law'.

31. An early team leader from the UN Special Commission in Iraq wrote that, 'In the face of the highly efficient Iraqi deception, the inspection could not have gone forward without

accurate intelligence.' (D. Kay, 'Arms Inspections in Iraq:
Lessons for Arms Control', *Bulletin of Arms Control* (Council
for Arms Control/Centre for Defence Studies, London) no. 7
(August 1992), pp. 6–7. For a more complete account see
Tim Trevan, *Saddam's Secrets: The Hunt for Iraq's Hidden
Weapons* (HarperCollins, London, 1999).
32. As early as 1971 the Secretary-General complained of the
'lack of authoritative information, without which the
Secretary-General cannot speak' (U Thant letter of 30 March
1971, quoted by A.W. Dorn, 'Keeping Tabs on a Troubled
World: UN Information-Gathering to Preserve Peace', *Security
Dialogue*, vol. 27, no. 3 [1996]). The theme was taken up
again in the early days of intervention in the former Yugoslavia
in statements such as 'intelligence is a vital element of any
operation and the UN needs to develop a system for obtaining
information without compromising its neutrality' (a British
admiral: *RUSI Journal*, vol. 139, no. 1 [February 1994],
p. 35), and 'I have asked for numerous reforms in the
structure of the UN in Yugoslavia, especially in the use of
information, the capacity to analyse and reflect' (a French
general, quoted in *The Independent*, 31 January 1994).
33. 'Aerial photographs and phone intercepts are giving
instant evidence of atrocities' (Anthony Lloyd, *The Times*
[14 May 1999]).
34. GCHQ graduate careers brochure (1996).
35. As in its (reported) refusal to provide satellite results
during the period of disunity before mounting IFOR.
36. J. Keegan, *Daily Telegraph* (4 June 1999).
37. DFID Policy Statement *Poverty and the Security Sector*,
the basis of an address at the Centre for Defence Studies
(9 March 1999), p. 6.
38. As in the TV programmes about British Cold War observations from trawlers in northern waters.
39. For this legal position, see B. Jasani, 'Civil Radar

Observation Satellites for IAEA Safeguards', *Journal of the Institute of Nuclear Weapons Management*, vol. 27, no. 2 (Winter 1999). UN resolutions such as A/RES53/76 have, however, stressed the need for transparency on the use of outer space and the avoidance of a space arms race.

40. For a brief description, see *British Defence Doctrine* (JWP 0–01) (1996), Annex B. 6.

41. Though for many years a British protest group has alleged that the American SIGINT station at Menwith Hill in northern England is intercepting British communications.

42. The well-attested American U-2 observations of Anglo-French preparations in Cyprus for the Suez operation perhaps entailed overflights of what was then British territory but might have been possible by oblique photography from outside territorial limits. On maritime collection, the relevant law is *United Nations Convention on the Law of the Sea 1982*, articles 19 and 29. 'Innocent passage' excludes 'collecting information to the prejudice of the defence or security of the coastal state' (19.2(c)).

43. For a summary, see Dick Nelson and J. Koenen-Grant, 'A Case of Bureaucracy in Action', *International Journal of Intelligence and Counterintelligence*, vol. 6, no. 3 (Fall 1993).

44. O. Gordievsky, *Next Stop Execution* (Macmillan, London, 1995), pp. 257–8.

45. D.R. Herspring, 'The Cold War: Perceptions from the American Embassy, Moscow', *Diplomacy and Statecraft*, vol. 9, no. 2 (July 1998), p. 200.

46. For Soviet activities, see D. Ball, *Soviet Signals Intelligence (Sigint)* (Papers on Strategy and Defence No 47, Australian National University, Canberra, 1989), pp. 38–70.

47. *Vienna Convention 1961*, Articles 3.1 and 41.3.

48. A Soviet defector, himself betrayed by Ames, claimed that up to forty-five CIA agents had been identified (*The Times* [18 February 1997]). Other press reports quoted lower figures.

49. B.L. Gerber, *A Discussion of Intelligence Ethics*, (paper at International Studies Association Convention, Toronto, March 1997), p. 6.

50. Compare with S. Cohen, *Folk Devils and Moral Panics: The Creation of the Mods and Rockers* (Blackwell, Oxford, 1987 edition).

51. The liberal view also includes the belief that the agent can be induced to 'betray obligations of loyalty which may be legitimately demanded of him' (Lustgarten and Leigh, *In from the Cold*, p. 225). (This assumes, of course, the regime spied upon deserves loyalty.) Other elements are the risks to the agents and the corrupting effects on the officers running them; according to a former CIA General Counsel, 'the constant pressure of the clandestine life can try the moral ballast of the most honest man or woman' (quoted by Gerber, *Intelligence Ethics*, p. 30).

52. Thus China and Iran, in signing the Comprehensive Test Ban Treaty, made separate declarations that verification should not be interpreted as including the results of 'espionage or human intelligence' (see also note 30).

53. G. Best, *War and Law Since 1945* (Oxford University Press, Oxford, 1994).

54. The second of these incidents, of KAL-007 in September 1983, also exacerbated a period of high East-West tension.

55. Major C.B. Brackenbury, 'The Intelligence Duties of the Staff Abroad and at Home', *RUSI Journal*, vol. 19, no. 80 (1975), p. 265.

56. Lustgarten and Leigh, *In from the Cold*, p. 496.

57. Security Council Resolution 699 (1991).

58. Accusations by Scott Ritter, reported for example in *The Guardian* (30 March 1999).

59. See R.J. Aldrich, *Espionage, Security and Intelligence in Britain 1945–70*, (Manchester University Press, Manchester, 1998), pp. 33–4, 100–1, 103–4. For intelligence cases and

diplomatic expulsions as an irritant in Anglo-Soviet relations, see Anne Deighton, 'Ostpolitik or Westpolitik? British Foreign Policy, 1968–75', *International Affairs*, vol. 74, no. 4 (October 1998), p. 896.

60. The official history of the Crimean War is said to have concluded that 'the gathering of knowledge by clandestine means were [*sic*] repulsive to the feelings of an English Gentleman' (quoted by B. Parritt, *The Intelligencers* [Intelligence Corps Association, Ashford, Kent, 2nd edition 1983], p. 80). On the other hand, Lord Salisbury wrote in 1875 that 'we receive pretty constantly copies of the most important reports and references that reach the Foreign Office and War Office at St Petersburg' (from J. Ferris, quoted by the author in *Intelligence Power in Peace and War*, p. 22). For 'reading each other's mail', see correspondence in *Intelligence and National Security*, vol. 2, no. 4 (October 1987).

61. For Vadim Bakatin's handover of bugging details, see J.M. Waller, 'Russia's Security Services: A Checklist for Reform', *Perspective*, vol. 8, no. 1 (September-October 1997). Earlier reports of the handover were confirmed, with disapproval, by the Director of the Russian codebreaking organisation in a Russian television interview of 25 October 1997. For statements by V.A. Kirpichenko, SVR Director, see *Krasnaya Zvezda* (30 October 1993), p. 6.

62. Reuters, quoted by *Jane's Intelligence Watch Report* (1 July 1997).

63. J. Ferris, 'Intelligence after the Cold War: A Global Perspective', in A. Bergin and R. Hall (eds), *Intelligence and Australian National Security* (Australian Defence Studies Centre, Canberra, 1994), p. 8.

64. Quoted from Professor D. Ball in *Far East Economic Review* (9 June 1997). Chinese and North Korean reactions are referred to in VERTIC *Trust and Verify*, No. 83 (November 1993), p. 6.

65. A. James, 'Diplomacy', *Review of International Studies*, vol. 19, no. 1 (January 1993), p. 95.
66. Not limited to the alleged Chinese nuclear espionage. A Chinese academic had previously been arrested on his return from Stanford University and accused of betraying Chinese secrets (*Newsweek* [29 March 1999]).
67. *Rossiyskaya Gazeta*, Moscow, laid surprising emphasis on defence against 'leaks of important political, economic, scientific-technical and military information', 'the threat of foreign intelligence services' agent and operational-technical penetration of Russia', and the need for 'information security'; far more than in any comparable Western statement of national security policy.
68. *British Defence Doctrine* (JWP 0–01) (HMSO, London, 1997), p. 310.
69. For some time Israeli courts approved the use of 'moderate physical pressure' in such circumstances (Gerber, *Discussion of Intelligence Ethics*, p. 7), but this was overtaken by a Supreme Court decision in 1999 (*The Guardian* [7 September 1999]).
70. R. Cohen, 'Diplomacy 2000 BC–2000 AD' (paper delivered to the British International Studies Association annual conference, 1995), p. 1.
71. The Russian national blueprint cited in note 67 also highlights 'the objective and comprehensive analysis and forecasting of threats to national security'.
72. S. Turner, *Secrecy and Democracy* (Harper and Row, NY, 1986), pp. 280–5; W.E. Colby 'Reorganising Western Intelligence', in C.P. Runde and G. Voss (eds), *Intelligence and the New World Order* (International Freedom Foundation, Bustehude, 1992), pp. 126–7.
73. 'To the extent prudent, US intelligence today is . . . being used in dramatically new ways, such as assisting the international organisations like the United Nations . . . . We will

share information and assets that strengthen peaceful relationships and aid in building confidence.' (*National Security Strategy of the United States*, White House, Washington, DC, [January 1993], p. 18).

74. Concluding words in J. Keegan, *War and Our World* (Hutchinson, London, 1998; Reith Lectures 1998), p. 74.

75. For accusations and counter-accusations, see N. Farrell, 'Hark Who's Talking (and Listening)', *The Spectator* (21 November 1998).

76. For a survey of the issues and of US thinking, see L. Johnson, *Secret Agencies: US Intelligence in a Hostile World* (Yale University Press, New Haven, 1996), ch. 6; also D. Clarke and R. Johnston, 'Economic Espionage and Interallied Strategic Co-operation', *Thunderbird International Business Review*, vol. 40, no. 4 (July/August 1998).

77. US objectives are regularly aired by holders of the DCI office and through Congressional reports and special investigations. The annual reports of the Parliamentary Intelligence and Security Committee now provide a British viewpoint.

78. The US-USSR Incidents at Sea agreement of 1972 also had some implications for intelligence collection at close quarters.

79. *The Economist* (16 January 1999), p. 28.

80. *Sunday Times*, World News (25 July 1999), p. 21.

81. Russian accounts of the press conference refer to 'total mutual understanding' having been reached on 'one sensitive topic,' and existing agreements 'to work in a fairly correct sort of way' (FBIS and BBC translations of 28 and 29 July items).

82. M.E. Bowman, 'Intelligence and International Law', *International Journal of Intelligence and Counterintelligence*, vol. 8, no. 3 (Fall 1995), p. 330.

83. Best, *War and Law since 1945*, p. 7.

INDEX

Moscow: European, KGB
SIGINT penetration 6;
French, KGB SIGINT pene-
tration 6; US, Soviet/Russian
penetration 4–5, 298, 303
Soviet in London 298
Empta 259, 285n76
ENIGMA 103
Ermath, Fritz 112
Ernst, Maurice C. 279–80n28,
282n41
espionage *see* covert intelligence
espionage agents
advantages and disadvantages
103–4
British Stasi agents 86, 91
Cambridge 'Magnificent Five'
agents 16, 44, 89, 91
collection of material by 102–4
KGB agents in Italy 6
Soviet agents in USA 7
see also HUMINT (human
intelligence); intelligence officers
ETA (Basque group) 54
ethics and morals
consequences of covert intelligence 289
economic espionage 273
ethical foreign policies, intelligence services and xxii–xxiii,
287–305
honesty, role in covert intelligence 64
intelligence activities 296–302,
315, 319
intelligence gathering xxii–xxiii,
274, 288–9
international morality, intelligence and 288
le Carré, John 321n11
moral cost of intelligence services 67–8, 85, 91–2
of professional objectivity 292
see also just espionage
ethnic unrest 75
need for intelligence sharing on
175

Europe: non-Alliance countries, and
intelligence sharing 185
European Commission
Monitoring Mission 186
proposal for European GPS
185
European Union
assessment of candidates for
admission 187
Cologne Declaration 185, 200
Common Foreign and Security
Policy 181, 184–5, 305
information for United Nations
195
intelligence dependence on
United States 295
intelligence and OSINF 193
members' spying activities 303
and NATO 200
relationship with United States
183–4
sharing of intelligence 184–8
supranational intelligence
agency, possibility of 183
supranational intelligence
assessment 307
targetting of other members
304
UK conflict of interest over
intelligence 9, 183
European Union, Western *see* WEU
evaluation of information *see* analysis
expenditure on intelligence
Far East 303–4
UK/US 66, 288, 320n3, 4
see also costs
export controls
and Economic Espionage Act
250
opposition to 216
and proliferation of WMD 207,
212, 220

facts: acquisitions 101–2
Factual-Technical Warning 101
Falklands conflict 123–4
fanaticism and power 48, 52

raw intelligence
for decision-makers 162
Stalin and 22, 41
Reagan, Ronald 49
administration: and intelligence
services 139-41, 171*n*28; on
military security 240
rebel groups *see* non-state actors
recruitment: present needs 58
Red Army: SIGINT units 4
Redesdale, Lord 27
regional intelligence services 87
future 73
Reiss, H. 321*n*17
religious sects *see* non-state actors
Richelson, Jeffrey T. 277*n*5
Risen, James 284*n*65
Ritter, Scott 325*n*58
rogue states 53–4, 78, 218, 300–1,
302
Rolls-Royce 41
Romania: Russian threat in 1945 37
Roosevelt, Franklin D. 13
Roper, John 182–8, 200
Rowen, Henry 139
Rumsfeld Commission 120
Russia
abortive 1991 coup 106, 111
assessment methods 105–6
code-breaking organisation,
ethics of 297
Cold War influence on
US/NATO relationships 305
economic espionage 249, 268,
269–70
economic future, US intelligence 251
and EU IMF loans 187
Federal Security Service, intelligence, intercepting 303
Foreign Intelligence Service
(FIS) 148, 150–3, 167
glasnost and intelligence services
152–3
intelligence *détente* 303
intelligence officers as Prime
Ministers 165–6
intelligence problems 109

links with Western intelligence
309–10
national security policy 327*n*67,
71
need for focus on 52, 53
need for unfettered intelligence
309
non-military covert intelligence
308
post-Cold War, US intelligence
and 239
proposal to ban information
warfare 310
Security Council 147–8
underground construction 11
US Co-operative Threat
Reduction Programme 232
US espionage 298–9
and US mutual reductions in
espionage 310
WMD proliferation and 231
Rwanda 241, 243
international tribunal 178
suppression of information
176

S & T intelligence
and industrial intelligence
273–4
Soviet use of 17–18
SADC (South African Development
Committee) 198–9
St Antony's College, Oxford xiii–iv
St Malo, Declaration of 185
Sakharov, Andrei 20
SALT agreement 15
sanctions *see* economic sanctions
Sanger, David E. 281*n*35, 283*n*51
Sargent, Sir Orme 30, 34, 37
satellite imaging xx, 295
ethics 297
high resolution, OSINF and
193, 217
information from commercial
sources 194, 200, 217, 276
see also IMINT
satellites
Corona satellites 115